TOTAL QUALITY CULTURE
IN
TEACHER TRAINING COLLEGES

TOTAL QUALITY CULTURE IN TEACHER TRAINING COLLEGES

By

Dr. Noorjehan N. Ganihar

&

Dr. Vinayak Krishna Bhat

DISCOVERY PUBLISHING HOUSE

NEW DELHI-110002

First Published-2006

ISBN 81-8356-086-5

Published by

DISCOVERY PUBLISHING HOUSE
4831/24, Ansari Road, Prahlad Street,
Darya Ganj, New Delhi-110002 (India)
Phone: 23279245 • Fax: 91-11-23253475
E-mail:dphtemp@indiatimes.com

Printed at
Arora Offset Press
Laxmi Nagar, Delhi–92

Preface

The strength of an educational system depends largely upon the quality of its teachers. So, the teacher education in real sense calls for systems moulding and the most competent and dedicated teachers to meet the challenges of the advancement of society for mutual benefit. Current trends in teacher education system show a declining importance given to this moulding process. Nowadays teacher education institutions have a greater responsibility in producing quality teachers, lest the future of our nation is at stake.

Usually educational institutions are rated on the basis of their performance related to the quality parameters, like examination results, students employment after graduation, reputation of the institution based on external reports, etc. Though there may be different degrees or grades in quality, broadly it could mean that quality is the difference between the average and the excellent. It is the difference between failure and success. "Quality as a value based, information driven management process through which the minds and talents of people at all levels are applied fully and creatively to the organizations continuous improvement".

Total Quality Management (TQM) requires a change culture. This is notoriously difficult to bring about and takes time to implement. It requires a change of attitudes and working methods. The staff in institutions need to understand and live the message if TQM is to make an impact. The latter is characterised by an understanding that people produce quality. Two things are required for staff to produce quality. First, staff need a suitable environment in which to work. They need the roots of the trade and they need to work with systems and procedures, which are simple in doing their jobs.

The modern world is one in which the only constant is change. Change is a precarious matter. Implementing total quality of management is secondary teacher education colleges requires coping with change in a positioned constructive manner. Secondary teacher education institutions must be redesigned so as to be consistent with the total quality culture that helps to create a congenial atmosphere for management.

Quality models for education have been developed and debated by many researchers. Models have been widely accepted in Western Countries. However, in a developing country like India, having deep-rooted traditional practices accepting these models will be a difficult task. Moreover total quality needs an ongoing level of research investment to continue to perfect and advance the state of quality art.

For the last few years there has been no research on total quality culture in the field of secondary teacher education programme. The major concern in secondary teacher education course should be educational excellence for which teacher education colleges have to be total quality driven. The research in secondary teacher education colleges, total quality culture would go a long way in making the colleges quality driven and quality borne.

Dr. Noorjehan N. Ganihar

Dr. Vinayak Krishna Bhat

Contents

The Problem

Introduction

The teacher education institutions have vital role in improving the standards of the system of education by preparing competent and effective teachers. It has generally been agreed that the quality of a nation is judged by the quality of its citizens. The latter is mostly determined by the educational system in the nation which, in turn, is decided by the quality of teachers it has. Thus, the real dynamic force of the educational system is the teacher.

After independence strenuous efforts have been seriously and continuously made for expansion and qualitative improvement of teacher education. For the qualitative improvement of education in general and teacher education in particular various committees and commissions were formed. Among the commissions the Kothari Commission (1964-66), which dealt extensively with all aspects of education is worthy of mentioning, which said: "A sound program of professional education of teachers is essential for the qualitative improvement of education". But it pointed out that "unfortunately, the professional education of teachers has been comparatively neglected in the post independence period". In their opinion, "The quality of training institutions remains, with a few exceptions, either mediocre or poor".

Preparation of qualified and able teaching personnel is one of the most significant functions of our teacher education institutions. Realising the fact National Policy on Education (1986), places complete trust in the teaching community and has suggested a variety of steps to improve the status of teachers with effective teacher accountability. The policy envisages teacher education as a continuous process and its pre-service and in-service components are inseparable. The quality of teacher education would largely depend upon the effectiveness of teacher education institutions. The latter is mostly judged by its infrastructure, competent faculty, dynamic curriculum, the input, process, products, community interaction and innovativeness etc. Investments, facilities and all other factors become meaningless if the real functionaries (teacher educators) fail to support and implement the new reforms.

The Origins of the Quality Movement

It is from industrial practices that the language, concepts and methodology of Total Quality Management (TQM) are derived.

There has always been a need to ensure that products conform to their specification and give customer satisfaction and value for money. Achieving consistent quality allows consumers to have confidence in a product and its producers. However, quality becomes an issue with the advent of industrialisation. Prior to this craftsmen set and maintained their own standards on which their reputations and livelihoods depended. The advent of mass-production, the breaking down of work into narrow and repetitive tasks, took away from the worker the possibility of self-checking quality. The responsibility of the worker for the quality of the product was lost when goods were mass-produced. New production methods, associated with the scientific approach to management and the name of F W Taylor, at the turn of the last century, reduced many in the work force to human components in the process of manufacturer. A strict division of labour developed from it and necessitated the expansion of the system of inspection known as 'quality control'.

Quality control and inspection are processes to ensure that only products meeting their specifications leave the factory gate. Quality control thus is an after-the-event process, and is divorced from the people who produce the product. Inspection and quality control detect defective quality products. They are not means of assuring that the workforce care about quality. They are necessary processes under mass production, but they are often wasteful and expensive, involving considerable amounts of scrap and reworking Quality control and inspection, by themselves, are increasingly being seen as uneconomic. Many companies are replacing or augmenting them with methods of quality assurance and quality improvement that seek to build quality into the process by returning to the workers their responsibility for quality.

Notions of quality improvement and quality assurance began to average after the Second World War. However, in Britain and the USA they began to attract attention on a large scale in the 1980's as companies started to ask questions about the Japanese capturing a larger share of world markets.

Total Quality Movement in Management

Quality is realised and maintained not by adopting a program or project, but by creating a new quality culture in the organisation, a new philosophy of action practiced not by an individual or a few functionaries, but the totality of the organisation. Every individual, every group, every division in enterprise will be active participants for the common objective of the goal of quality. That is the significance of the word total in Total Quality Management.

Total Quality Management, by its very nature is dynamic and vibrant. It is not a finite program, which can be realised by a target date. Total Quality Management (TQM) is a management philosophy for the pursuit of excellence in the organisation.

The quest for perfection and excellence is a continuing activity. The goal is ever widening and not static.

There is no standard definition for Total Quality Management (TQM). The United States Department of Defense uses the following definition for Total Quality Management (Smith 1994).

"Total Quality Management is both a philosophy and a set of guiding principles that represent the foundation of a continuously improving organisation. Total Quality Management is the application of quantitative methods and human resources to improve the material and services supplied to an organisation, all the processes within the organisation, and the degree with which the needs of customer are met, now and in the future. Total Quality Management integrates fundamental management techniques, existing improvement efforts, and technical tools under a disciplined approach focused on continuous improvement." Or more simply "systematically and continuously improving quality of products, service and life using all available human and capital resources".

What is Total Quality Management?

Total Quality Management is essentially a philosophy of continuous improvement, constantly trying to upgrade the quality of a product, to the satisfaction of the customers. Here customer is sovereign. It is the approach popularised by Peters and Waterman in (excellence published in 1982), and which has been constant theme of Tom Peters writing since. Many Japanese, American and British Companies have been pursuing this approach for a number of years. It is about providing the customer with what they want, when they want it and how they want it. It involves moving with changing customer expectations and fashions to design products and services that meet and exceed their expectations. Only by delighting customers will they return and tell their friends about it. (This is sometimes called the 'sell-on' definition of quality). The perceptions and expectations of the customers are recognized as being short term and fickle, and so organisations have to find ways of keeping close to their customers to be able to respond to their changing tastes, needs and wants.

Juran (1989), one of the exponents of Total Quality Management uses the Japanese word Kaizen to explain that Total Quality Management means step by step improvement. He emphasises the major role of the Management in tackling problems relating to quality. Crosby (1961), another prominent exponent of Total Quality Management, states that the first step in quality improvement program, is the commitment of the management to quality improvement. Crosby is also remembered for his concept of "Zero Defects", which implies that in a perfect quality product there should be no defects in production process. Deming (1951), another philosopher of Total Quality Management, also gives importance to the role of the management. According to him the problem of quality lies primarily with the management.

Total Quality Management Implies Following 'Pancha Sutras'. (five aphorisms)

1. Serious concern for improving quality at all levels.
2. Giving utmost importance for the customers demands, treating the customer as sovereign and trying to satisfy the customer completely.
3. Management's total commitment for enhancing the quality of the products.
4. Setting up goals and planning in advance for upgrading quality.
5. Removing the defects in the process of production and improving the process at all levels.

Rhodes (1992) in his article "on the road to quality" defined total quality as a "value based, information-driven management process through which the minds and talents of people at all levels are applied fully and creatively to the organisation's continuous improvement".

Total Quality Management (TQM) in the Context of Education

Quality has to be universal, it cannot be had in isolation. Quality must permeate into every activity of society. Education is no exception. In fact education is at the root of all programs.

It is not difficult to implement the general principles of Total Quality Management in educational institutions as outlined above, Modifications or alterations to suit the educational organisations can be made for achieving the best results. Even in industry and business, there is no rigid or single model of Total Quality Management. Depending on the situations prevailing in each organisation, the concepts of Total Quality Management are applied. Hence it can be said that, the theory of Total Quality Management can be adapted in general to the advantage of the educational institutions, to improve the quality of education.

Sallis (1996) in his book "Total Quality Management in Education" emphasised that, "Total Quality Management is a philosophy of continuous improvement, with a set of practical tools for meeting and exceeding the present and future customers' needs, wants, and expectations". Habbard (1994) in a paper "Total Quality Management in Higher Education-Learning from the Factories", asks, "If American industries can dramatically improve their effectiveness through their application of Total Quality Management principles would similar improvements result if education adopted the same approach?". The answer to the question is in the affirmative and he explains in his paper, in detail, the experience of his university (North-West Missourie State University) in implementing the Total Quality Management approach.

When the principles of Total Quality Management are adopted to suit the educational organisations, the following important steps could be followed.

1. Creating quality consciousness among all connected with the educational institutions, viz., management, faculty, students, parents and the society at large.
2. Total commitment of the management be it government, university, or private aided or unaided body, for providing quality education.
3. Treating the students as the sovereign authority and creating a feeling amongst the faculty that the institution exists for the students and not for the staff. Students are not the only customers of an educational organisation; the parents, employers, and the society in general are also the consumers. Since students are the primary and direct customers of an educational institution, students should get the best from them.
4. Setting up of short-term and long-term goals for improving the quality of education and preparing plan of action for achieving the goals.
5. Monitoring the quality improvement programs at frequent intervals and making suitable alterations wherever necessary in the programs.
6. Motivating the staff to work with enthusiasm and dedication to achieve the goals set.
7. Provide effective and dynamic leadership to the institution for successfully implementing the Total Quality Management programs.

8. To pay attention for improving the entire process of teaching-learning and the environment in the institution, to bring out the best from the students.

Good buildings with well furnished and well maintained classrooms, well-equipped laboratories, a good library with ample facilities for students, well-qualified and committed faculty and an environment which facilitates the prevalence of an effective teaching-learning process, are all important sources of quality. Of all the ingredients of qualitative education mentioned above, the most important is the dedicated faculty. A school, college or university may not have good buildings, furniture, play grounds and even well-equipped laboratories and libraries, but if the teachers there are enthusiastic, highly motivated and committed to their task, the students are likely to have the best education. That is why Perry (1994) in "what is quality in higher education?" appropriately writes "teachers who feel enthusiasm for their job and who are well qualified and experts in what they teach are the only essential ingredients in teaching quality".

While judging the quality of education imparted in an institution, we should assess not only the knowledge gained by the students, but should also estimate the personality of each student in terms of his/her participation in extra-curricular activities like debates, cultural activities, games and sports and social service programs, because education is not mere acquisition of knowledge but is a process of developing one's personality.

Tribus (1990) in "Total Quality Management in Education," while answering the question, what should good education provide for learners, mentions that good education should provide for knowledge—which enables to understand, know how—which enables to do, wisdom—which enables to set priorities and character which enables to "co-operate, to preserve and to become respected and trusted members of society".

Total Quality Management in Teacher Education

If quality is to be universal, perhaps the best way to go about it is to begin with educational institutions. Teaching institutions in general and professional schools in particular can contribute to the quality movement by preaching quality and even more by practicing total quality.

Quality of teacher education is an integral part of quality education system. Teacher education institutions have a greater responsibility in producing quality teachers, lest the future of our nation is at stake. University Education Commission (1948-49) opined that the objectives of teacher education should be formulated, keeping in view of the following tasks of teacher.

"The right kind of teacher is one who possesses a vivid awareness of his mission. He not only loves his subject, but he loves also those whom he teaches. This success will be measured not in terms of percentage of pass alone, not even by the quantity of original contribution of knowledge—important as they are; but equally through the quality of life and character of men and women whom he taught".

Education Commission (1964-66) popularly known as Kothari Commission devoted one complete chapter on teacher education and detailed various recommendations for the improvement of its quality. They emphasised that the essence of teacher education is 'quality' and in its absence, teacher education becomes not only a financial waste but a source of overall deterioration in educational standards. They suggested that objectives of teacher education be formulated on the basis of some broad principles listed as under.

1. Re-orientation of subject knowledge.
2. Vitalization of professional studies.
3. Improvement in methods of teaching and evaluation.
4. Improvement of student teaching.
5. Development of special courses and programs.
6. Revision and improvement of curricula.

Further the committee on plan projects (1963) of the planning commission studies at length the issues and problems of teacher education and stated in their draft report as under.

Modern education aims at education of the whole person. So every teacher should have a deep knowledge and understanding of children and skill in applying that knowledge and understanding. These cannot be acquired by rule of the thumb and very often an untrained teacher has to learn the job by an arduous and long practice during which it is not impossible that young children might be exposed to irreparable harm, because the teacher has not used the skills and knowledge which he should have. To argue that a few teachers are born and not made, would have its counter argument that one swallow does not make a summer and the overwhelming majority of the men and women can ably become good teachers if their training program is built on a sound foundation of the theoretical knowledge and supervised practical work. This is what a training institution is designed to provide but admittedly, like all academic institutions of same kind, no teacher training institute can produce teachers towards cent per cent efficiency.

Quality Control in Teacher Education

Whitty (1991) emphasised that quality teacher education requires:

(i) A genuine partnership between the various stake holders (training institutions, schools, etc) in all routes to Qualified Teacher Status.

(ii) A clearer definition of competencies (or core professional skills) required by teachers as reflective practitioners.

(iii) Monitoring of academic validation through a quality assurance system.

(iv) Administration of professional accreditation through a Council for the Accreditation of Teacher Education (CATE) or through General Teaching Council (GTC), with strong extra-professional representation to ensure public accountability.

(v) Sensitively to local and sectional needs within this national framework.

With such a framework, teacher education could both control and assure quality.

According to Sallis (1996) education is also recognizing the need to pursue quality and to deliver it to their pupils and students. He said that, the source of quality in education is a well maintained building, outstanding teachers; high moral values; excellent examination results; specialisation; the support of parents, business and the local community; plentiful resources; the application of the latest technology; strong and purposeful leadership; the care and concern for pupils and students; a well balanced curriculum, or some combination of these factors.

Barlosky and Lawton, (1995) noticed four quality imperatives, which are the drivers for motivating forces that challenge any institution that seeks to take a proactive stance on quality issues, they are

1. The Moral Imperative—the Link with Customers

The moral imperative lies behind the proposition that customers and clients of education service (students, parents, the community, etc.) are deserving of the best possible quality of education. It is the duty of educational professionals and administrators to have an overriding concern providing the very best possible educational opportunities. As Burnham (1992) has put it, 'it is difficult to conceptualise a situation where anything less than total quality is perceived as being appropriate or acceptable for the education of children'.

2. The Professional Imperative—the Link with the Professional Role of Educators

Closely linked to the moral imperative is the professional imperative. This represents the duty of all of those involved in the service to strive to provide high standards of tuition to learners. Professionalism implies a commitment to the needs of students and an obligation to meet their needs by employing the most appropriate pedagogic practices. Educators have a professional duty to improve the quality of education and this, of course, places an enormous burden on teachers and administrators to ensure that both classroom practice and the management of the institution are operating to the highest possible standards.

3. The Competitive Imperative—the Link with Competitors

Competition is a reality in the world of education. Falling enrollments can mean staff redundancies and ultimately the viability of the institution is under threat. In the new educational market place educationalists must meet the challenge of competition by working to improve the quality of their products, services and delivery mechanisms. The importance of Total Quality Management (TQM) to survival is that it is a customer-driven process, focusing on the needs of clients and providing mechanisms to respond to their needs and wants. The deregulation of such educational provision requires competitive strategies that clearly differentiate institutions from their competitors. Quality may some times be the only differentiating factor for an institution. Focusing on the needs of the customers, which is at the heart of quality, is one of the most effective means of facing the competition and surviving.

4. The Accountability Imperative—the Link with Constituent Groups

Schools and colleges are part of their communities and as such they must meet the political demands for education to be more accountable and publicly demonstrate the high standards of their products (for example curriculum, learning, graduates) and services. Total Quality Management (TQM) supports the accountability imperative by promoting objective and measurable outcomes of the educational process and providing mechanisms for the improvement of those outcomes. Quality improvement becomes increasingly important as institutions achieve greater control over their own affairs. Greater freedom has to be matched by greater accountability. Institutions have to demonstrate that they are able to offer a quality education to their learners.

Failure to meet even one of these imperatives can jeopardize institutional well being and survival. If they fail to provide the best services they risk losing clients who will opt for their competitors. By regarding these 'drivers' as any thing less than imperatives we risk the integrity of our profession and the future of our institutions.

Total Quality Culture

Total Quality Management requires a change culture. This is notoriously difficult to bring about and takes time to implement. It requires a change of attitudes and working methods. The staff in institutions need to understand and live the message if TQM is to make an impact. The latter is characterised by an understanding that people produce quality. Two things are required for staff to produce quality. First, staff need a suitable environment in which to work. They need the roots of the trade and they need to work with systems and procedures which are simple in doing their jobs.

Total Quality Management involves a system composed of three subsystems held together by Total quality. The three sub-systems are managerial, social, and technical.

The social system includes factors associated with the formal and informal characteristics of the organisation (1) organisational culture; the values, norms, attitudes, role expectations, and differentiation that exist in each organisation (2) quality of social relationships between individual members and among groups, including reward structures and symbols of power; and (3) behavioural patterns between members including roles and communication. It is the social system that has the greatest impact on such factors as motivation, creativity, innovative behaviours and teamwork.

To achieve total quality, a social system must be developed in which customer satisfaction continuous improvement, management based on facts, and genuine respect for people are accepted practices. Frequently this requires a substantial change in the social system, and change does not come easily.

Quality culture is influenced mostly by six factors, namely (1) environment (2) product or service (3) methods, (4) people, (5) organisational structure and (6) mindset of the people for total quality improvement.

The Problem

The modern world is one in which the only constant is change. Change is a precarious matter. Implementing Total Quality of Management in secondary teacher education colleges requires coping with change in a positioned constructive manner. Secondary teacher education institutions must be redesigned so as to be consistent with the Total Quality Culture that helps to create a congenial atmosphere for management.

Quality models for education have been developed and debated by many researchers. Models have been widely accepted in Western Countries. However, in a developing country like India, having deep rooted traditional practices, accepting these models will be a difficult task. Moreover total quality needs an ongoing level of research investment to continue to perfect and advance the state of quality art.

The major concern is secondary teacher education course should be educational excellence for which teacher education colleges have to be total quality driven. The research in secondary teacher education colleges, total quality culture would go a long way in making the colleges quality driven and quality borne.

The research studies on Total Quality Culture in India are very rare and are very few abroad. Studies on Organisational Health are done at school level only. So far no studies have been carried out in India involving study of the variables Quality of Work-Life, Student Teachers' Commitment to Course, Student Teachers' Involvement in College Activities and Change Facilitator Styles of Principals at secondary teacher education college level. Hence, the present work intends to study the correlates of Total Quality Culture in teacher education colleges especially in Karnataka State. The study of this kind would highlight the dimensions, which can be manipulated to increase the Total Quality Culture of teacher education colleges. This may also help in planning the resources to be tapped, and further the management and principals concerned to understand the instrumental and expressive managerial behaviour.

The present study aims at identifying certain variables related to total quality culture in teacher education colleges.

The Objectives

The present study has the following objectives to study the relationship between:

A. Total Quality Culture and

(a) Organisational Health.

(b) Quality of Work -Life of Teacher Educators.

(c) Student Teachers' Involvement in College Activities.

(d) Change Facilitator Styles of Principals.

(e) Student Teachers' Commitment to Course.

(f) Sex of College.

(g) Type of Management of College.

B. Organisational Health and

(a) Quality of Work- Life of Teacher Educators.

(b) Student Teachers' Involvement in College Activities.

(c) Change Facilitator Styles of Principals.

(d) Student Teachers' Commitment to Course.

(e) Sex of College.

(f) Type of Management of College.

C. Quality of Work Life and

(a) Student Teachers' Involvement in College Activities.

(b) Change Facilitator Styles of Principals.

(c) Student Teachers' Commitment to Course.

(d) Sex of College.

(e) Type of Management of College.

D. Student Teachers' Involvement in College Activities and

(a) Sex of College.

(b) Type of Management of College.

Limitations of the Study

1. The present study is limited to the Karnataka State only.
2. This study is restricted only to the Secondary Teacher Education Colleges.

2

Theoretical Background

Total Quality Management

Total Quality Management (TQM) is total in three senses: it covers every process, every job, and every person. First, it covers every process, rather than just manufacturing or production. Design, construction, R&D, accounting, marketing, repair, and every other function must also be involved in quality improvement. Second, total quality is total in that it covers every job; as opposed to only those involved in making the product. Secretaries are expected not to make typing errors, accountants not to make posting errors and presidents not to make strategic errors. Third, total quality recognized that each person is responsible for the quality of his or her work and for the work of the group.

Total quality also goes beyond the traditional idea of quality, which has been expressed as the degree of conformance to a standard or the product of workmanship. Enlightened organisations accept and apply the concept that quality is the degree of user satisfaction or the fitness of the product for use. In other words, the customer determines whether or not quality has been achieved in totality.

This same measure—total customer satisfaction—applies throughout the entire operation of an organisation. Only the outer edges of the company actually have contact with customers in the traditional sense, but each department can treat the other departments as its customer. The main judge of the quality of work is the customer, for if the customer is not satisfied, the work does not have quality. This coupled with the achievement of corporate objectives, is the bottom line of total quality.

In that regard, it is important, as the Japanese say, to "talk with facts and data". Total quality emphasised the use of fact-oriented discussions and statistical quality control techniques by everyone in the company. Everyone in the company is exposed to basic quality control ideas and techniques and is expected to use them. Thus, total quality becomes a common language and improves "objective" communication.

Total quality also radically alters the nature and basic operating philosophy of organisations. The specialised, separated system developed early in the twentieth century is replaced by a system of mutual feedback and close interaction of departments. Engineers, for example, work closely with construction crews and storekeepers to ensure that their knowledge is passed on to workers. Workers, in turn, feed their practical experience directly back to the engineers. The information interchange and shared commitment to product quality is what makes total quality work. Teaching all employees how to apply process control and improvement techniques makes them party to their own destiny and enable them to achieve their fullest potential.

However, total quality is more than an attempt to make better products; it is also a search for better ways to make better products. Adopting the total quality philosophy commits the company to the belief that there is always a better way of doing things, a way to make better use of the company's resources, and a way to be more productive. In this sense, total quality relies heavily upon value analysis as a method of developing better products and operations in order to maximize value to the stakeholder, whether customers, employees, or shareholders.

Total quality also implies a different type of worker and a different attitude toward the worker from management. Under total quality, workers are generalists, rather than specialists. Both workers and managers are expected to move from job to job, gaining experience in many areas of the company.

History of Quality

Deming (1951) is generally recognized as the "father of quality". He was first introduced to the basic tenets of traditional management principles in the late 1920s, as a summer employee at Western Electric's famous Hawthorne plant in Chicago. This experience led him to ask, "How can firms best motivate their employees?" Deming found the traditional motivation system in use at the time to be degrading and economically unproductive. Under that system, work incentives were linked to piecework to maximize worker output, followed by an inspection process in which defective items were subtracted from the worker's piecework credits.

Deming (1930) collaborated with Shewhart, a statistician working at Bell Telephone Laboratories, to develop statistical control techniques that could be applied to management processes. Deming recognised that a statistically controlled management process gave the manager a new found capacity to systematically determine when to intervene and, equally important, when to leave a process alone. During World War II, Deming got his first opportunity to demonstrate to the government how Shewhart's statistical quality control methods could be taught to workers and put into practice in the nation's busy war plants.

At the conclusion of World War II, Deming left government service and set up a private consulting practice. The State Department, one of his early clients, sent Deming to Japan in 1947 to help prepare a national census in that country. American managers soon forgot their wartime quality control lessons and returned to their pre-war traditional management practices. However, Deming's evolving quality control methods received a warm reception in Japan. The Japanese attribute their economic success to Deming's quality methodology.

Deming's philosophy is prone to put quality in human terms. When a firm's work force is committed to doing a good job and has a solid managerial process in which to act, quality will flow naturally. A more practical, composite definition of quality might read: Quality is a predictable degree of variation for adopted standards and dependability at low cost. Quality is customer driven and market focused. The methodological core of Deming's quality management approach is the use of simple statistical techniques to continuously improve output. Only through statistical verification can the manager know that he or she has a problem and find the causes of the problem.

Some of Deming's key principles as applied to education are:

- School board members and administrators must make the pursuit of quality an educational goal
- Emphasis should be placed on preventing students from failing instead of detecting failure after the fact
- The use of statistical control methods, if rigorously applied, can help to improve administrative and student outcomes.

Juran (1989) is also recognised as one of the "fathers of quality". Juran received his education in engineering and law. Like Deming, Juran is a distinguished statistician. Juran defines quality as "fitness for use" and maintains that the basic quality mission of a school is "to develop programs and society." Furthermore, Juran states that "fitness for use" is properly determined from the viewpoint of the user as opposed to the provider.

Juran's (1989) quality outlook reflects a rational, matter-of-fact approach to business organisation and is heavily dependent on sophisticated "shop floor" planning and quality control processes. The focal point of his quality management philosophy is the organisation's belief in the productivity of the individual. Quality is ensured by making sure that each individual has the building blocks necessary to do his or her job properly. With the proper tools, workers will produce products and services that consistently meet customer expectations.

Like Deming, Juran also played a significant role in rebuilding Japan after World War-II. He was recognised by the Japanese for the development of quality control in Japan and the facilitation of a friendship between the United States and Japan. His search for the underlying principles of the management process led to his focus on quality as the ultimate goal.

Some of Juran's points include:

- The pursuit of quality is a never-ending process
- Quality improvement is an ongoing process, not a one-shot program
- Quality requires hands-on leadership by school board members and administrators
- Massive training is a prerequisite of quality
- Everyone in a school must be trained.

If the teachings of Deming and Juran seem familiar, they should. Much of their thinking has been adopted and adapted by many organisations in America. The point is that the establishment of quality as the basic educational principle for schools is grounded in the proven track record and results that others have achieved with similar philosophies and strategies.

Juran predicted the success of the Japanese in 1966 in a speech to the European Organisation for Quality Control. He said:

"The Japanese are headed for world quality leadership and will attain it in the next two decades because no one else is moving towards it at the same pace."

Defining Total Quality

First and foremost, "total quality is a set of philosophies by which management systems can direct the efficient achievement of the objectives of the organisation to ensure customer satisfaction and maximize stakeholder value". This is accomplished through the continuous improvement of the quality system, which consists of the social system, the technical system, and the management system. Thus, it becomes a way of life for doing business for the entire organisation.

Quality has been defined in a variety of ways. Crosby (1979) defined Quality in terms of 'conformance to requirements' of the customers. Juran (1988) defined Quality in terms of 'fitness of use'. According to Macdonald and Piggott (1990), 'Quality is defined as delighting the customer by continuously meeting and improving upon agreed requirements' (Malhotra, 1993). Total quality is also defined as 'Customer satisfaction at competitive cost' (Udupa, 1992).

Quality is a process of continuous improvement and is not something absolute but relative. The key to quality improvement is to focus on the process and not the product or the outcome (Barry, 1996).

Total quality management is a holistic approach and consists of three essential components:

- Customer focus,
- Employees' involvement, and
- Continuous improvement.

The House of Quality

The metaphor used here to present the basic concepts and principles associated with total quality is the House of Quality (Figure 2.1). As in a well-built house, the major components of the House of Quality are (1) the *roof*, or superstructure, consisting of the social, technical, and management systems; (2) the *four pillars* of customer satisfaction, continuous improvement, speaking with facts, and respect for people; (3) the *foundation* of four managerial levels-strategy, process, project, and task management; and (4) the *four cornerstones* of mission, vision, values, and goals and objectives.

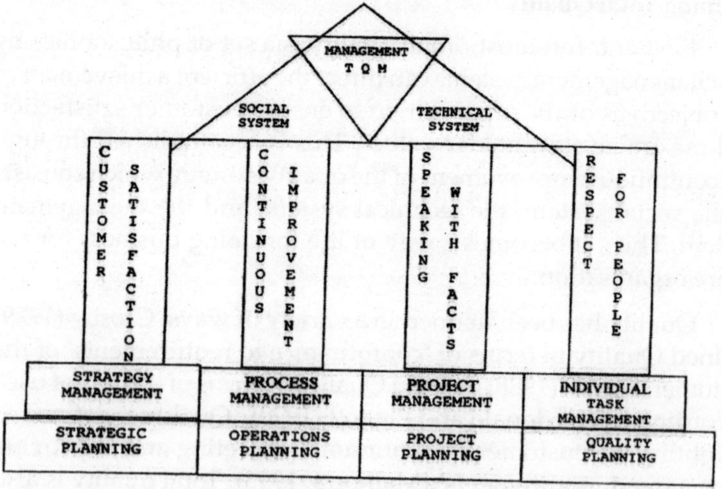

Fig. 2.1: House of Quality

As in building any house, the plans must be developed first, usually by experienced individuals working together-as a team. Once the plans are approved, construction (implementation) can begin.

Total quality efforts frequently fail because the individuals responsible for the efforts (i.e. management) are unable to carry out their responsibilities. They do not recognise the importance of systems thinking and do not have a well-defined purpose and process to follow.

- Recognise quality improvement as a system
- Define it so others can recognize it, too
- Analyse its behaviour
- Work with subordinates in improving the system
- Measure the quality of the system
- Develop improvements in the quality of the system
- Measure the gains in the quality, if any, and link these to customer delight and quality improvement
- Take steps to guarantee holding the gains
- Attempt to replicate the improvements into other areas of the organisation
- Tell others about the lessons learned.

These guidelines, when implemented, will assure success because of their impact on all aspects of the college or university. They are also reflected in the House of Quality, which illustrates the universality of the basic principles and procedures for carrying out total quality.

The Pillars of Total Quality Management

Total quality management in any organisation is supported by four driving forces, or pillars, that move the organisation towards the full application of quality service. The four pillars of the House of Quality are customer service, continuous improvement, processes and facts, and respect for people. All are distinct, but equal in potential strength. All four must be addressed; minimizing one weakens the others. By not addressing one, the entire House of Quality will fall. Figure 2.2 presents the pillars of Total Quality Management.

Organisational Vision: All achievements arise out of vision-vision of a leader, a prophet or a thinker. This vision is the polestar that gives direction and purpose to an organisation. In a Total Quality Management (TQM) organisation this vision focuses on quality and excellence. The framework that the vision creates guides the enterprise beliefs and values.

Customer focus: A TQM organisation believes that the customer is supreme. It is not a slogan to be just displayed, but an article of faith. TQM considers that companies become successful as a result of satisfied and loyal customers. The customer is the ultimate judge of the quality. Obviously customer expectations are highly dynamic and the successful companies must manifest foresight dynamism and flexibility of approach in its functioning.

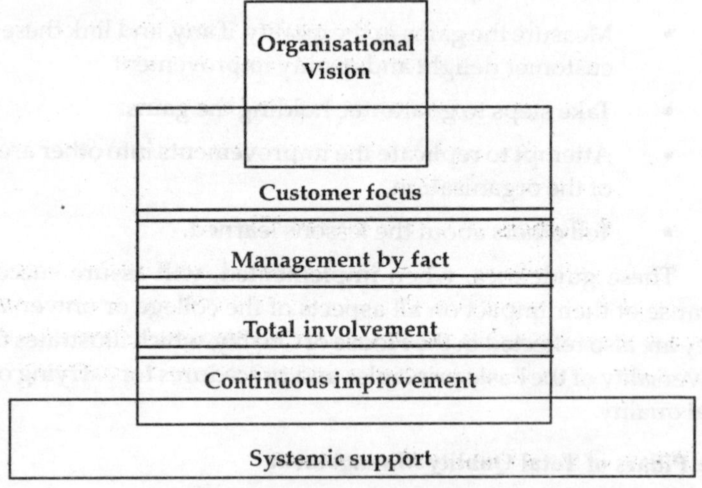

Fig. 2.2: Pillars of Total Quality Management

Management by Fact: The framework of the organisation its processes and resources, its goals and objectives must be based on facts and hard data. Opinions not supported by data have no place in TQM. Assessment of performance is based on measured performance, which is a continuing activity.

Total Involvement: This factor is perhaps the key for organisational success in TQM. In such an organisation, every one from the chief executive to the junior most employee has dynamic and meaningful roles to play in fulfilling the mission of the enterprise. Hierarchy and bureaucracy have lost their traditional significance. TQM believes every individual to be a centre of skill, innovation and intelligence and when properly nurtured through training, motivation, trust and empowerment can contribute enormously for fulfilling the mission of the organisation.

Continuous Improvement: Continuous improvement is virtually a synonym for Quality. In TQM these changes are improvements for greater customer satisfaction, driven by improvements in technology, human expectations and the need to excel. The dynamic processes of improvement are not by accident but planned improvement process nurtured by TQM. Eventually TQM aims at eliminating defects and errors altogether.

Systemic support: An organisation can be only as good as the management system it practices. The individuals work within the boundaries of its systems. Therefore the operating systems, procedures and practices in a TQM organisation must be in tune with the organisational vision and the principles of TQM which the organisation professes. The processes within the organisation must be subjected to constant scrutiny and these must be re-engineered in the interests of the objectives of TQM.

Systems and Total Quality

The superstructure for the House of Total Quality involves a system composed of three sub-systems held together by total quality (Figure 2.3). The three subsystems are management, social, and technical. The successful implementation of total quality and continuous improvement efforts requires the redefinition of management to recognise the importance of the systems. Deming states; "The people work in a system. The job of the manager is to work on the system, to improve it continuously, with their help". Within the House of Quality the manager must work on the three systems.

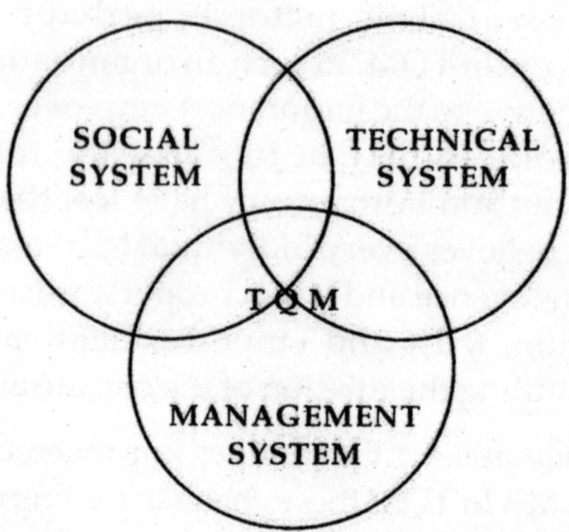

Fig. 2.3: Total Quality as a Management System

The Social System

The social system includes factors associated with the formal and informal characteristics of the organisation: (1) organisational culture (the values, norms, attitudes, role expectations, and differentiation that exist in each organisation); (2) quality of social relationships between individual members and among groups, including reward structures and symbols of power; and (3) behavioural patterns between members, including roles and communication. It is the social system that has the greatest impact on such factors as motivation, creativity, innovative behaviour, and teamwork. Managers have a major responsibility for the nature and character of the social system.

The social system may or may not have a planned function within the organisation. Many managers would like to deny, or at least ignore, the existence of cultures, roles or organisational values. However, social systems exist, and they exert influence, both positive and negative, on the activities of an organisation.

To achieve total quality, a social system must be developed in which constituent or customer satisfaction, continuous improvement, management based on facts, and a genuine respect for people are accepted practices of the college or university. Frequently this requires a substantial change in the social system, and change does not come easily for most colleges and universities. Change usually occurs when the cost (disadvantages, lost opportunities) of remaining the same becomes greater than the benefit of an alternative condition. Several characteristics of higher education encourage resistance to change, many of which are both intellectually correct and philosophically appropriate.

The Technical System

According to Tribus, (1990) "The technical system includes all the tools and machinery, the practice of quality and the quantitative aspects of quality. If you can measure it, you can probably describe and perhaps improve it using the technical systems approach." The technical system is concerned with the flow of work through the organisation. It is driven by two primary guides: fulfillment of its mission and service to the customer.

The expected benefits from analyzing and improving the technical system(s) are to:

- Reduce (eliminate) waste and rework
- Reduce (eliminate) negative variation
- Increase learning
- Reduce (eliminate) interruptions and idle time
- Save time and money
- Increase employee control over the work process
- Reduce bottlenecks and frustration
- Improve safety and quality of Work-Life
- Increase speed and responsiveness
- Improve customer satisfaction.

The Management System

The management system includes factors associated with (1) the organisational structure (formal design, policies, division of responsibilities, and patterns of power and authority); (2) the mission, vision, and goals of the institution; and (3) administrative activities (planning, organising, directing, co-ordinating, and controlling organisational activities). Management provides the framework for the policies, procedures, practices, and leadership of the organisation. The management system is deployed at four levels:

strategy, process, project, and personal management. These comprise the foundation of the House of Quality.

Organisational Culture

Fixing the vision sets the direction for the organisational ship. Then it is upon the sea of organisational culture that quality improvement efforts must sail if they are to be successful. Organisational culture refers to the patterned ways of feeling, thinking, and acting that are shared by members of the organisation. The specific dimensions of culture include systems and structures, actions, roles, behaviours, attitudes, norms, and values. These dimensions provide the basic assumptions and attitudes on which members operate. They are often so well internalised that they are taken for granted.

Debate exists among academics as to whether organisations have cultures. One should believe that the organisational culture is to be addressed a total quality improvement efforts are to be successful and another believable fact that culture of most colleges and universities are to be transformed if quality improvement efforts are to be made.

The implementation of total quality will call for a major transformation of organisational values, norms, structures and processes. This transformation does not mean that the sequential values of academic freedom, intellectual creativity and the new wisdom must be sacrificed. Old habits based on debated needs will have to be discarded.

If cultural transformation is required, as it is in most cases, then there must be a plan to achieve the transformation. There are nine key steps in cultural transformation process:

* Planning for cultural change
* Assessing the cultural "baseline"
* Training managers and the workforce
* Management adopting and modeling new behaviour
* Making organisational and regulation changes that support quality action.

* Redesigning individual performance appraisal and monetary reward systems to reflect the principles of total quality management.
* Changing budget practices.
* Awarding positive change
* Bring communication tools to reinforce TQM principles.

Several of these steps need to be emphasised. Assessing the culture "baseline" is critical because it provides the data needed to establish priorities for change.

The factors involved in creating an organisational culture are part of a causal hierarchy that initiates and ultimately leads to changing the culture. These are discussed below and presented in figure 2.4.

* *Change in System and Structures:* Modify or change systems and structures to be consistent with the principles of total quality improvement.
* *Change in Actions:* Action should be based on both achieving the vision and mission of the college and university and on the principles of total quality improvement.
* *Changes in Roles:* Management must assume new roles as a facilitator, supporter, provider, creator and promoter.
* *Change in Behaviour:* The changes in the roles of management must be evident in the daily behaviours of the managers, i.e., they must facilitate, support, provide, create and promote.
* *Change in Attitudes:* Behavioural change produces attitudinal change. If you want people to think differently, get them to behave differently first.
* *Change in Norms:* Overtime, changes in roles, behaviours, and attitudes will be collected in changes in personal and organisational norms.
* *Change in Values:* Ultimately, the collective change will affect the values of the organisation and the people who are a part of the organisation.

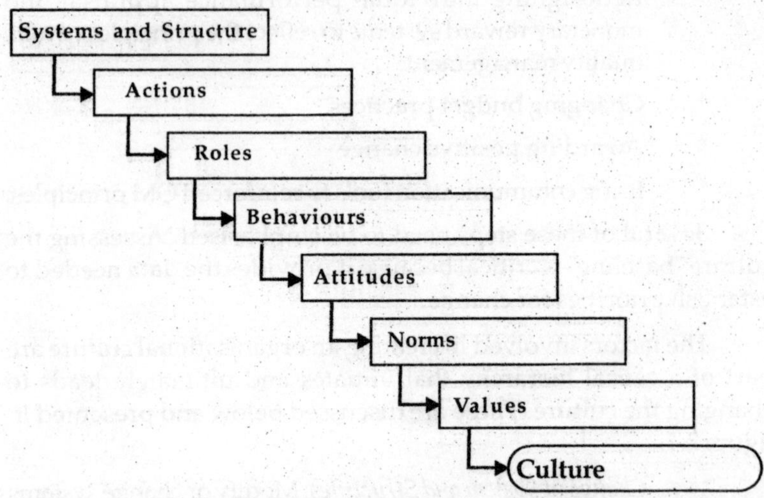

Fig. 2.4: Specific Issues to Address in Transforming the Culture

Total Quality Culture

Management is solely responsible for the transformation of the social system, which is basically the culture of the organisation. It is the social system that has the greatest impact on teamwork, motivation, creativity, and risk taking. How people react to one another and to the work depends on how they are managed. If they enter the organisation with poor attitudes, managers have to re-educate, redirect, or remove them. The social system includes the reward structure, the symbols of power, the relationships between people and among groups, the privileges, the skills and style, the politics, the power structure, the shaping of the norms and values, and the "human side of enterprise", as defined by McGregor (1960).

If a lasting culture is to be achieved, where continuous improvement and customer focus are a natural pattern, the social system must be redesigned so as to be consistent with the vision and values of the organisation. Unfortunately, the social system is always in a state of flux due to pressure from ever-changing influences from the external physical and technological environments. The situation in most organisations is that the impact of total quality is not thought through in an organised manner. Change occurs when the pain of remaining as the same dysfunctional unit becomes too great and a remedy for relief is sought.

There are six areas of strategy must be addressed in order to change and transform the culture of an organisation to a quality-driven organisation as shown in Figure 2.5. These six areas of strategy are considered as dimensions of total quality culture in the present study.

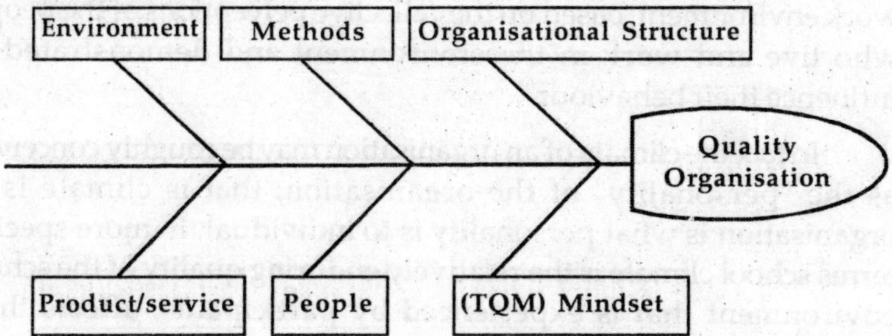

Fig. 2.5: Strategic Areas for Cultural Transformation

- Environment
- Product or Service
- Methods
- People characteristics
- Organisational structure and
- Total Quality Management Mindset (TQM).

Organisational Health

Total Quality Management is apparently related to the nature of work place in educational organisations. The notion of the feel of the work place has been referred to and studied under the concept of climate originated in the late 1950s as social scientists studied variations in work environments. Although researchers interested in educational organisations (Halpin & Croft, 1963; Pace & Stern, 1958) made the initial efforts to define and measure dimensions of organisational climate, usefulness of the concept soon was recognised by scholars of business organisations (Tagiuri, 1968).

Climate initially was used as a general notion to express the enduring quality of organisational life. A particular configuration of enduring characteristics of the ecology, milieu, social system would constitute a climate as much as a particular configuration of personal characteristics constitute a personality. Gilmer (1966) specified organisational climate as "those characteristics that distinguish the organisation from other organisations and that influence the behaviour of the people in the organisation", Lithwin and Stringer (1968) suggested that perception is a critical ingredient of climate and defined it as "a set of measurable properties of the work environment, based on the collective perceptions of the people who live and work in the environment and demonstrated to influence their behaviour".

In fact the climate of an organisation may be roughly conceived as the "personality" of the organisation; that is climate is to organisation is what personality is to individual. In more specific terms school climate is the relatively enduring quality of the school environment that is experienced by participants, affects their behaviour, and is based on their collective perception of behaviour in schools.

Halpin and Croft (1962) viewed organisational climate using a personality metaphor, in which openness of the organisation is analyzed on the basis of distinctive characteristics like high degree of thrust and esprit and low disengagement. Here both the principal and faculty are genuine and open in their interactions. The principal leads by example (thrust), providing the proper blend of direction and support depending on the situation. Teachers work well together (esprit) and are committed to the task at hand (low disengagement). Given the "reality-centered" and considerate leadership of the principal as well as the commitment of the faculty, there is no need of burdensome paper work (hindrance), close supervision (production emphasis), or impersonality and plethora of rules and regulations (aloofness). Leadership develops easily and appropriately, as it is needed. In brief, behaviour of both the principal and faculty is authentic.

Another way of viewing the organisation is by using a health metaphor, in which the general well being of the interpersonal relationships in the organisation is the main consideration. The health metaphor initially was used by Miles (1965) to examine the property of schools. A healthy organisation is one that not only survives in its environment, but continues to grow and prosper over the long term. An organisation on any given day may be effective or ineffective but healthy organisations avoid persistent ineffectiveness.

Miles (1965) developed a configuration of healthy organisation that consists of 10 important properties. The first three aspects reflect the task needs of a social system; the second set of properties describes maintenance needs; and the final group of characteristics are growth and development needs.

First the task needs are (1) Goal Focus (2) Communication Adequacy and (3) Optimal Power Equalisation.

The second set of properties describes maintenance needs (4) Resource utilisation (5) Cohesiveness and (6) Morale.

Finally there are four more properties of organisational health; (7) Innovativeness (8) Autonomy (9) Adaptation and (10) Problem Solving Adequacy.

Healthy organisations have a *Goal Focus*. Participants understand the goals of the organisation and accept them as realistic ends. *Communication Adequacy* is critical in healthy organisations. Information of needs is to travel reasonably well. The system relatively is distortion-free with members easily receiving the information they need to function efficiently.

In healthy organisations there is *Optimal Power Equalisation*. That is, the distribution of power and influence is equitable. The exertion of influence, however, rests on competence and knowledge rather than position, charisma or other factors not related to the problem at hand. Collaboration rather than coercion imbues the healthy organisation.

Healthy organisations has proper *Resource Utilisation*, especially their personnel effectively, There is minimal internal strain; the people are neither overloaded not idle. People in healthy organisations like their jobs and have a positive sense that they are learning and growing as they contribute to the organisation.

Cohesiveness refers to a clear sense of identity participants have with the organisation. Healthy organisations have members who are attracted to the organisation, take pride in their membership and wish to remain. They are proud of the organisation and glad they are a part of it.

Morale is a group concept. It is the sum of individual sentiments, centered on feelings of well being and satisfaction as contrasted with feelings of discomfort and dissatisfaction. In healthy organisations the dominant personal response of organisational members is a sense of well being.

Innovativeness is the organisations ability to invent new procedures, move to new goals and objectives and become more differentiated over time.

Autonomy describes the organisation's relationship with its environment. Healthy organisations use the environment constructively.

Adaptation is closely related to autonomy. Healthy organisations have effective contacts with their surroundings. The organisation has the ability to bring about corrective changes in itself.

All organisations have problems and strains. *Problem-solving Adequacy* describes the way organisations handle their difficulties.

Thus Miles (1965) postulated that healthy organisations are characterized by the ten properties mentioned above.

Attempts have been made to operationalise Miles dimensions of organisational health. But the attempts were unsuccessful in determining the school effectiveness. Then the authors Hoy, Tarter and Kottakamp turned their attention to the theoretical analyses of Parsons, Bales and Shils (1953) and Etzioni (1975) as well as the empirical literature on school effectiveness for a scheme to conceptualise and measure school health. All social systems must solve four basic problems, if they are to survive, grow and develop. In brief healthy schools effectively meet the instrumental needs of adaptation and goal achievement as well as expressive needs of social and normative integration, that is they mobilise their resources to achieve their goals as well as infuse common values into the work group. On the basis of sound theory and as noted by Parsons

(1967), the authors evolved three distinct levels of responsibility and control over these needs (instrumental and expressive). They are (i) Technical Level, (ii) Managerial Level, and (iii) Institutional Level. In the opinion of Parson a healthy school is one in which the Technical, Managerial and Institutional levels are in harmony and the school is meeting both its instrumental and expressive needs as it successfully copes with disruptive external forces and directs its energies towards its mission. In more specific terms seven dimensions (Academic emphasis, Morale, Principal influence, Principal Consideration, Principal Initiating Structure, Resources Support and Institutional Integrity) of school health were conceptualized using Parsonian frameworks.

In the present investigation these seven dimensions and organisation control are used to study the organisation health of teacher education colleges.

Quality of Work-Life

Hersey and Blanchard (1984) in their book 'Management of Organisational Behaviour' defined Quality of Work-Life (QWL) as "the quality of the relationship between employees and the total working environment, with human dimensions added to the usual technical and economic dimensions". As the definition of Quality of Work-Life (QWL) and its characteristics make clear, the goal of Quality of Work-Life (QWL) is the creation of organisational conditions that foster individual learning and development, that provide individuals with substantial influence and control over what they do and how they are to do it, and that provide individuals with interesting and meaningful work that serves as a source of personal satisfaction and a means to valued personal rewards.

Advocates of Quality of Work-Life (QWL) do not believe that the provision of a high quality of Work-Life for members of the organisation must be achieved at the expense of the productivity and effectiveness of the organisation. In fact, the argument made in favor of enhancing the quality of Work-Life is quite the contrary. Quality of Work-Life (QWL) advocates believe that the factors leading to a poor quality of Work-Life for the employees of an organisation are precisely the same factors that account for the declining productivity and effectiveness of many modern organisations.

Characteristics of a High Quality of Work-Life

- Security
- Equitable pay and rewards
- Justice in the workplace
- Relief from bureaucratic and supervisory coercion
- Meaningful and interesting work
- Variety of activities and assignments
- Challenge
- Control over self, work and workplace
- Own area of decision making (or responsibility)
- Learning and growth opportunities
- Feedback, knowledge of results
- Work authority—authority to accomplish that for which one is held responsible
- Recognition for contributions—financial, social and psychological rewards, status, advancement
- Social support—reliability of others when needed; mutual expectation of sympathy and understanding when needed
- Futures that are viable (no dead-end jobs)
- Ability to relate one's work and accomplishments to life outside the workplace
- Options or choices to suit the individual's preferences, interests, and expectations.

Advocates of Quality of Work-Life (QWL) argue that organisations setting out to provide a high quality of Work-Life for their members will, at the same time, be designing organisations more likely to be effective and to succeed in the modern era of rapid change, unpredictable events, and increasing foreign competition. But how are organisations to accomplish this? How are they to go about establishing a higher quality of work-life for their members, and in the process, more effective and adaptive systems of management?

First, management must seek to establish a good fit between the technical and the social aspects of the organisation. It is no longer acceptable for new technological systems to be designed and implemented without consideration for the impact of the new technology upon the people in the organisation and the nature of their work. If optimal benefit is to be achieved from technological advances, the implementation of new technology must take into account the nature and the needs of the people who will be operating the technological systems. Organisational effectiveness requires that the organisation's technical and social systems be planned and designed in concert with one another.

Organisations must also be designed to permit maximum *adaptability* to changing conditions and to maximize the *motivation* of members to perform effectively. The route to both adaptability and motivation advocated by Quality of Work-Life (QWL) is the use of autonomous or self-managing work groups as the primary basis for performing the work of the organisation. The use of such autonomous work groups can facilitate motivation since the members of the group will experience a high degree of freedom and personal responsibility, and also will perform a variety of challenging tasks in order to complete the overall primary task for which they are responsible. Adaptability is increased since the groups are self-managing and contain individuals with many different skills.

Finally, the Quality of Work-Life (QWL) approach emphasises that organisational effectiveness is dependent upon a high degree of commitment on the part of everyone in the organisation to the attainment of organisational goals. Achieving this commitment requires a managerial approach stressing open lines of communication and a high level of participation in the decision-making process by all members of the organisation.

The implementation of Quality of Work-Life (QWL) requires management to adopt a new role and new attitudes towards employees. A High Quality of Work-Life cannot be established in a climate of mistrust and adversarial relationships. High Quality of Work-Life demands that management view employees as cooperating members of a single team. The manager must become less a directive supervisor and more a coach or helper available to provide assistance and support when these are required.

Change Facilitator Styles of Principals

Lieberman and Millez (1981) observe that without question in efforts to improve the quality of schooling "the principal is the critical person in making change happen".

Reinhard et al. (1980) studied the behaviour of principals who supported or hindered a change, which had been government funded. They examined four distinct phases of the change process: planning and initiation, building a temporary operating system for the project, developing and implementing, and institutionalising the change. During the first phase, the principals' agreement with the project was crucial. It was also imperative that the principals communicate their enthusiasm to others. Successful projects were characterised by the principal being actively involved and positive in selling the project. The main role of principals in the development and implementation phase was the demonstration of interest, the making of suggestions for problem solution, and the gradual turnover of responsibility for the project to others. Institutionalisation occurred only when the principals demonstrated continued commitment and provided adequate resources.

Change Styles of Principals

Extensive research related to the role of the principal as change facilitator has been conduced in the University of Texas Research and Development Center for Teacher Education (Hale et al., 1983; Rutherford et al., 1982). These researchers have adopted a category system developed by Thomas (1978) of the behaviour of principals related to the facilitation of alternative programs. The three styles identified were:

Detector: the principal who makes the procedural and substantive decisions in the school at both the classroom and school level and who involves the teacher in decision making in a consultative manner while always retaining the final decision-making authority.

Administrator: the principal, who separates procedural from substantive decisions, allows teachers autonomy in their classrooms but makes those decisions, which affect the whole school himself. This principal tends to identify more with district management than with the staff.

Facilitator: the principal who perceives support of the staff as the primary function. Concern is more with process than with procedures. Collegial relationships with the staff are crucial and, therefore, staff members are actively involved in the decision-making process. The University of Texas Researchers investigated the categories as they emerged in various innovation efforts and identified three distinct styles of facilitating change.

Responder: allows opportunities for teachers and others to take the lead. They perceive their primary role to be maintaining a smooth-running school by keeping up with administrative tasks and treating students and teachers well. These principals believe their teachers are professionals who know how to do their jobs. They frequently give people the opportunity to make decisions. Their own decision-making focus tends to be short-ranged rather than long-termed. They like to please people and are frequently limited in their ability to see the future of their school.

Manager: responds to situations and initiates changes. Their response to change is related to their rapport with teachers and central office as well as the relative importance of the change effort. They work behind the scenes to provide the resources their teachers need to bring about the change and keep their teachers well informed of decisions. They become involved with their teachers to meet demands from central office and try to shield them from undue stress. They do not, however, typically initiate attempts to go beyond what is imposed.

Initiator: are characterized by clear long-ranged policies and goals, which go beyond but include the specific program change. Decisions are made on their view of what will create the best school in the future in light of student teacher abilities and interests. They have high expectations for students and staff. They actively seek changes in program policy or reinterpret it to meet the needs of their school. They seek input from teachers in decision making but final decisions are made in terms of the goals of the school. (Hall et al., 1983, 1984). The initiators are those who effect more successful changes in their schools.

Student Teachers' Commitment to Course

In general terms, commitment refers to the degree that an individual internalises organisational values and goals and feels a sense of loyalty to the workplace. This type of commitment reflects an alignment between individual and organisational needs and values, thereby resulting in a strong unity of purpose among workers and work groups. Katz and Kahn (1978) discussed commitment as an intrinsic motivation factor where the internalisation of organisational values represents a more powerful source of employee motivation than rule compliance or extrinsic rewards. Commitment does not depend on coercive control or a continual stream of rewards but is self-sustaining once it is achieved.

Etzioni (1961) made an important conceptual distinction between two types of commitment: "calculative" commitment and "moral" commitment. Calculative commitment embodies cognitive decision processes of weighting alternatives and costs/benefits in individual decisions to stay with or leave the organisation. Becker's (1960) notion of "side bets" is often discussed here. Side bets are perceived individual investments in an organisation (for example; salary, pension, and status) that figure in considerations to stay or leave. Moral commitment, on the other hand, is a distinct attitudinal component addressing the individual's internalisation of organisational values. This idea of the individual internalising organisational values provides an important perspective on employee motivation, particularly in organisations like schools where normative and symbolic control take precedence over material incentives and rewards (Meyer & Rowan, 1978; Weick, 1976; Weiner, 1982).

Much of the research on organisational commitment has used a three-part definition of the construct developed by Porter and his colleagues (Mowday et al. 1982; Mowday, Steers, & Porter, 1979; Porter, Steers, Mowday, & Boulian, 1974). These components are (a) the willingness of the individual to exert effort on behalf of the organisation, (b) a desire to stay with the organisation, and (c) acceptance of its major values and goals. The first component is almost synonymous with the idea of work motivation (see Campbell & Pritchard, 1977) and clearly places commitment within the motivational domain. The second component describes loyalty and, like the first, hints of behavioural intentions rather than attitudes per se. Finally, the third component describes an alignment between individual and organisational values and goals that allows the organisation to achieve its ends.

The research on organisational commitment has covered a range of occupations and job levels in both public and private organisations. Human service and public service workers, such as nurses, mental health workers, and federal employees, have received particular attention because these are occupations bearing some resemblance to the occupation of school teacher. A study by Hrebiniak and Aluto (1972) compared the organisational commitment of elementary and high school teachers to that of nurses and found identical levels of commitment and no moderating effects of occupation on relationships between commitment and antecedent variables. Hence, even though this body of research does not focus heavily on school teachers, it does have some relevance to the extent that findings generalise across similar occupational types. The researches tended to be correlational, focusing on relationships between organisational commitment and hypothesized antecedents and outcomes.

Organisational commitment is a highly appropriate school effectiveness construct, especially for urban schools serving disadvantaged students. Teacher organisational commitment addresses three important facets of an effective school: the teachers' work effort required to successfully teach students who do not easily learn, the staff loyalty needed to create an enduring school culture of teacher professionalism and academic excellence, and staff agreement about the school's basic educational values and goals. Organisational commitment represents a powerful motivational force in schools given that other motivational means, such as extrinsic rewards or bureaucratic rules, are not very feasible.

In summary, commitment to student learning is grounded in the ideas of high teacher efficacy and high expectations, while adding a third supporting dimension of teacher willingness to exert effort on behalf of low-achieving students. The efficacy and expectations researches provide support for a linkage between commitment to student learning and student achievement, although the causal direction of this relationship is open to question. Like organisational commitment, commitment to student learning is a school effectiveness variable deserving further study. What this facet of teacher commitment adds is a stronger focus on students, teaching, and the central student achievement mission of schools.

The central premise of this study is that organisational commitment and commitment to student learning address distinct but equally important teacher attitudes for an organisationally effective school, an idea that has some support in the literature but requires further empirical validation. There are at least three theoretical linkages between these commitments and school organisational effectiveness. First, both commitments reflect teacher willingness to go beyond the minimum role requirements of the job, to seek solutions to educational problems, and to ensure that all students succeed. Second, commitment to student learning should result in more effective instructional behaviours, increased student commitment to school, and, ultimately, higher student achievement. Third, organisational commitment should result in reduced staff turnover and, consequently, a strong school culture rather than a school fragmented by changing actors and shifting values and goals, which is often the situation many schools.

It is an important ingredient for successful training program. Conceptually, this type of commitment speaks to increasing teacher trainees engagements in training course and academic achievement. The present study focuses on teacher trainees work effort, work attitude, engagements, participation in co-curricular activities at the college and practicing schools, and loyalty to college work.

The succeeding chapter gives details of the previous studies.

3

Review of Related Literature

Introduction

A wide survey has been made on the area of Total Quality Culture, Organisational Health, Quality of Work-Life, Students' Involvement, Students' Commitment and Change Facilitator Styles of Principals. While surveying it was found that the previous studies on Organisational Health, Total Quality Culture, Quality of Work-Life, Students' Involvement, Students' Commitment and Change Facilitator Styles of Principals were very meager and hence the researcher has made a survey of the related fields. They are presented in the form of abstracts in the present chapter chronologically.

Previous Studies

Franklin (1975) in his study on "Organisational Climate and Teacher Morale in Colleges of Education in Gujarat" arrived at the following findings.

(i) The openness of climate in contrast to closedness of the climate did not lead to 'high' or 'low' effectiveness of the teacher education program. However, the dimension "Esprit" indicated a significant effect on the low side.

(ii) The background of the teacher educators in colleges of education in Gujarat did not show any marked difference under the six climate categories, viz. the open, the autonomous, the controlled, the familiar, the paternal and the closed.

Gupta (1977) studied "Some Inputs for Improving Education of Secondary School Teachers (B.Ed. level) in Punjab".

The study covered all the seventeen colleges of education in the state of Punjab and one of the important objectives was to locate and select the tools to assure the selected inputs, viz. Organisational climate of colleges of Education. It was found that the inputs of organisational climate, leadership style and teacher morale in the colleges of education were not in perfect health.

Sharma (1982) conducted a study on "Management of Education Systems with Special Reference to Decision Making and Organisational Health". He selected the educational systems of a Technological University, and Indian Institute of Technology, for his study.

The Study Revealed

(i) relationship between organisational health and existing decisional participation of faculty members was significant.

(ii) there was no significant relationship between organisational health and expected decisional participation.

(iii) factor Analysis revealed that all the ten divisions of organisational health questionnaire were related with one another; only one dominant factor was found out, which was named as organisational effectiveness.

Hall and Guzman (1984) conducted a study on "Sources of Leadership for Change in High Schools".

In examining the dynamics of change processes in high schools, this study makes initial interpretations about school officials who serve as change facilitators. The researchers found that a trend exists for the source of change to come from outside the high school. Principals, assistant principals, and department heads as well as central office staff and teachers are obvious roll groups to take the lead in implementing change in high schools. Some principals do act as a active change facilitators. Department heads, in most cases do not facilitate change implementation. The role assistant principals' play in facilitating change is defined by the principal. If principals are passive than assistant principals maintain the status quo; when active principals involve assistant principals there tends to be a dynamic change facilitating team. The dynamic of the central office is similar to that within the school; if the superintendent or the assistant sets a priority for change, then the central office staff is active in that direction. In general, teachers rarely act as change facilitators.

Mistry (1985) studied the "Quality of School Life as a Function of Organisational Climate and Pupil Control Ideology". He concluded that quality of school life was found to be directly proportional to their climate.

Huling and others (1985) conducted a study on "High school Principals; Their Role in Guiding Change".

This study, focuses on activities of principals in guiding and facilitating change, on leadership configurations found in high schools, and on how principals interact with other change facilitators during the change process. They found that Principals most often performed a role related to vision and goal setting and least often related to the role of "structuring of the school as a workplace". Schools that were more actively involved in change showed greater principal involvement with structuring the process. Data related to configurations of leadership and the change facilitating roles of principals support the contention that, despite the myriad roles that principals assume, they are capable of maximizing their time and decision making opportunities.

Evans (1988) conducted a study on "Teachers' Perceptions of Principals' Change Facilitator Styles in Schools that Differ According to Effectiveness and Socio-economic Context".

The purpose of this study was to investigate the various ways principals provide leadership for school improvement efforts and the relationship of these styles to school effectiveness in various socio-economic contexts.

The instrument used for data collection, "Indicators of Change Facilitator Style of Principal" by Bost and Ruch (1995), consists of thirty six items directly related to the change facilitator style model developed by Hall (1983). It measured teachers' perceptions of principals' change facilitator styles. The sample for the study included a random sample of teachers in 19 school districts in Louisiana who participated by completing the indicators of Change Facilitator Style of Principal Questionnaire.

Results indicated that in less effective schools there were significantly more principals than expected who displayed the Responder change facilitator style. Principals in more effective schools were perceived as exhibiting more initiating behaviours than principals in less effective schools. Results also suggest that a continuum exist between the three styles—Initiator, Manager, and Responder.

Podgurski (1991) conducted a study on "Schools Effectiveness as it Relates to Groups Consensus and Organisational Health of Elementary Schools". When isolated characteristics of schools are studied by researchers or used by administrators to initiate strategies for organisational change, the results are often inconsistent from setting to setting. What works in one setting does not necessarily work in another setting. The complexity of schools calls for the auditing of broad patterns of school processes and careful documenting of contexts. The application of the concept of 'climate' to the assessment of schools provides a holistic framework appropriate to the subject.

Rossmiller (1992) conducted a study on the "Secondary School Principals and Teachers' Quality of Work-Life".

They study shadowed and interviewed eight high school principals to identify and describe how the administrators' actions influenced teachers' quality of working life. Principals positively influenced the respect accorded to teachers, teacher participation in decisions, professional collaboration and interaction, use of skills and knowledge, and the teaching/learning environment.

Larkin (1994) conducted a study on "Faculty Integration in International Schools: An Application of the Organisational Health Inventory to the East Asia Regional Council of Overseas Schools".

The study found that the schools studied succeeded in creating very healthy school environments; on an average the schools were one standard deviation above the U.S. norms in the measure of school health. The two factors most strongly influencing school health were resource support and academic emphasis. The two dimensions most limiting to positive school health were institutional integrity and initiating structure. The investigation of the faculty sub-groups revealed significance in three areas. The results of the Wilks Lambda test for variance indicated that most national teachers view the school environment more positively than do expatriate teachers (F= 3.903, df 7/440, p<0.000). The study concludes that the school environments of international schools contain a variety of factors which promote positive school health and that the faculty sub-groups which promote positive school health in international schools view their schools differently.

Barnes (1994) conducted a study on "The Organisational Health of Middle Schools".

Six dimensions of organisational health in schools became evident after factor analysis. Those factors were identified as: teacher affiliation, collegial leadership, resource support, academic emphasis, institutional integrity and principal influence. The Organisational Health Inventory—(Rutgers Middle OHI-RM) had high reliability and construct validity. The relationships between the various dimensions of middle school organisational health and faculty trust, and faculty decision deprivation were investigated.

Middle school organisational health was found to be positively related to faculty trust in the principal and in colleagues and inversely related to faculty decision deprivation in the classroom and in management decisions.

Smith (1994) conducted a study on "Teacher Quality of Work-Life According to Teacher: the case of High Schools."

Qualitative analyses of 82 teacher interviews conducted during case studies of eight restructuring high schools are drawn on to develop a teacher driven conception of quality Work-Life. A convergence framework of organisational attributes persistently discussed by teachers is constructed. At an elementary level-shared convictions indicate the importance of school organisations that renounce highly bureaucratic postures, procedures and responses. More specifically they suggest categories of organisational conditions which affect teachers' work. These are: conditions conferred upon teachers by others, conditions co-created by teachers and administrators, and conditions teachers develop and sustain themselves. The categories convey teachers' beliefs about where the capacity and responsibility for identified conditions are located and are supportive of restructuring strategies emphasising actionable knowledge for school reform. It is significant that two of the categories indicate that ways quality of Work-Life is shaped by teachers' own attitudes and actions. The framework developed may facilitate school level analysis of teacher quality of Work-Life that progresses beyond extrinsic measures to consider teacher engagement.

A second set of findings addresses divergence within teachers' views. Analyses of divergence reveals how working conditions can support or constrain particular conceptions of teaching and the purpose of high schools. The most striking divergence suggested by the interview data reflects competing conceptions of teachers as either individualistic specialists or as members of collaborative teaching communities. The original convergence framework is modified to illustrate the affect of these conceptions on ideal organisational conditions and norms. Because patterns of conceptual orientations along lines of teacher gender and student socio-economic status are suggested it is recommended that future researches investigate the distribution of conceptual orientations among high school teachers and school communities.

Giard (1994) conducted a study of the "Relationships between the Components of Students' Involvement and Educational Outcomes with the Prospect of Improving Achievement in Québec Cégeps".

This study is concerned with the large numbers of students who failed to reach educational goals, leaving the system without having completed a given cycle, or not meeting expected standards in spite of having obtained a diploma. This study focussed on student involvement as a comprehensive construct mediating relationships between student characteristics and educational outcomes.

Results confirm student involvement provides a plausible explanation for how differently involved students reach different levels of attainment. Students prior performance in secondary school, value attributed to learning, encouragement from parents were found to be positively associated with student involvement, while spending a lot of time on work for pay proves to be negatively associated with the same variable. Time on task, grade expectancies and instruction on study skills were identified as exerting significant influence on the level of participation in college activities, which in turn increases the levels of process and satisfaction reported by students. It was also established that academic performance and persistence in college could be predicted from some preliminary and self-assessment variables, as well as from study compartment, but neither was found directly related to total participation in college activities.

Kells (1994) conducted a study on "Perceptions of Quality of Working-Life in Two Ontario Colleges of Applied Arts and Technology".

This study examined reward characteristics conceptualised by college academic faculty as being important to their quality of life, and perceptions of their actual work conditions. Comparison with conceptualisations and perceptions of faculty Work-Life by college administration were examined and the resulting interrelationships and consequences to the organisation were assessed. The effects of demographic/biographic variables as determinants of faculty work attitudes were explored.

The results indicated that the reward characteristics desired by faculty were predominantly intrinsic in nature, and associated with the demographic organisational processes and values, while their actual work conditions were felt to be those associated with an hierarchical organisation; also, faculty perceptions were significantly different to those of administrative staff.

Jeannett (1995) conducted a study on "Organisational Health and Leadership in Educational Administration".

The purpose of the study was to investigate organisational health as understood and developed by today's administrative leaders. This study focused on six high school principals who were identified as leaders of excellence.

The results revealed principals of excellence as developers of organisational health. These principals attributed meanings to organisational health. Twelve aspects of organisational health were identified. Ten aspects were similar to Miles' (1975) ten dimensions of health. Two additional aspects of trust and humanness were identified. The principals described numerous processes that they used to develop organisational health. Fifty-six themes were identified of which forty-seven were parallel to Miles' (1975) ten dimensions of health. Nine additional themes were identified, which included pro-active leadership, modeling, managing perceptions, using basic operating principals and the importance of building a core team. Maintaining organisational health was described as a process of on going development and change. The principals in this study asserted leadership responsibility for developing the dimensions of health that they identified. This study affirms the importance of principals as leaders in the development of organisational health.

Alkire (1995) conducted a study on "Principal as a Cultural Leader and The Change Process: Elements and Tools that Contribute to Shaping the Elementary School's Organisational Culture".

The purpose of the study was to examine and describe the impact of the application and implementation of organisational cultural elements and shaping techniques on elementary schools by the principals two years or more after the principals had been trained in this approach at the California School leadership academy (CSLA).

Findings: (1) The principals' mean ratings of the application and implementation of the seven elements of organisational culture were significantly higher two or more years after the CSLA training than the mean ratings given prior to the training. (2) the three highest ranked elements contributing the most were "shared values and beliefs", "communication network", and "rules, rewards (norms) sanctions". The three easiest ranked elements were "communication network", "rules, rewards (norms), sanctions", and "physical environment". The top three culture-shaping tools were "managing the communication network", "modeling, teaching, coaching", and "allocating resources, time rewards, and recognition". The same three tools that contributed the most to shaping the schools' culture were the easiest ones to use.

Conclusions: (1) The ratings of the principal's perceptions demonstrated that the application and implementation of the seven elements of the organisational culture had a significant effect in changing their school's organisational culture. (2) The principal's rankings of the elements that "contributed the most" and those "easiest to use", indicated that those that were most productive were also the ones easiest to implement. (3) The data suggested that the principals perceived their training in organisational culture to have been a positive professional experience and enhanced leadership skill. (4) The training in organisational culture was an effective and productive experience regardless of the principals' years of experience.

Babione (1995) conducted a study on "Interaction between Organisational Culture and Process of Continuous Quality Improvement in the Community College Environment".

The purpose of the study was to investigate the interaction of the organisational culture of a community college with the implementation of a program of continuous quality improvement (CQI). The culture frame was used because it provides a useful lens for examining how organisations create social order to manage their external and internal environments.

The results indicated that the existing culture is characterized by the passive mistrust among college personnel due to cultural fragments from and conflicts among sub culture members. This mistrust has evolved over a number of years. Efforts to change behaviours by changing instructional structures have been minimally successful.

Hillman (1995) conducted a study on "Total Quality Reform (TQR): Restructuring Teacher Education Through the Infusion of Technology and Total Quality Management".

The purpose of the study was (a) to examine the perceived computing and related technology skills of those students completing their student teaching experience at Mississippi state university, (b) to examine and describe the infusion and integration of various technologies into teacher preparation programs, and (c) to examine and describe the use of TQM principals as an underlining management and decision-making process for teacher preparation programs.

The research found the students at MSU who graduated in the spring of 1993 had experiences throughout their course work not unlike those experiences of other students in most colleges of education. Approximately 80% of those students felt it would have benefited them to have more technology experiences integrated throughout their course work.

The researcher concluded that more teacher education faculty teaches about technology than with it. One conclusion drawn was teacher education programs must take heed to the fact that perk-12 teachers need consistent, pragmatic training in the use of various technologies for instructions.

Baughman (1995) conducted a study on "The Contributing Effect of Organisational Health to Organisational Climate in Explaining Public Secondary School Teacher Job Satisfaction (Work Atmosphere)".

The purpose of this study was to examine if organisational health provided a unique contribution to organisational climate in explaining secondary school teacher job satisfaction. Independent variables included organisational health and climate, age, gender, years of teaching experience, educational level, school expenditures per pupil, teacher salary level, socio-economic status and school size.

Results indicated only organisational climate and health were significant in accounting for variance in job satisfaction of secondary teachers ($R^2 = 59.7\%$, $p < \$.001$). Five factors of the work atmosphere were significant in explaining teacher job satisfaction including three from climate: engaged teacher, low frustrated teacher and supportive principal, and two health factors: morale and academic emphasis. The two health factors contributed 7.1% to the cumulative explained variance not explained by factors of climate alone. When controlling for each main independent variable, health ($R^2 = 0.188$) accounted for more of the variability in teacher job satisfaction than climate ($R^2 = 0.122$).

This study supports the potential powerful effect of the work atmosphere on teacher behaviour as well as the distinctiveness and importance of utilising the organisational health construct in describing the school environment. Implications of the findings suggest that the school principal can improve teacher job satisfaction by: (a) being supportive of teachers' social and task needs; (b) eliminating unnecessary non-teaching duties for faculty; (c) providing teachers with autonomy and treating them as professionals; (d) trusting staff; and (e) establishing a serious and orderly learning and teaching environment by setting high expectations for staff and students.

Kyle (1995) conducted a study on "Visionary Leadership and Total Quality Management in Higher Education Administration".

To examine TQM in higher education, the effect of the visionary leader on the TQM culture was studied. The visionary leader was measured by the Leader Behaviour Questionnaire developed by Sashkin. The TQM culture was measured by the TQM Assessment Inventory developed by Sashkin and Kiser.

The study results did not show a strong relationship between the visionary leader and the Total Quality Culture. The literature and personal interview with experts suggest this is effected by a dispersion of leadership throughout the organisation.

In conclusion, proper resources must be allocated by higher education institutions and accurate measurements for progress, must be used to determine if TQM can make higher education more effective and efficient.

Dhiman (1995) conducted a study on "Leadership Implications of Total Quality Management in Higher Education".

The study started with the hypotheses (a) the environment of higher education has changed; (b) the current management paradigm does not work; (c) a new paradigm (TQM) may enable higher education to rely more on performance and less on resources; (d) leadership plays a critical roll in pursuing a new paradigm; it also explored the leadership issues involved in facilitating the transformation from current management paradigm to TQM managed paradigm in order to respond effectively to the changed environment.

The study brought out the following key challenges; (1) unfamiliar business language of TQM; (2) inveterate resistance by the faculty; (3) individualistic reward / evaluation system in higher education; (4)departmental separatism; (5) higher education is trading-based and is resistant to large scale change; (6) TQM is pursued as downsizing measure.

Kehoe (1995) conducted a study on "An Investigation of the Relationship Between the Organisational Structure of the Middle School and School Health".

This study examined the relationship between the structure of a middle school and its organisational health. Schools must take the most effective component of bureaucracy and strike the balance between the organisation's structure and those who work in it. If schools dramatically create a climate that is too formal and centralizes the decision-making power, then that climate may prove to be an unhealthy one.

Robinson (1996) conducted a study on "Total Quality Management in Education: The Empowerment of School Community".

The purpose of the study was to investigate the role of leadership and training and development in the implementation of Total Quality Management, philosophy, and practice in an Australian elementary school.

The focus of the school was quality teaching and learning. A visionary and collaborative leadership style modeled by the principal and leadership team provided the context for teaching and learning programs. Leadership strategy included a team approach to problem solving, collaborative decision making, trust, empowerment, delegation of roles and responsibilities, the provision of opportunities for leadership, continuous improvement of process, and training and development programs for staff and parents. There was a strong evidence to support TQM philosophy, as well as visionary leadership, customer focus, collaborative decision making and empowerment for stakeholders as characteristics of TQM. However, there was insufficient evidence to support continuous improvement of processes, decisions based on facts and data and the provisions of relevant tools as significant issues within leadership practice.

Chang (1996) conducted a study on "Organisational Culture and Total Quality Management".

The researcher used a practical and promising model developed by Quinn (1988) to study the cultural characteristics, which support and facilitate TQM implementation.

The results of this research show that the link between organisational culture and TQM performance is less straightforward than what many studies have suggested. Although different culture profiles are identified in the sample, there is no strong evidence indicating that these cultural groups are significantly different in TQM performance measures.

Gordon (1996) conducted a study on "Readiness for Change Among Urban School Principals: Leadership Style and Other Potential Influences".

This study examined the leadership style and readiness for change exhibited by elementary school principals in two urban school districts. More specifically, the study examined leadership style and four demographic variables; gender, age, highest academic degree earned, and years of principal experience.

The results revealed that significant relationship (alpha level of 0.05) existed between personal readiness for change and leadership style (p=0.009), and also between personal readiness for change and highest earned academic degrees (p=0.019). Principals with a considerate leadership behaviour and those holding a doctorate degree appeared more ready for change. The remaining independent variables gender (p=0.394), age (p=0.350), and years of administrative experience (p=0.801) were not found to be significant with respect to personal readiness for change.

Mazula (1996) conducted a study on "Pupil Control Orientation and Organisational Health in Special Education Schools: A Comparative Analysis".

The purpose of the study was to compare school health and pupil control orientations of regular secondary schools with those of special education schools, schools that educate emotionally disturbed students.

Two hypotheses and one research question relating school type to school organisational health and pupil control orientation were proposed and subjected to statistical analyses. Neither the hypotheses, nor the research questions were confirmed in the study. Special education schools were not shown to be more custodial or less organisationally healthy than regular education schools. Further, there were no relationship between custodialism and organisational health. Alternative explanations were offered regarding the findings of this research.

McDonald (1996) conducted a study on "Total Quality Management: A Case Study of the Cherry Hill Public School's Cherry Hill, New Jersey".

This case study was designed to investigate the New Jersey Cherry Hill Public School implementation of a Total Quality Management (TQM) approach throughout its school organisation.

The data for the study were collected through a variety of techniques using a triangulation approach combining three basic processes: (a) quality self-assessment survey (b) interviewing, and (c) document review.

A major conclusion of the study was that the core values and components of TQM are reflected in the Cherry Hill strategic planning process. Staff perceptions, however, differ regarding the deployment of quality practices.

Wenbourna (1996) conducted a study on "Perceptions of Principal Change Facilitator Style in California Distinguished Schools and Non-Distinguished Schools".

The purpose of the study was to identify which Principal Change Facilitator Style (CFS) is perceived most often by principals and teachers in California Distinguished (CDS) and Non-Distinguished schools (Non-CDS). It was hypothesized that congruence between these perceptions may lead to organisational fitness and school-wide effectiveness. Twenty-six principals (17 CDS and 9 Non-CDS), representing five counties and 13 school districts, participated in this study.

Results indicated that the most frequent change facilitator style across school status is manager. Significant differences were noted between CDS and Non-CDS principals in secondary leadership styles. A greater congruence was noted between principals and teachers in CDS than in Non-CDS schools. The study concluded that congruence has an impact on organisational fitness and school-wise effectiveness.

Chirichello (1997) conducted "A Study of the Preferred Leadership Styles of Principals and the Organisational Climates in Successful Public Elementary Schools in New Jersey".

The purposes of the study were to analyze and identify the preferred leadership styles of principals in successful public elementary schools in New Jersey, and to analyse and identify the organisational climates in the selected schools. The researcher concluded that each principal's preferred leadership style had a tendency to exhibit many of the characteristics of transformational leadership, and each principal had an understanding about cultural leadership. Three principals exhibited some characteristics of transactional leadership. This study also examined the relationship between the preferred leadership style of principal in successful public elementary schools and the teacher's perceptions of the organisational climate in the selected schools. In all six cases, where the preferred leadership style of the principal appeared to be transformational, the school climates were not disengaged or closed. In five schools the climate was open and in one school the climate more engaged than open. Teachers perceived themselves as more intimate or collegial than disengaged. They perceived four principals as more supportive than directive or restrictive. Two principals were perceived as more directive than restrictive.

Pletnick (1997) conducted a study on "Relationship between the Leadership Styles of Middle School Principals and the Stages of Development of Interdisciplinary Teams".

The findings of the study did indicate linkages existing between the principal style and the hierarchical stages of team development.

Sweeney (1997) conducted a study on "The Effects of Self Determination Training on Student Involvement in the IEP Process".

The purpose of the study was to examine the effect of a popular, research-based self-determination curriculum on student involvement in various aspects of the IEP process. The major findings in the study were: (1) Students in the training group attended IEP conferences at greater proportional levels than students in the comparison group, (2) Students in the training group could report a greater number of IEP goals, (3) Students in both the training groups as well as comparison group expressed interest in a wide variety of post school outcomes. The training groups had overall grater per cent agreements between expressed post school outcomes and the returns from IEP.

Shear (1997) conducted a study on "Measuring Student Involvement and Participation in Decision-Making in Public Schools".

The results indicated that the higher a students grand mean on the student involvement and participation scale (SIPS), the more likely he or she is to be satisfied with his/her education and his/her treatment. Approximately, ninety percent of the students stated that they are somewhat very satisfied with their education. Yet, only sixty five percent of the student felt they were treated good to excellent by adults in their school. SIPS revealed that ninety percent of the students believe that increased student involvement will result in some to great improvement in their school.

Tolbart (1997) conducted a study on "Principals as Change Agents".

The primary focus of the study is on understanding what it is to be an urban middle school principal who had the multiple and varied tasks of changing how services are rendered to students, involving teachers in the decision-making process, providing support for teachers as they take on additional responsibility in the school, establishing support systems that encourage teachers to engage in discussions with each other about teaching and learning practices and issues, and organising the organisational structures of the schools to support change intiatives.

The study found that principals who functioned as change agents in their schools derived their understanding of their responsibilities as educational leaders from their personal vision rather than from their professional training. The principals in the study tried to replicate those experiences in their lives that they considered important in their educational development. The principal used the reform initiative as a means of accomplishing the goals derived from their personal vision.

Binkley (1997) conducted a study on 'Implementing the Total Quality Management Philosophy in an Elementary School'. This descriptive case study examined Garden view elementary school which answered this call through the use of total quality philosophy. The implementation of this philosophy is examined through the rules, roles and relationships, which have occurred as a result of the transformation.

Many of the tenets of the Total Quality Philosophy can be viewed at the site. Staff members share in the decision making process of the school, articulate the school's vision, have sought the training needed to make educationally sound decisions based upon current research findings, are not afraid to make mistakes, and participate in the leadership of the business.

While there is confusion as to what constitutes total quality and the tools and techniques are not labeled or used, the essence of continuous improvement is evident at Garden view. A through knowledge of philosophy itself, would improve the understanding of how to implement it on aspects of the school, including the classroom. A formal program for sharing the structures and philosophy with new staff members is needed to sustain the change.

Julia (1997) conducted a study on "Beginning Teachers and Learning in the Work Place".

This study examines the experience of twenty-five beginning teaches over a period of three years in order to find out more about teacher learning. It investigates the issue from three perspectives: teacher as learner; teachers' networks for learning; and the school as a work and learning environment for teachers.

Findings from this study have implications for teacher education and learning in the work place. The study revealed that teachers consistently felt they needed to know more about teaching instructional strategies, subject matter, discipline and students. Both groups reported the need to learn more about instructional strategies. Initially, college-based teachers felt they needed to know more about subject matter whereas, alternate route teachers felt they needed to know more about discipline and students.

In their efforts to know more about teaching, teachers developed a variety of networks, which include other teachers, relatives, school administrators, and even students. Other teachers, however, were their primary resource for learning in the work place.

With regard to school settings more college-based teachers felt their schools were supportive than alternate route teachers. Supportive schools were described as schools that had supportive administrators opportunities for professional growth and development, and opportunity to interact with other teachers in the school.

The study has implications for teacher education, school settings and adult learning. Teacher preparation must be viewed as a long-term process, which spans both the formal teacher preparation phase, and the early ears of teaching when teachers are developing as professionals.

Chenoweth (1997) conducted a study on "Organisational Culture in School Districts: A Phenomenological Perspective".

The purpose of the study was to examine the organisational culture of one school district and the impact of that culture on school district members.

The findings indicated six major themes that serve to describe the culture and the impact of that culture on school district members. The six themes include A Historical View, Leadership, Mission and Focus, Isolation, Ability to Influence the Culture, and Defining the District Culture.

Ethel (1997) conducted a study on "The Principal's Role in Educational Change".

This study is an investigation to identify the behaviours that are perceived by the principal and teachers (in his/her building), as indicators that an innovation should be implemented. The sample of the study was an elementary school principal and the teachers who were implementing the innovation.

The results of this study indicated that change can occur in the elementary school. For change to be successful the principal must have an active role in the change process and support the innovation. The principal must be an effective communicator and have the support and trust of his/her staff. The principal must have a second change facilitator to assist him/her in this process as the principal cannot effect change alone.

Joseph (1997) conducted a study on "The Relationship Between the Quality of School Life and Students' Perception of Power in Middle School".

The study was conducted to determine whether the concept of quality of school life of middle school students' is related to students' perception of their own level of empowerment and students' perception of the kinds of power used in the classroom by their teachers.

The results indicated that (1) there was a statistically significant positive correlation between students perception of their own empowerment and quality of school life (2) students whose teachers used low degrees of both personal and positional power perceived lower quality of school life than students whose teachers used high personal power (with either low and high positional power). (3) students perceived more learner empowerment in the classroom when they perceived their teachers relying more on personal power than positional power.

Ronald (1997) conducted a study on "Organisational Commitment, Professional Commitment and Union Commitment of Teachers in Public Schools in Saskatchewan".

The researcher found evidence, which supported both the presence of the three dimensions of teacher commitment (organisational commitment, professional commitment, and union commitment) as well as the presence of simultaneous commitments to more than one dimensions.

Elizabeth (1997) conducted a study on "A Comparison of Organisational Culture Between Academic Affairs Administrators and Student Affairs Administrators at Selected Institutions of Higher Education".

This study examines the organisational culture through two administrative sub cultures, the academic affairs division and student affairs division, on three different types of campuses.

The conclusions of the study included the following: (a) student affairs administrators generally rated their cultural elements higher than did academic affairs administrators; (b) there were a high number of cultural similarities among the three student affairs divisions; (c) there were few cultural similarities among all the three academic affairs divisions; (d) academic department chairs did not view themselves as part of the academic administrative culture; (e) the primary customer of student affairs divisions was students, whereas the primary customers for academic affairs divisions were the faculty and academic programs; and (f) the qualitative and quantitative inquiry methods complemented each other and allowed for comparison of the administrative sub cultures.

Graham (1997) conducted a study on "Teacher Perceptions and Total Quality Management Teaching Strategies".

The purpose of this study was to examine and determine teacher perceptions of Total Quality Management as they relate to teaching strategies and practices.

Twenty teachers actively involved in their school system's Total Quality Management/Learning Lab Project were interviewed face to face. Initially, a total of ten in-depth questions addressing the incorporation of TQM methods and principals were asked. All 20 teachers agreed that the strategies enhanced their teaching; in turn, student success resulted from positive attitudes, collaboration, and activity variety. Though the methods presented minor difficulties and challenges to one or two teachers, all teachers believed that the use of the methods would only help improve teaching strategies.

Mouristen (1997) conducted a study on "The Development and Application of a Model Total Quality Education Approach in Utha School District".

The costs of Quality Improvement Model was developed and applied to the 40 schools in Utha using financial and enrollment data from the 1994-95 academic year to provide support for Total Quality Education programs.

As findings from the study, the descriptions of the activities that drive the costs of programs related to prevention, testing, at-risk students, and adult/dropouts were compiled. The result showed that districts spending a higher percentage on prevention activities often registered lower overall costs as a percentage of total budget on activities related to quality improvement as defined in the study.

Nielson (1997) conducted a study on "Student Involvement in Graduate Education: Comparison of African, American and White Students".

This study explored the association between race (African, American versus White American) and graduate students' level of involvement in mentoring, networking, and professional development activities as well as the subsequent effect of such student involvement and general satisfaction with campus environment. African, American students in master's and doctoral programs in the colleges of education and Liberal Arts and Sciences at a pre-dominantly white, mid western research university were matched by gender and degree with white students in similar programs. Students were surveyed about the frequency of their participation in various activities typically believed to lead toward professional socialisation, the level of support they received from peers and faculty/professionals in their graduate preparation, presence of a mentor who supported their graduate studies, and their satisfaction with several aspects of the campus environment.

No differences were found in the presence of a mentor by race, gender, or degree objective; approximately half of all students within each category reported having a mentor. Results from the analyses of variance supported the presumption that presence of a mentor and higher degree objective (doctorate) were associated with higher levels of professional support and participation in professional development activities. However, no race or gender differences were found in these areas. White students reported more peer support than African, American students, but no differences were found related to gender or degree objective. Results of the multiple regression analysis supported the conceptual model of student involvement, which suggests that the higher levels of involvement in the educational process are associated with greater satisfaction with the overall campus environment. Also students who reported higher levels of professional support were more satisfied with campus life, and finally, as expected, African, American students reported lower overall satisfaction with campus life than did white students.

Bauerly and Michelle (1997) conducted a study on "The Implementation of Total Quality Management Principals in Minnesota Schools: Evidence From the Field".

This research examined Total Quality Management (TQM) as it is being applied in selected Minnesota high schools. The concepts used to define TQM include: continuous Improvement, Customer Focus, Data Based Decision Making, Leadership, Studying and Evaluating Process, Systems Thinking, and Training. The study was designed to answer the following research questions: (1) To what degree are the principles of TQM being implemented in Minnesota schools? (2) What are the barriers or obstacles preventing implementation of the quality principles? What are the aids to implementation?

The findings of the research led the author to three main conclusions: (1) The seven principles of TQM are been implemented in Minnesota schools, but in varying degrees. Full implementation of all seven principles has not being achieved in any of the site study. (2) some of the principles are not being fully implemented due to lack of training and common understanding about the meaning of the concepts. Training has been fragmented and insufficient in most sites and has therefore not been a significant aid to implementation. The gap in training between administrator and staff is evident in the level of implementation of the principles. (3) the aids to implementation have been leadership and attitudes of the staff. The barriers have been time, staff issues (attitude), and training.

Davis (1997) conducted a study on "The Relationship Between West Virginia Early and Middle School Principal's Leadership Style and School Culture".

This study was designed to investigate the relationships between early and middle school principals' leadership style and school culture, controlling the variable: enrollment, school type, age, gender, years of experience and county. The sample population for principals leadership style was faculty from 97 early and middle schools, in one district from each of the eight West Virginia regions. Each principal of the same schools was surveyed for demographic data. Data were obtained through the faculty completion of a 40 items Leader Behaviour Description Questionnaire, a 38 items Schools Culture Survey, and a research designed Questionnaire.

The study indicated that early and middle school principals' leadership style has profound effect on level of school culture. Initiating structure was strongly associated with a strong school culture. Conversely, a negative association existed between consideration leadership and school culture. Principals' age was also negatively associated with school culture. An ancillary finding showed that males are more likely than females to produce initiating structure leadership.

The findings from the study and resulting conclusions indicated that early and middle school principals' leadership impacted level of school culture. A task-oriented leadership style resulted in a strong school culture. While the reverse was indicated for the relations-oriented leadership.

Gatto (1997) conducted a study on "A Description of the Influence of Culture on the Change Process at Central High".

The purpose of this case study is to examine and report on the change process at Central High. Instead of a traditional schedule a block-schedule format is used to study the change process. This study was completed at a large Mid-western public high school with information gathered during the 1995-96 and 1996-97 academic years. This study identifies the need for those involved in any change efforts to view the change through the lens of the school's organisational culture. The results reveal several components of Central High's culture, including characteristics of the setting and people involved, along with descriptions of steps taken by staff members to work toward improving student learning.

Lok (1997) conducted a study on the influence of "Organisational Culture, Sub Culture, Leadership Style and Job Satisfaction and Organisational Commitment".

The aim of this study is to examine the effects of both organisational culture and sub culture on organisational commitment. Other measures, which have been shown to be related to either organisational commitment or organisational culture, are also included in the study. These are leadership style, job satisfaction and demographic variables such as age, education, years in position and years of experience. A questionnaire survey was used which was complemented by semi-structured interviews. It was found that organisational sub culture had a greater impact on commitment than organisational culture. Innovative and supportive sub cultures had a positive effect on commitment and a bureaucratic sub culture had a negative effect on commitment. The leadership style variable, consideration, also exerted a relatively strong influence on commitment when compared with other variables included in the study.

The results of the study also revealed that the job satisfaction dimensions with significant associations with commitment were control, professionalism and interaction. The effect of the culture and leadership style variables on commitment was found to be significantly reduced, but not totally eliminated, after statistically controlling for job satisfaction variables. Age showed a direct positive influence on commitment. However, the level of education, years in position and years of experience failed to show any impact on commitment.

Thomas (1997) conducted a study on "Perceived Levels of Success of a Total Quality Management Program in an Institution of Higher Learning".

The purpose of the study was to provide the base line data and information on the perceived levels of success of Total Quality Management (TQM) efforts at a university that is currently employing the process. An analysis was conducted to determine if faculty members and administrators differed significantly in their perception of the efficacy of these TQM efforts. Additional analyses were accomplished to determine if the differences in perceptions were a function of various demographic characteristics of the respondents.

A stratified random sample consisting of 285 faculty members and 186 administrators was drawn to insure a 95% confidence level. Respondents were asked to complete the University Quality Profile which is based on the seven Malcolm Baldrige National Quality Award indices for measuring quality in education. In order to test the null hypotheses a multivariate analysis of variance (MANOVA) was used. The MANOVA indicated that none-of the Baldrige sub scales were significantly different overall accept for the Customer/Student Focus and Satisfaction category. Administrators perceived a higher level of success than did faculty members.

Joffres (1998) conducted a study on "Beyond Organisational Commitment: Selected Elementary School Teachers' Work Commitments".

The purpose of the study was to better understand the experiences of commitment of selected elementary school teachers participants were full time teachers and worked in elementary schools. Fourteen teachers (three males and eleven females) participated in the study.

Teachers indicated that they experienced multiple commitments. They suggested that their main commitments were to the children, their growth and learning, their colleagues, the children's parents, the their administrators. Nonetheless, commitments varied in foci and intensity throughout the teachers' careers. The rise and fall of the story tellers' commitments were influenced by the teachers' experience of positive and negative events, and degree to which they felt successful in their work communities.

Commitments to teaching was influenced by the story tellers' feelings of performance efficacy and their relationship with the community members. When teachers experienced high feelings of efficacy and deep feelings of community with the community members, their commitment to teaching increased, along with their commitments to the community members and work communities. Alternately, when story tellers felt unsuccessful (e.g., low feelings of performance efficacy and poor relationship with the community members) and when they attributed their lack of success to specific community members, their commitments to these community members and work communities decrease. Story tellers suggested that their commitment to teaching only decreased when they felt powerless to influence the children's learning and other community members and when they experienced deep feelings of hopelessness.

Carey (1998) conducted a study on "Total Quality Management in Higher Education: Why it Works; Why it Does Not".

The purpose of the study was to analyze the rationale expressed by presidents of four year, public colleges and universities in the United States for deciding to implement Total Quality Management (TQM) on their respective campuses.

The researcher concluded that external environmental inputs in the form of both demands and supports influenced presidents to implement TQM programs on their campus. Both forms of inputs emanated from the state governing bodies, which demanded increased accountability while simultaneously decreasing institutional funding. Further, the internal factors of dissatisfaction with past management practices and declining budgets within the political system also influenced the presidents to implement quality initiatives.

Frueauff (1998) conducted a study on "Organisational Health and the Influences that Enable and Constrain the Development of Healthy School".

The purpose of the study was to determine what enables and what constrains the development of healthy schools. Two widely divergent schools were selected from among five schools following an analysis of the Organisational Health Inventory that was administered to teachers in those schools. The qualitative component of the study examined these two schools through open-ended interviews with 12 teachers in each school. The school found to be the most healthy exhibited the following enabling conditions: extensive support by parents and community; a strong system of communication within the school and outside the school; a welcoming school atmosphere; a supporting environment for staff; a pro active problem solving process; a collegial workplace; provision of adequate supplies and materials; a tone of trust, loyalty and commitment; an ability to influence superiors; and focus on the academic purpose of the school. The school found to be the least healthy exhibited conditions that inhibited or constrained the development of good health.

Ford (1998) conducted a study on "A Multi-Site Case Study of Total Quality Management within a Texas School District".

Procedure: Using a multi-site case study methodology, this investigation examined administrator and teacher concerns regarding the impact of Total Quality Management on three campuses within the McKinney independent school district. The sites studied were McKinney High school, Webb Elementary school, and a Valley Creek Elementary school.

Findings: Using a pattern-matching of the stages of concern questionnaire, interviews, and participant-observer observations, the investigation found evidence of high 'awareness' of Total Quality Management principles and concepts among staff of sites studied. The respondents communicated low levels of collaboration on the stages concern questionnaire.

Turan (1998) conducted a study on "A Study of Organisational Climate and Organisational Commitment in Human Organisations".

The purpose of the study is to examine the relationship between organisational climate and organisational commitment of teachers in secondary public schools in the city of Bursa in Turkey. Specifically the objectives of this study was to determine the strength of the relationship between each dimension of organisational climate (supportive principal behaviour, directive principal behaviour, engaged teacher behaviour, frustrated teacher behaviour, and intimate teacher behaviour), as measured by the Organisational Climate Description Questionnaire for secondary schools. (OCDQ-RS), and Organisational Commitment of teachers, as measured by the Organisational Commitment Questionnaire (OCQ).

The study concludes that there is a significant relationship between organisational climate of the school and teachers' organisational commitment. Furthermore, this study conforms that OCDQ-RS and OCQ are stable across cultural settings. Organisational Climate of the school provides an overall information about the nature of the leadership behaviour (supportive and directive) and teacher behaviour (engaged, frustrated, and intimate) that can be used to describe the quality of life and teachers' identification with their schools.

McMillan (1998) conducted a study on "Total Quality Management in Higher Education: A Study of Senior Administrators Perceptions About Total Quality Management in Institutions of Higher Education in Ohio".

The central goal of this study is to determine and compare senior administrators' knowledge, participation, and attitudes about TQM. A secondary function is to determine and compare to what extent senior administrators perceive TQM to be relevant and useful in solving some of higher education's salient issues and problems. The existence of TQM in institutions in Ohio was also explored within the scope of the study.

Findings of the study revealed that the implementation of TQM recently started in higher education in Ohio. Senior administrators in Ohio possess very positive attitude towards TQM, were moderately highly knowledgeable about TQM, and found TQM to be moderately to highly relevant to higher education's issues and problems. However, they had very low TQM participation rates. Institutions of higher education in Ohio have moderately participated in TQM and senior administrators perceived the president's or chancellor's endorsement and support of TQM from below. TQM program existence and participation rates were highest at two-year community colleges, four-year public institutions, two-year technical colleges, and four-year private institutions respectively.

Millard (1998) conducted a study on "Perspective of Leaders in Educational Change".

This study focuses on the perceptions and experiences of six leaders in education change, administrators who have been placed in positions that required them to provide leadership to many people. They provide leadership beyond one school site, either at a school jurisdiction level or at provincial level.

Paul (1998) conducted a study on "The Relationship Between the Principles of Total Quality Management and School Climate, School Culture and Teacher Empowerment".

The purpose of the study was to investigate the relationship among the principles of Total Quality Management and (a) school climate, (b) school culture, and (c) teacher empowerment.

Findings: Eleven of the fourteen principles of total quality management showed high correlations with school climate and teacher empowerment sub-scales. Nine of these principles had strong correlations with school climate sub-scales. Strong predictive relationships were found between the principles of Total Quality Management and each of the dependent variables.

Rodgers (1998) conducted a study on "Teacher Perceptions of Total Quality Management Practices in Elementary Schools".

The purpose of the study was to explore the extent of Total Quality Management practices in Maricopa County public schools. The second purpose was to determine if total quality management practices have an impact on public schools in the following areas: (1) strategic planning, (2) data analysis, (3) staff training, (4) faculty and staff involvement, (5) employee satisfaction, (6) student involvement (7) evaluation of services, (8) customer satisfaction (9) student achievement. The study found that one of the 56 public school districts in Maricopa county was implementing total quality management practices. There was a significant difference between teachers' perceptions in a Total Quality School versus teachers in a non-total quality schools in all nine surveyed areas. Total Quality Management teachers report high morale and job satisfaction.

Students are aware of their learning outcomes and are able to assess their accomplishments. Evaluation of services is carried out by the faculty.

Obisesan (1998) conducted a study on "Quality Management and System Change in Three Suburban Public School Districts".

Quality Management (QM) is a problem-solving and systems approach to the change process that promotes communication among members and enhances leaders' commitment to continuous improvement, efficiency of operations, increased productivity. Although QM of Deming has been successfully implemented in Japan as well as in the United States manufacturing industry, its potential for improving the educational systems has not been widely examined. Research suggests that the traditional ways of managing schools can not help schools survive in the next century. This study use the qualitative methods to examine the extent to which QM enhances system change through the analysis of implementation of the philosophy in three suburban school districts in the north-eastern part of the United States. Specifically, they:(a) assessed the impact of QM on the productivity and efficiency of the three school districts, (b) validated the potential of QM in sustaining systemic changes in the school organisations, and (c) ascertained whether or not QM can be extended to mean the needs of other school districts. The study used a 3x6 comparative matrix case design and examined the leadership efforts and the implementation styles of QM, issues amenable to QM, analysis of communication and collaboration on the QM process, and the quality outcomes to assess the difference between the past and the present. The study covered a 12-month period and used interviews, observation and document analysis of the Miles and Huberman data collection, and the Strauss comparative method of analysis.

The results indicated that: (1) QM influenced leadership motivation for change and fostered three different collaborative implementation styles. (2) QM was found to be adaptable to improving key school issues: human resource development, academics, discipline, budget, and social association based on team efforts and problem-solving approaches and practices. (3) It facilitated communication within organisations, including sharing of information through regular accountability, assessment, and planning team meetings. (4) QM team structure facilitated collaboration among different members, departments, and buildings that evolved in to relationship development. (5) QM fostered teachers' expansion of knowledge based on collaborative experiences resulting in quality teaching: students' attitude change, high student achievement, and yearly increases in graduation rate. (6) QM helped people think to operative efficiently, resulting in improved budgetary management.

Finkelstein (1999) conducted a study on "The Effects of Organisational Health and Pupil Control Ideology on the Achievement and Alienation of High School Students".

This researcher focused on how two dimensions of school climate, organisational health and Pupil Control Ideology, affect a school's primary beneficiaries, the students. Further the research sought to establish the usefulness of the dimensions as predictors of selected student outcomes.

The school was the unit of analysis in the study. The sample consisted of 41 New Jersey high schools. These schools represented wide range of socio-economic status as well as rural, and urban, and sub-urban areas. Data were collected from each faculty at a regularly scheduled faculty meeting and survey forms with instructions were placed in their mailboxes. The faculty members, selected at random filled out either the Organisational Health Inventory, Pupil Control Ideology form or the student control ideology form, a revision of the PCI. Each of these instruments was designed to measure selected dimensions of school climate.

Eight hypotheses were tested in the study. Three were supported by the data; organisational health is related to student achievement, organisational health and pupil control ideology are related to student alienation and an inverse relationship between organisational health and pupil control ideology. As health rises, custodiolism decreases. There was no relationship found between pupil control ideology and student achievement, and student control ideology did not correlate with either pupil control ideology or organisational health.

Richardson (1999) conducted a study on "Perceptions of the Preparedness of Teacher Educator Students for Teaching: A Case Study".

The focus of the study is to understand dimensions of the sense of preparedness that relate to the experiences of student teachers and their supervisors at completion of their student teaching experience. The student teachers participating in this study were involved in completing the requirements for baccalaureate degrees in elementary education at Ohio University's College of Education. The study enabled the researcher to examine the abilities of two prospective teachers their perceptions related to their sense of preparedness. The researcher also examined the perceptions of preparedness of personnel critical to the student teaching experience. In this case, two co-operating teachers and university supervisor.

The study was explanatory in nature and investigated the phenomenon associated with two pre-service teachers selected from different preparation programs, and their sense of preparedness for beginning their professional careers. The beliefs of the two student teachers selected for this study with regard to their sense of preparedness were determined by conducting two-hours semi-structured interviews with each student teacher. Questions were asked to elicit information with respect to beliefs about one's ability to teach elementary education subjects.

As a result of the study several pertinent issues emerge as worthy of being investigated. There is a viable evidence that indicates students in Ohio University's College of Education are well-prepared in content knowledge. They complete student teaching successfully and feel confident to enter their professional careers.

One of the conclusions of the study is that concentrated practical classroom experiences equip the pre service teacher with a greater sense of preparedness. This sense of preparedness is perceived prior to student teaching, and is reaffirmed during the student teaching experience.

Holt (1999) conducted a study on "Relationship Between the Organisational Health of Selected Public Schools in Texas and Strategies for Communicating With the Public".

The purpose of the study was to determine if there is a relationship between the schools' organisational health as perceived by the principals and the strategies utilised by the schools to communicate with various stake holders about school reform.

A survey containing 26 questions based on a 5-point Likert rating scale was utilised. The survey was responded to by 101 elementary principals from 26 school districts reflective of the varied demographics in the state of Texas. SPSS a statistical package, was use to create, administer, and analyze the survey.

This study determines the degree to which principals perceived they utilized the following 12 indicators of organisational health: goal focus, communication, enterprise wholeness, power equalisation, human resources utilisation, cohesiveness/morale, innovativeness, diversity, autonomy, adaptation, accountability, and problem-solving. The scores for these indicators were totaled for each school, rank-ordered, and divided in to quartiles representing four levels of organisational health. Significant differences in relation to the degree of organisational health were exhibited between all groups.

Colegrove (1999) conducted a study on "Total Quality Management at a Southwest School District: A Case Study of Practicing Educators".

This study examined the perceptions of practicing educators in a school district that had used Total Quality Management. The research used information from practicing educators to discern how Total Quality Management affected the following factors in schools: school climate, relationships between administration and teachers, and decision-making. The research also discussed what practicing educators felt were the benefits and what they felt were less successful aspects of Total Quality Management.

Critchley (1999) conducted a study on "The Nature and Extent of Student Involvement in Educational Policy Making in Canadian School Systems".

The study examines the nature and extent of student involvement in educational policy-making in Canadian education systems in order to find out how much of a role students have in helping to shape the education systems that serve them. Participants for the study consists of ministers of education (or their designates,) directors of education or school district superintendents at the school district level, high school principals and high school students from across Canada. All participants contributed to the data collection for this study by completing a written questionnaire.

The study shows that education system across Canada do involve students in policy-making at the department, school district and school levels, but only in an advisory capacity. The study shows that although there is a favourable reaction by stakeholders across Canada to student involvement in educational policy-making, student involvement is restricted to providing policy-makers with information. Students do not have a formal role to play in policy-making at the department, school district, and school.

Ronne and Jeffry (2000) conducted a study on "The Urban School Leader as a Change Agent: Case Studies of Three Urban School Principals".

The purpose of the study was to discover the critical dimensions of leadership demonstrated by three urban school principals who have successfully facilitated change in their schools, and the strategies and the skill they practice to create that change. Case studies of three urban school principals, utilising qualitative and quantitative methods of research, were used to investigate the research question. The principals identified for these case studies were selected because they have been recognised as outstanding urban school principals. A survey tool was administered to teachers in each school in order to identify critical dimensions of leadership, and the following qualitative methods were used to reveal the skills and the strategies practiced by each principal that facilitate change: principal and teacher interviews, observations, and document analysis.

The study led to the conclusion that a strong commitment to personal vision drives school visions and facilitates change. It was also concluded that each of the seven dimensions of the leadership, as well as the emergent critical dimension, builds external support, and is critical to creating change, and that despite differences in personality and leadership style each principal demonstrated successful practices within each critical dimension of leadership.

Watson (2000) conducted a study on "Total Quality Education: A School District's Beliefs, Behaviours, and Outcomes".

The researcher in this phenomenological study examined the perspectives of six key informants concerning the beliefs, behaviours, and outcomes of school system that immersed itself in to Total Quality Education (TQE). The informants were a superintendent, board member, principal, classroom teacher, business/ industry executive, and university representative. The data analysis process began with in-depth interviews of each participant. These interviews were audio taped and transcribed verbatim. The transcriptions were then analysed using a four-step phenomenological process. This process resulted in an understanding of the meanings developed by the key informants. The researcher used nine basic principles of quality that were embedded in the research questions. The nine principles were (a) systems thinking, (b) customer focus (c) leadership, (d) management by fact, (e) continuous process improvement, (f) participatory management, (g) human resource development, (h) team work, and (i) long-term commitment. The study found that the nine basic principles were interrelated. The researcher found that significant cultural changes were identified in the way school district operates as a result of the TQE initiative. The researcher also found many previous methods procedures of operation in the school district had changed as a result of implementing the quality principles and these changes were continuing to evolve.

Astone (2000) conducted a study on "Commitment to College: What it Means and How it Changes, From the Community College Student Perspective".

Students commitment to college is examined through multiple, in-depth interviews with eleven 18-to-20-year-old, U.S.-born students. Interviews were conducted at a large urban community college over the course of students' first two semesters. Interview data are supplemented with college records relating to academic background, basic skills test scores, and first-year performance and progress outcomes. The satisfaction and success of students enrolled in learning communities, curricular structures that actively promote student integration, compared to regular, stand-alone courses, were also examined.

The study finds that students' social capital-in particular, their attitudes and beliefs about learning and themselves as learners, and factors associated with socio-economic status and prior education were related to college commitment. Scarce personal and academic resources were cumulatively and negatively associated with both the nature and quality of initial commitment, and with the quality of academic and social interactions after enrollment. The study suggests that in learning communities, curricular were integrated, active learning strategies were employed, and collaborative, supportive, and community-like atmosphere among teachers and student prevailed, and some performance and progress outcomes and the social integration of participating students were better.

Conclusions

The previous studies on Total Quality Culture, Organisational Health, Quality of Work-Life, Students' Involvement in College Activities, Students' Commitment to Course and Principal's Change Facilitator Styles revealed as below;

Studies on Total Quality Culture emphasised the following facts that are:

(i) continuous qualitative improvement in the organisational culture is based on how organisations create social order to manage their external and internal environments.

(ii) for effective and efficient working of educational organisations the role of visionary leadership has a strong relationship with the Total quality culture.

(iii) the staff perception and their deployment in the strategic planing process of quality practices.

(iv) rules formulated, roles to be played by each members and the relationships maintained within the members helps for the attainment of organisational goals.

(v) implementation of total quality management model in education approach geared the cost effectiveness of education in organisation.

(vi) the rationale to implement total quality management in the campus of an organisations are environment, inputs, political systems, outputs and feed-back.

(vii) the successful implementation of total quality management in teacher education training program emphasised the fact that teacher trainees need consistent pragmatic training in the use of technologies for instruction.

(viii) understanding about the concept and principles of total quality management for staff members, administrators and their attitudes show that there is a need of proper training.

(ix) there is a strong predictive relationship between the principles of total quality management and school climates, school culture and teacher empowerment.

The studies on organisational health revealed that the factors like leadership style, teacher morale and faculty trust in the principal and in colleagues are most important in the development of organisational health in an institution.

Findings on quality of Work-Life conclude that it is directly related to the ideal organisational conditions and norms of the teacher working conditions.

Findings from the studies on students' involvement reveal that the higher levels of involvement in the educational process are associated with greater satisfaction with the overall campus environment.

Organisational commitment in learning communities integrated with curricular active learning strategies, collaborative, supportive and community like atmosphere among teacher and students, some performance and progress outcomes and the social integration of participating students were better.

The studies on change facilitator style of principal reveal that a strong commitment to personal vision, drives school visions and goal setting. A task oriented leadership style resulted in a strong school culture. For change to be successful the principal must have an active role in the change process and support the innovation. He must be an effective communicator and have the support and trust of his/her staff.

Research investment is needed to find out the worth of 'money and time' invested to bring quality culture in education. The research studies undertaken in India on total quality culture are nil and only a few studies are conducted abroad.

Hence, the present investigation aims to study the correlates of total quality culture in teacher education college.

Research Procedure

Introduction

A research study cannot be evaluated unless its procedure is reported in sufficient detail. The investigator should adopt a systematic and appropriate procedure in conducting the research. A careful consideration is being given in the selection of tools, collection of data and analyses of data. The accuracy, reliability and validity of the research findings depend on the correct and careful choice of the tools. The details regarding the choice of the tools, selection of the sample, collection and analysis of data are outlined in this chapter.

Research Design

The present study is a normative survey (ex-post-facto) type research. The research design specifies the questions to be investigated, the process of sample selection, methods of procedure to be followed, measurements to be obtained and comparison and other analyses to be made. The research design of the study is presented in Table—4.1.

The Problem

Correlates of Total Quality Culture in Teacher Education Colleges.

Table—4.1

Research Design

S. No.	*Variable Studied*	*Tools Used*	*Sample*	*Statistics used*
1.	Total quality culture of Teacher education colleges	Total quality culture assessment form	45 teacher education colleges, 260 teacher educators and 31 principals	Descriptive and differential
2.	Organisational health of teacher education colleges	Organisational health inventory	45 teacher education colleges, 260 teacher educators	Correlation ANOVA
3.	Quality of work-life of teacher educators in teacher education colleges	Quality of work-life inventory	45 teacher education colleges, 260 teacher educators	Multiple regression Factor analysis
4.	Student teachers' involvement in colleges activities	Student teachers' involvement in college activities questionnaire	45 teacher education colleges, 260 teacher educators	
5.	Change facilitator styles of principles in teacher education colleges	Change Facilitator Styles of principals inventory	45 teacher education colleges, 260 teacher educators	
6.	Student teachers' commitment to course in teacher education colleges	Student teachers' commitment to course questionnaire	45 teacher education colleges, 900 student teachers	

The Objectives

The present study has the following objectives to study the relationship between:

A. Total Quality Culture and
   (a) Organisational Health
   (b) Quality of Work -Life of Teacher Educators
   (c) Student Teachers' Involvement in College Activities
   (d) Change Facilitator Styles of Principals
   (e) Student Teachers' Commitment to Course
   (f) Sex of College
   (g) Type of Management of College

B. Organisational Health and
   (a) Quality of Work- Life of Teacher Educators
   (b) Student Teachers' Involvement in College Activities
   (c) Change Facilitator Styles of Principals
   (d) Student Teachers' Commitment to Course
   (e) Sex of College
   (f) Type of Management of College

C. Quality of Work-Life and
   (a) Student Teachers' Involvement in College Activities
   (b) Change Facilitator Styles of Principals
   (c) Student Teachers' Commitment to Course
   (d) Sex of College
   (e) Type of Management of College

D. Student Teachers' Involvement in College Activities and
   (a) Sex of College
   (b) Type of Management of College

Hypotheses

Differential Hypotheses

The differential hypotheses of the study are stated below:

Hypothesis 1

Teacher educators of different age groups differ in their perception of Total Quality Culture as a whole and in the following dimensions of Total Quality Culture

(a) Environment

(b) Product and Service

(c) Methods

(d) People Characteristics

(e) Organisational Structure

(f) Total Quality Mindset

Hypothesis 2

Teacher educators of different age groups differ in their perception of Organisational Health as a whole and in the following dimensions of Organisational Health

(a) Institutional Integrity

(b) Initiating Structure

(c) Principal Influence

(d) Resource Support

(e) Consideration

(f) Morale

(g) Academic Emphasis

Hypothesis 3

Teacher educators of different age groups differ in their perception of Quality of Work-Life as a whole and in the following dimensions of Quality of Work-Life

(a) Autonomy

(b) Personal Growth Opportunity

(c) Workspeed and Routine

(d) Work Complexity

(e) Task-Related Interaction

Hypothesis 4

Teacher educators of different age groups differ in their perception of Student Teachers' Involvement in the College Activities

Hypothesis 5

Men and Women teacher educators differ in their perception as a whole and in the dimensions of following variables

(a) Total Quality Culture
(b) Organisational Health
(c) Quality of Work-Life
(d) Student Teachers' Involvement in College Activities

Hypothesis 6

Teacher educators with different specialisation differ in their perception as a whole and in the dimensions of the following variables

(a) Total Quality Culture
(b) Organisational Health
(c) Quality of Work-Life
(d) Student Teachers' Involvement in College Activities

Hypothesis 7

Teacher educators with different designations differ in their perception as a whole and in the dimensions of the following variables

(a) Total Quality Culture
(b) Organisational Health
(c) Quality of Work-Life
(d) Student Teachers' Involvement in College Activities

Hypothesis 8

Teacher educators with different years of teaching experience differ in their perception as a whole and in the dimensions of the following variables.

(a) Total Quality Culture

(b) Organisational Health

(c) Quality of Work-Life

(d) Student Teachers' Involvement in College Activities

Hypothesis 9

Teacher educators working in different college sex differ in their perception of as a whole and in the dimensions of the following variables

(a) Total Quality Culture

(b) Organisational Health

(c) Quality of Work-Life

(d) Student Teachers' Involvement in College Activities

Correlational Hypotheses

The correlational hypotheses of the study are stated below;

Hypothesis 1

Total Quality Culture and its dimensions significantly correlate with

(a) Organisational Health and its dimensions

(b) Quality of Work-Life and its dimensions

(c) Student Teachers' Involvement in College Activities

(d) Student Teachers' Commitment to Course

Hypothesis 2

Organisational Health and its dimensions significantly correlate with

(a) Quality of Work-Life and its dimensions

(b) Student Teachers' Involvement in College Activities

(c) Student Teachers' Commitment to Course

(d) Change Facilitator Styles of Principals

Hypothesis 3

Quality of Work-Life and its dimensions significantly correlate with:

(a) Student Teachers' Involvement in College Activities

(b) Student Teachers' Commitment to Course

Tools

The tools that are used for the present study are described in detail in the following pages.

Total Quality Culture Assessment Form

This inventory is developed and standardised by Lewis and Smith (1994). It consists of seventy one items under six dimensions, to be responded on a five point scale as 1-definitely applies, 2-some what applies, 3-neutral, 4- does not apply, 5-definitely does not apply.

The details regarding six dimensions and number of items under each are given in Table—4.2.

Table—4.2

Dimensions of Total Quality Culture

	Dimensions	*Number of Items*
A	Environment (ENV)	11
B	Product & Service (PS)	05
C	Methods (MET)	08
D	People Characteristics (PEO)	10
E	Organisational Structure (OS)	10
F	Total Quality Mindset (TQM)	13
	Total	**57**

The investigator has modified the tool and reduced the number of items to fifty-seven. This inventory has been revalidated by calculating validity and reliability coefficients. It was administered to all teacher educators and Principals of teacher education colleges.

Reliability and Validity

In the present study the reliability of the tool was established by test and retest method and the correlation between the two tests worked out to be 0.71. The validity was established by taking the square root of reliability and it was 0.87. Thus this tool is found to be reliable and valid.

Organisational Health Inventory

Organisational Health Inventory of Hoy and Feldman (1987) is a four point Likert type rating scale. The OHI contains forty four statements, whereas in the present study only thirty nine statements are considered and are modified. It covered all the seven dimension of Organisational Health. The details regarding the dimensions and number of items under each are given in Table—4.3.

Table—4.3

Dimensions of Organisational Health in Terms of Organisational Levels and Functions

Levels	*Functions*	*Dimensions*	*Number of Items*
Institutional	Instrumental	Institutional Integrity (II)	06
Managerial	Instrumental	Initiating structure (IS)	04
	Instrumental	Resource Support (RS)	04
	Instrumental	Principal influence (PI)	05
	Expressive	Consideration (CON)	05
Technical	Instrumental	Academic Emphasis (AE)	08
	Expressive	Morale (MO)	07
		Total	**39**

Institutional Integrity is the colleges ability to cope with its environment in a way that maintains the educational integrity of its program. Teacher educators are protected from unreasonable community and parental demands.

Institutional integrity serves as an indicator of health at the institutional level. Principal Influence, Consideration, Initiating Structure and Resource Support provide measures of the health of the managerial system. Morale and Academic Emphasis are the indices of health at the technical level. The response to the items is on four point scale (RO=Rarely occurs, SO=Some times occurs, O=Often occurs, VFO=Very frequently occurs). Weighted scores 4,3,2 and 1 are associated to the responses and reverse scoring is adopted for negative items.

Reliability and Validity

Test-retest reliability was computed for the Inventory and it worked out to be 0.72. The validity of the tool was measured by square root of reliability and it was 0.85. Thus this tool is found to be reliable and valid.

Quality of Work-Life Inventory

It was developed by Marshall Shashkin and Joseph Lengerman (1984). It is a four point Likert type rating scale. The QWLI contains twenty five statements. All the statements were modified and administered to teacher educators. The teacher educators were asked to indicate their responses on a four point scale namely, "A" for All the times (score four), "M" for Most of the time (score three), "P" for Part of the time (score two), "N" for Never (score one). They are keyed to identify the following five dimensions of Quality of Work-Life given in Table—4.4.

Table 4.4

Dimensions of Quality of Work-Life

	Dimension	*Number of Items*
1.	Autonomy (AT)	05
2.	Personal Growth Opportunity (PGO)	05
3.	Work speed and Routine (WSR)	05
4.	Work complexity (WCO)	05
5.	Task Related Interaction (TRI)	05
	Total	**25**

Reverse scoring was adopted for negative items.

Reliability and Validity

The researcher established the reliability of the tool by test-retest method and the correlation between two tests worked out to be 0.58. The validity of the tool was measured by computing square root of reliability and it was 0.76. Thus tool is found to be reliable and valid.

Student Teachers' Involvement in College Activities Questionnaire

To collect the relevant data from teacher educators the Students Involvement Questionnaire, a four point Likert type rating scale developed by Selvaraju was used.

Initially twenty-four statements were listed out. After the jury opinion sixteen statements were modified and retained. The scale measures the following four dimensions of Students' Involvement in College Activities. The dimensions and number of items under each are given in Table—4.5.

Table—4.5

Dimensions of Student Teachers' Involvement in College Activities

Sl. No	*Dimensions*	*No. of items*
1.	Discipline	04
2.	Willingness to work	04
3.	Organisation Ability	04
4.	Participation in extra-curricular activities	04
	Total	**16**

This inventory has been revalidated by calculating the validity and reliability coefficients.

Reliability and Validity

Reliability of the tool has been established by test-retest method and it worked out to be 0.693 and the validity as measured by the square root of reliability is 0.86. Thus this tool is found to be reliable and valid.

Change Facilitator Styles of Principals Inventory

To collect the relevant data from teacher educators the Change Facilitator Style Inventory of Hall and Rutherford (1983) was used. This tool is modified and adopted. This inventory consists of thirty seven items relating to three change facilitating styles of Principals namely 'Responder', 'Manager' and 'Initiator'. The details regarding their dimensions and number of items under each are given in Table—4.6.

Table—4.6

Change Facilitator Styles of Principals

Sl. No.	*Principal Behaviour's*	*Number of items*
A.	Vision	03
B.	Structuring the college as a work place	05
C.	Structuring involvement with change	06
D.	Sharing of responsibility	03
E.	Decision Making	03
F.	Guiding and Supporting	06
G.	Structuring his/her professional role.	11
	Total	**37**

This inventory has been revalidated by calculating the validity and reliability coefficients.

Reliability and Validity

Reliability of the tool has been established by test-retest method and it worked out to be 0.695 and the validity as measured by the square root of reliability is 0.87. Thus this tool is found to be reliable and valid.

Student Teachers' Commitment to Course Questionnaire

To collect the relevant data from student-teachers the Student's Commitment Index, a four point Likert type of rating scale was developed adopting of Ladewing and White (1984) Job Commitment Index.

This scale contains sixteen items about how teacher trainees feel about their job in the training course. Respondents have to indicate the extent to which he/she agrees or disagrees with each item. Item numbers 6, 8 and 16 are reverse scored. The scores will range from a low of 16 to a high of 64. The higher the score the higher is the level of commitment. This inventory has been validated by calculating the validity and reliability coefficients.

Reliability and Validity

Reliability of the tool has been established by test-retest method and it worked out to be 0.692 and the validity as measured by the square root of reliability is 0.83. Thus this tool is found to be reliable and valid.

Sample

The data for the study were gathered using a sample of 260 teacher educators, 35 Principals and 900 teacher trainees randomly from 45 colleges of secondary teacher educators out of 66 secondary teacher education colleges coming under six universities in Karnataka. The teacher educators were selected from each college giving due representation to the age, sex, qualification, designation, teaching experience and type of management. Similarly, Principals were also selected from 45 colleges giving due representation to the age, sex, qualification, managerial experience and type of management. In case of student-teachers due representation was given to the arts and science group. The Table—4.7 given below furnishes the details of the sample selected.

Table—4.7

Details of Sample Selected

Universities	*Types of College*			*Sex of College*		*Principal*		*Teacher Educators*				*Student Teachers*			
	AID	*UAID*	*GOVT*	*COED*	*WOED*	*Male*	*Female*	*Science*		*Arts*		*Science*		*Arts*	
								Male	*Female*	*Male*	*Female*	*Male*	*Female*	*Male*	*Female*
Karnataka	1	11	3	14	1	13	2	24	10	38	13	70	70	70	70
Bangalore	6	4	–	9	1	8	2	17	17	12	17	50	50	50	50
Mysore	3	1	1	5	0	4	1	5	7	6	11	25	25	25	25
Mangalore	1	–	1	1	1	2	1	8	4	5	4	15	15	15	15
Gulburga	1	6	1	6	2	7	1	13	4	18	6	40	40	40	40
Kuvempu	3	2	–	5	–	5	–	9	1	7	4	25	25	25	25
Total	**15**	**24**	**6**	**40**	**5**	**39**	**7**	**76**	**43**	**86**	**55**	**225**	**225**	**225**	**225**
	45			45		46		260				900			

AID – Aided College
UAID – Un-Aided College
GOVT – Government College
COED – Co-Education College
WOED – Women Education College

Data Collection

The investigator personally collected the data from 45 teacher education colleges out of 66 teacher education colleges affiliated to six universities in Karnataka State namely Karnatak University, Bangalore University, Mysore University, Mangalore University, Gulburga University and Kuvempu University. Principals and individual teacher educators were personally administered the tools. Clear cut instructions were given to fill up the responses to the items in the tools. The filled in proformas were collected. Questionnaires were given to the current batch of student teachers selected randomly. From each batch, ten student teachers from Arts group and ten student teachers from Science group were randomly selected to rate their commitment to the course on a four-point scale. The student-teachers were informed the purpose of the study. The confidentiality of the responses was assured. The filled in response sheets were collected immediately. It took about 20 minutes for the students to complete the ratings.

Data Analyses

For the analyses of data collected, descriptive, differential, correlation, multivariate and factor analysis statistics were used.

The succeeding chapter spells out the details of data analyses.

5

Data Analyses and Results

Introduction

However valid, reliable and adequate the data may be, it does not serve any useful purpose unless it is carefully processed, systematically classified and tabulated, scientifically analysed, intelligently interpreted and rationally concluded.

After the data had been collected, it was processed and analysed using Microsoft Excel-97 and SPSS Software to draw exact conclusions. In the present study correlates of total quality culture are measured using the relevant tools.

The data collected from the teacher educators, Principals and student teachers' with regard to Organisational Health, Total Quality Culture, Quality of Work-Life, Student Teachers' Involvement in College Activities, Student Teachers' Commitment to Course and Change Facilitator Styles of Principals of the teacher education colleges were analysed with reference to the objectives and hypotheses. The data have been subjected to the following statistical analyses, namely descriptive, differential, correlational, multiple regression and factor analyses. The results of statistical analyses have been summarized, tabulated and interpreted appropriately. Table—5.1 gives the descriptive statistics of the variables.

Table—5.1

Descriptive Statistics of Variables

Sample		*No.*	*Total Quality Culture Maximum Score = 600*		*Organisational Health Maximum Score = 700*		*Quality of Work Life Maximum Score = 100*		*Student Teachers' Involvement in College Activities Maximum Score = 80*	
			M	*SD*	*M*	*SD*	*M*	*SD*	*M*	*SD*
1		*2*	*3*	*4*	*5*	*6*	*7*	*8*	*9*	*10*
Teacher Educators Whole Sample		260	483.000	86.211	491.896	83.177	65.889	05.294	51.927	7.112
Age	up to 35 years	115	471.026	75.111	473.817	82.268	65.365	05.579	50.748	7.424
	Above 35 years	145	492.497	93.254	506.235	81.348	66.303	05.036	52.862	6.735
Sex 1. Male :	Teacher Educators	162	481.235	85.450	485.525	86.845	65.778	05.097	51.400	7.302
2. Female :	Teacher Educators	98	485.918	87.818	502.429	76.558	66.071	05.626	52.765	6.741
Specialisation :	Arts	141	487.667	84.099	494.603	84.943	66.135	05.170	52.248	7.198
	Science	119	477.471	88.686	488.689	81.275	65.597	05.444	51.546	7.020
Designation :	Lecturer/Sr. Lect.	212	485.043	78.732	489.623	82.281	65.797	05.253	51.613	7.263
	Reader/Lect.Sl.Gr.	48	476.979	114.135	501.938	87.207	66.292	05.508	53.313	6.288
Experience :	Up to 10 years	150	478.580	74.578	482.460	81.022	65.660	05.346	51.347	6.938
	Above 10 years	110	489.027	99.970	504.764	84.711	66.200	05.230	52.718	7.301

(Table Contd...)

1		2	3	4	5	6	7	8	9	10
Management :	1. Government	35	509.200	68.827	476.027	79.995	65.971	04.756	52.200	8.145
	2. Private Aided	86	473.174	103.660	512.244	86.149	66.267	05.603	53.721	6.817
	3. Private Un-aided	135	482.415	77.638	483.215	81.149	65.657	05.300	50.660	6.883
College Sex :	1. Co-education	240	480.463	87.849	491.929	84.139	65.867	05.401	52.021	7.203
	2. Women	120	513.450	56.385	491.500	72.513	66.150	03.870	50.800	5.961
Universities :	1. Karnataka	85	498.259	78.983	478.859	94.504	65.400	04.912	51.965	7.124
	2. Bangalore	63	471.619	103.760	489.127	80.975	66.905	06.712	53.175	6.987
	3. Mysore	29	474.207	86.593	523.690	68.801	66.759	04.050	53.690	5.977
	4. Mangalore	21	492.857	65.198	502.667	72.830	64.143	05.209	50.333	7.670
	5. Gulburga	41	458.024	84.317	472.854	68.460	65.049	04.577	48.951	7.701
	6. Kuvempu	21	506.429	65.113	523.048	72.542	67.000	04.313	53.000	5.630

Descriptive Analysis

Total Quality Culture

Whole Sample

The means and standard deviations for the whole sample in the various dimensions of Total Quality Culture are shown below.

Table—5.2

Means and Standard Deviations of Dimensions of Total Quality Culture

Dimension	*Mean*	*SD*	*Government*		*Private Aided*		*Private Un-Aided*	
			Mean	*SD*	*Mean*	*SD*	*Mean*	*SD*
Environment	81.323	14.734	80.829	12.517	79.998	17.720	82.356	13.125
Product & Service	85.062	14.831	90.400	9.059	83.349	17.665	84.889	13.854
Methods	79.004	16.741	85.00	14.194	78.349	18.550	77.941	16.051
People Characteristics	76.607	16.851	82.286	14.770	74.663	19.908	76.259	15.145
Organisational Structure	81.715	17.029	86.571	13.316	79.744	19.715	81.689	16.102
Total Quality Mindset	79.289	16.609	84.114	14.903	77.081	19.339	79.282	15.096

The results in Table—5.2 reveal that the means of Government colleges are above the grand means for the whole sample in the five of the six components namely Product and Service, Methods, People Characteristics, Organisational Structure and Total Quality Mindset. Within each type of colleges the highest mean is in the component Product and Service. This is presented in the Figure 5.1.

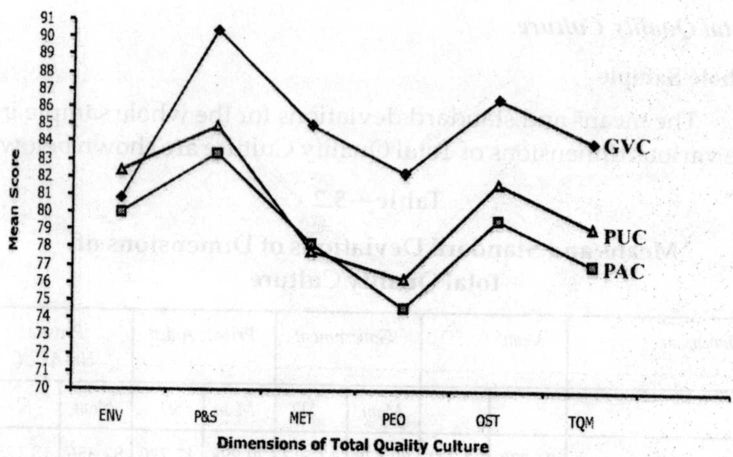

Legend: PAC-Private Aided College
PUC-Private Unaided College
GVC-Government College

Fig.: 5.1: Teacher Education Colleges Under Different Management

Total Quality Culture (TQC) was studied using 'Total Quality Culture inventory'. There are six dimensions namely, Environment (ENV), Product and Service (PS), Methods (MET), People Characteristics (PEO), Organisational Structure (OS), Total Quality Mindset (TQM). For each dimension separate scores are calculated and these scores are converted into percentages (%) of the maximum possible scores under each dimension. As there are six dimensions the maximum possible score for Total Quality Culture will be 600.

The means and the standard deviations for the whole sample and the sub samples divided on the basis of some selected variables are presented in Table—5.3.

Table—5.3

Means and Standard Deviations of Total Quality Culture

Variables			No.	Mean	SD
Whole Sample			260	483.000	86.211
Age :	Up to 35 Years		115	471.026	75.111
	Above 35 years		145	492.497	93.254
Sex :	1. Male:	Teacher educators	162	481.235	85.450
	2. Female:	Teacher educators	98	485.918	87.818
Specialisation :	Arts		141	487.667	84.099
	Science		119	477.471	88.686
Designation :	Lecturers/Senior Lecturers		212	485.043	78.732
	Readers/Lecturers Selection Gr.		48	473.979	114.135
Experience :	Up to 10 years		150	478.580	74.578
	Above 10 years		110	489.027	99.970
Management :	1. Government		35	509.200	68.827
	2. Private Aided		86	473.174	103.660
	3. Private Un-aided		135	482.415	77.638
College Sex :	1. Co-education		240	480.463	87.849
	2. Women		20	513.450	56.385
University :	1. Karnataka		85	498.259	78.983
	2. Bangalore		63	471.619	103.760
	3. Mysore		29	474.207	86.593
	4. Mangalore		21	492.857	65.198
	5. Gulburga		41	458.024	84.317
	6. Kuvempu		21	506.429	65.113

The results in Table—5.3 reveal that on Total Quality Culture teacher educators in women colleges have the highest mean score and those upto 35 years of age have the lowest mean of 471.026.

The means and standard deviations of Total Quality Culture dimensions are presented in the following tables.

Environment (ENV)

The means and standard deviations of the Total Quality Culture dimension, Environment, for the whole sample and the sub samples divided on the basis of some selected variables are presented in Table—5.4. The maximum score for this variable is 100.

Table—5.4

Means and Standard Deviations of the Dimension Environment

Variables			No.	Mean	SD
Whole Sample			260	81.323	14.734
Age	:	Upto 35 Years	115	80.739	12.964
		Above 35 years	145	81.786	16.028
Sex	: 1.	Male: Teacher educators	162	81.290	14.339
	2.	Female: Teacher educators	98	81.378	15.439
Specialisation	:	Arts	141	82.660	13.600
		Science	119	79.740	15.885
Designation	:	Lecturers/Senior Lecturers	212	81.561	13.490
		Readers/Lecturers Selection Gr.	48	80.271	19.440
Experience	:	Upto 10 years	150	81.240	13.191
		Above 10 years	110	81.436	16.671
Management	: 1.	Government	35	80.829	12.517
	2.	Private Aided	86	79.988	17.720
	3.	Private Un-aided	135	82.356	13.125
College Sex	: 1.	Co-education	240	80.971	15.053
	2.	Women	20	85.550	09.400
University	: 1.	Karnataka	85	83.082	13.320
	2.	Bangalore	63	80.683	17.349
	3.	Mysore	29	79.069	15.506
	4.	Mangalore	21	81.333	13.369
	5.	Gulburga	41	77.878	15.570
	6.	Kuvempu	21	85.952	08.009

The result in Table—5.4 reveals that on the dimension Environment, colleges in Kuvempu University have higher mean score than colleges in other Universities.

Product and Service (PS)

The means and standard deviations of the Total Quality Culture dimension, Product and Service, for the whole sample and the sub samples divided on the basis of some selected variables are presented in Table—5.5. The maximum score for this variable is 100.

Table—5.5

Means and Standard Deviations of the Dimension Product and Service

Variables				No.	Mean	SD
Whole Sample				260	85.062	14.831
Age	:		Upto 35 Years	115	82.713	12.994
			Above 35 years	145	86.924	15.939
Sex	:	1.	Male: Teacher educators	162	84.148	15.006
		2.	Female: Teacher educators	98	86.571	14.488
Specialisation	:		Arts	141	84.851	15.275
			Science	119	85.311	14.348
Designation	:		Lecturers/Senior Lecturers	212	85.245	13.601
			Readers/Lecturers Selection Gr.	48	84.250	19.516
Experience	:		Upto 10 years	150	84.373	13.281
			Above 10 years	110	86.000	16.733
Management	:	1.	Government	35	90.400	09.059
		2.	Private Aided	86	83.349	17.665
		3.	Private Un-aided	135	84.889	13.854
College Sex	:	1.	Co-education	240	84.767	15.227
		2.	Women	20	88.600	08.236
University	:	1.	Karnataka	85	85.977	15.087
		2.	Bangalore	63	82.921	17.498
		3.	Mysore	29	86.483	15.359
		4.	Mangalore	21	87.619	07.579
		5.	Gulburga	41	83.122	14.492
		6.	Kuvempu	21	87.048	09.790

The results in Table—5.5 reveal that on the dimension Product and Service Women Colleges have higher mean score than Co-education colleges.

Methods (MET)

The means and standard deviations of the Total Quality Culture dimension, Methods, for the whole sample and the sub samples divided on the basis of some selected variables are presented in Table—5.6. The maximum score for this variable is 100.

Table—5.6

Means and Standard Deviations of the Dimension Methods

Variables				No.	Mean	SD
Whole Sample				260	79.004	16.741
Age	:		Upto 35 Years	115	76.426	15.850
			Above 35 years	145	81.048	17.195
Sex	:	1.	Male: Teacher educators	162	78.296	17.115
		2.	Female: Teacher educators	98	80.174	16.121
Specialisation	:		Arts	141	79.028	16.879
			Science	119	78.975	16.647
Designation	:		Lecturers/Senior Lecturers	212	79.123	15.632
			Readers/Lecturers Selection Gr.	48	78.479	21.143
Experience	:		Upto 10 years	150	77.587	15.153
			Above 10 years	110	80.936	18.588
Management	:	1.	Government	35	85.000	14.194
		2.	Private Aided	86	78.349	18.550
		3.	Private Un-aided	135	77.941	16.051
College Sex	:	1.	Co-education	240	78.450	16.888
		2.	Women	20	85.650	13.496
University	:	1.	Karnataka	85	79.753	16.865
		2.	Bangalore	63	78.064	19.347
		3.	Mysore	29	79.172	14.575
		4.	Mangalore	21	80.429	12.968
		5.	Gulburga	41	75.317	16.928
		6.	Kuvempu	21	84.333	13.074

The results in Table—5.6 reveal that on the dimension Methods, Women colleges have higher mean score than Co-education colleges.

People Characteristic (PEO)

The means and standard deviations of the Total Quality Culture dimension, People Characteristic, for the whole sample and the sub samples divided on the basis of some selected variables are presented in Table—5.7. The maximum score for this variable is 100.

Table—5.7

Means and Standard Deviations of the Dimension People Characteristics

Variables			No.	Mean	SD
Whole Sample			260	76.607	16.851
Age :		Upto 35 Years	115	74.078	15.151
		Above 35 years	145	78.614	17.884
Sex :	1.	Male: Teacher educators	162	76.932	16.301
	2.	Female: Teacher educators	98	76.071	17.781
Specialisation :		Arts	141	77.738	16.562
		Science	119	75.269	17.160
Designation :		Lecturers/Senior Lecturers	212	76.793	16.071
		Readers/Lecturers Selection Gr.	48	75.792	20.113
Experience :		Upto 10 years	150	75.267	15.102
		Above 10 years	110	78.436	18.897
Management :	1.	Government	35	**82.286**	14.770
	2.	Private Aided	86	74.663	19.908
	3.	Private Un-aided	135	76.259	15.145
College Sex :	1.	Co-education	240	76.342	17.143
	2.	Women	20	79.800	12.747
University :	1.	Karnataka	85	81.424	14.775
	2.	Bangalore	63	73.619	19.520
	3.	Mysore	29	72.931	17.600
	4.	Mangalore	21	77.810	14.531
	5.	Gulburga	41	71.024	15.717
	6.	Kuvempu	21	80.857	14.305

The result in Table—5.7 reveal that on the dimension People Characteristic, Government teacher education colleges have higher mean score than colleges in other types of Management.

Organisational Structure (OS)

The means and standard deviations of the Total Quality Culture dimension, Organisational Structure, for the whole sample and the sub samples divided on the basis of some selected variables are presented in Table—5.8. The maximum score for this variable is 100.

Table—5.8

Means and Standard Deviations of the Dimension Organisational Structure

Variables				No.	Mean	SD
Whole Sample				260	81.715	17.029
Age	:		Upto 35 Years	115	80.330	15.374
			Above 35 years	145	82.814	18.213
Sex	:	1.	Male: Teacher educators	162	81.419	16.682
		2.	Female: Teacher educators	98	82.204	17.662
Specialisation	:		Arts	141	83.135	16.171
			Science	119	80.034	17.915
Designation	:		Lecturers/Senior Lecturers	212	82.519	15.588
			Readers/Lecturers Selection Gr.	48	78.167	22.167
Experience	:		Upto 10 years	150	81.760	15.445
			Above 10 years	110	81.655	19.051
Management	:	1.	Government	35	86.571	13.316
		2.	Private Aided	86	79.744	19.715
		3.	Private Un-aided	135	81.689	16.102
College Sex	:	1.	Co-education	240	81.050	17.346
		2.	Women	20	89.700	09.761
University	:	1.	Karnataka	85	85.153	15.876
		2.	Bangalore	63	78.762	20.184
		3.	Mysore	29	80.552	17.410
		4.	Mangalore	21	84.381	13.017
		5.	Gulburga	41	77.268	16.073
		6.	Kuvempu	21	84.286	13.730

The results in Table—5.8 reveal that on the dimension Organisational Structure Women teacher education colleges have higher mean score than Co-education colleges.

Total Quality Mind Set (TQM)

The means and standard deviations of the Total Quality Culture dimension, Quality Mindset, for the whole sample and the sub samples divided on the basis of some selected variables are presented in Table—5.9.The maximum score for this variable is 100.

Table—5.9
Means and Standard Deviations of the Dimension Total Quality Mindset

Variables			*No.*	*Mean*	*SD*
Whole Sample			260	79.289	16.609
Age	:	Upto 35 Years	115	76.739	15.450
		Above 35 years	145	81.310	17.261
Sex	:	1. Male: Teacher educators	162	79.148	15.837
		2. Female: Teacher educators	98	79.520	17.895
Specialisation	:	Arts	141	80.255	16.502
		Science	119	78.143	16.734
Designation	:	Lecturers/Senior Lecturers	212	79.802	15.715
		Readers/Lecturers Selection Gr.	48	77.021	20.130
Experience	:	Upto 10 years	150	78.353	15.235
		Above 10 years	110	80.536	18.314
Management	:	1. Government	35	84.114	14.903
		2. Private Aided	86	77.081	19.339
		3. Private Un-aided	135	79.282	15.096
College Sex	:	1. Co-education	240	78.883	16.783
		2. Women	20	84.150	13.812
University	:	1. Karnataka	85	82.871	14.634
		2. Bangalore	63	77.571	18.860
		3. Mysore	29	76.000	17.304
		4. Mangalore	21	81.286	12.370
		5. Gulburga	41	73.415	17.776
		6. Kuvempu	21	83.952	13.750

The results in Table—5.9 reveal that on the dimension Total Quality Mindset Women colleges have highest mean score.

Organisational Health (OH)

Organisational Health was studied using Organisational Health inventory. There are seven dimensions namely, Institutional Integrity (I I), Initiating Structure (I S), Consideration (CS), Principal Influence (PI), Resource Support (RS), Morale (MO) and Academic Emphasis (AE). For each dimension separate scores are calculated and these scores are converted into percentage (%) of the maximum possible scores under each dimension. As there are seven dimensions, the maximum possible score for total Organisational Health will be 700.

Whole Sample

The means and standard deviations of the Organisational Health for the whole sample in the various dimensions of Organisational Health are presented in Table—5.10.

Table—5.10

Means and Standard Deviations of Dimensions of Organisational Health

Dimension	*Mean*	*SD*	*Government*		*Private Aided*		*Private Un-Aided*	
			Mean	*SD*	*Mean*	*SD*	*Mean*	*SD*
Institutional Integrity	73.896	11.937	75.143	12.793	74.395	11.391	73.000	12.053
Initiating Structure	70.365	17.061	68.143	19.216	74.186	15.124	68.593	17.531
Consideration	65.635	19.275	63.286	16.713	66.977	20.512	65.407	19.365
Principal Influence	67.558	13.388	65.143	11.912	69.302	13.376	67.259	13.682
Resource Support	66.285	19.290	65.086	17.943	74.361	19.081	61.467	18.424
Morale	73.931	16.683	69.400	15.674	75.302	17.488	74.482	16.457
Academic Emphasis	74.227	15.970	69.829	17.316	77.721	15.074	73.007	15.872

The results in Table—5.10 reveal that the Aided colleges are at a higher level on the dimension Institutional Integrity than the other two types of colleges. This is presented in Figure—5.2.

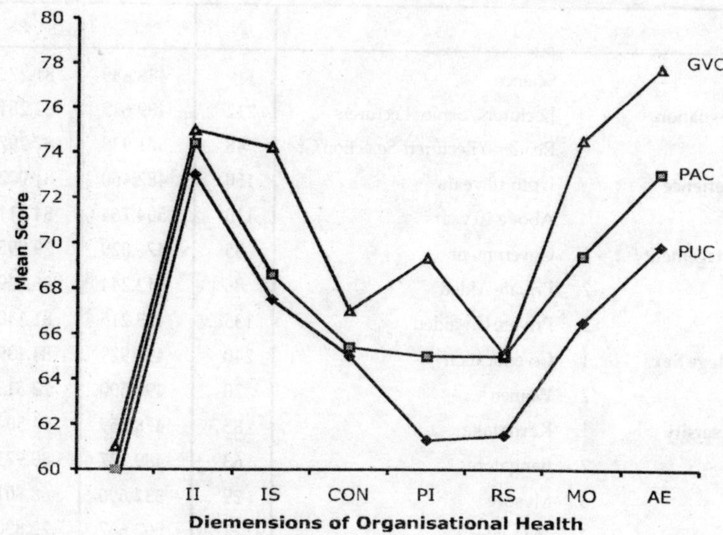

Legend: PAC- Private Aided College

PUC- Private Un-Aided College

GVC- Government College

Fig. 5.2: Teacher Education Colleges Under Different Management

The means and standard deviations for the whole sample and the sub-samples divided on the basis of some selected variables are presented in Table—5.11.

Table—5.11

Means and Standard Deviations of Organisational Health

Variables				*No.*	*Mean*	*SD*
1				*2*	*3*	*4*
Whole Sample				260	491.896	83.177
Age	:	Upto 35 Years		115	473.817	82.268
		Above 35 years		145	506.235	81.348
Sex	:	1. Male:	Teacher educators	162	485.525	86.545
		2. Female:	Teacher educators	98	502.429	76.558
Specialisation	:	Arts		141	494.603	84.943

(Table Contd...)

1				2	3	4
			Science	119	488.689	81.275
Designation	:		Lecturers/Senior Lecturers	212	489.623	82.281
			Readers/Lecturers Selection Gr.	48	501.938	87.207
Experience	:		Upto 10 years	150	482.460	81.022
			Above 10 years	110	504.764	84.711
Management	:	1.	Government	35	476.029	79.995
		2.	Private Aided	86	512.244	86.149
		3.	Private Un-aided	135	483.215	81.149
College Sex	:	1.	Co-education	240	491.929	84.139
		2.	Women	20	491.500	72.513
University	:	1.	Karnataka	85	478.859	94.504
		2.	Bangalore	63	489.127	80.975
		3.	Mysore	29	**532.690**	68.801
		4.	Mangalore	21	502.667	72.830
		5.	Gulburga	41	472.854	68.460
		6.	Kuvempu	21	523.048	73.542

The results in Table—5.11 reveal that on Organisational Health teacher education colleges in Mysore University have higher mean score than colleges in other Universities.

The means and standard deviations of Organisational Health dimensions are presented in the following tables.

Institutional Integrity (II)

The means and standard deviations of the dimension, Institutional Integrity, for the whole sample and the sub samples divided on the basis of some selected variables are presented in Table—5.12. The maximum score for this variable is 100.

Table—5.12

Means and Standard Deviations of the Dimension Institutional Integrity

		Variables	*No.*	*Mean*	*SD*
Whole Sample			260	73.896	11.937
Age	:	Up to 35 Years	115	72.130	12.017
		Above 35 years	145	75.297	11.727
Sex	:	1. Male: Teacher educators	162	73.735	12.012
		2. Female: Teacher educators	98	74.163	11.869
Specialisation	:	Arts	141	73.383	11.919
		Science	119	74.504	11.982
Designation	:	Lecturers/Senior Lecturers	212	74.467	11.695
		Readers/Lecturers Selection Gr.	48	71.375	12.779
Experience	:	Upto 10 years	150	73.847	11.886
		Above 10 years	110	73.964	12.061
Management	:	1. Government	35	75.143	12.793
		2. Private Aided	86	74.395	11.391
		3. Private Un-aided	135	73.000	12.053
College Sex	:	1. Co-education	240	74.342	11.453
		2. Women	20	68.550	16.099
University	:	1. Karnataka	85	75.000	09.751
		2. Bangalore	63	74.778	12.775
		3. Mysore	29	76.035	09.977
		4. Mangalore	21	77.381	12.396
		5. Gulburga	41	70.585	14.736
		6. Kuvempu	21	66.809	10.520

The results in Table—5.12 reveal that Colleges under Mangalore University have the highest mean score on the dimension Institutional Integrity.

Initiating Structure (IS)

The means and standard deviations of the Organisational Health dimension, the Initiating Structure for the whole sample and the sub samples divided on the basis of some selected variables are presented in Table—5.13. The maximum score for this variable is 100.

Table—5.13

Means and Standard Deviations of the Dimension Initiating Structure

			Variables	*No.*	*Mean*	*SD*
Whole Sample				260	70.365	17.061
Age	:		Upto 35 Years	115	67.957	17.269
			Above 35 years	145	72.276	16.708
Sex	:	1.	Male: Teacher educators	162	68.272	18.206
		2.	Female: Teacher educators	98	73.827	14.409
Specialisation	:		Arts	141	70.106	17.893
			Science	119	70.672	16.089
Designation	:		Lecturers/Senior Lecturers	212	69.670	17.152
			Readers/Lecturers Selection Gr.	48	73.438	16.476
Experience	:		Upto 10 years	150	69.300	17.301
			Above 10 years	110	71.818	16.697
Management	:	1.	Government	35	68.143	19.216
		2.	Private Aided	86	74.186	15.124
		3.	Private Un-aided	135	68.593	17.531
College Sex	:	1.	Co-education	240	70.854	17.096
		2.	Women	20	64.500	15.886
University	:	1.	Karnataka	85	67.882	19.811
		2.	Bangalore	63	72.143	15.906
		3.	Mysore	29	**77.069**	13.331
		4.	Mangalore	21	72.619	14.630
		5.	Gulburga	41	64.878	14.769
		6.	Kuvempu	21	74.286	15.913

The results in Table—5.13 reveal that teacher education colleges in Mysore University have a higher mean score on the dimension initiating structure than colleges in other Universities.

Consideration (CON)

The means and standard deviations of the Organisational Health dimension, Consideration, for the whole sample and the sub samples divided on the basis of some selected variables are presented in Table—5.14. The maximum score for this variable is 100.

Table—5.14

Means and Standard Deviations of the Dimension Consideration

Variables			*No.*	*Mean*	*SD*
Whole Sample			260	65.635	19.275
Age :		Upto 35 Years	115	62.391	18.759
		Above 35 years	145	68.207	19.353
Sex :	1.	Male: Teacher educators	162	65.093	18.943
	2.	Female: Teacher educators	98	66.531	19.876
Specialisation :		Arts	141	66.489	19.353
		Science	119	64.622	19.213
Designation :		Lecturers/Senior Lecturers	212	65.425	19.210
		Readers/Lecturers Selection Gr.	48	66.563	19.737
Experience :		Upto 10 years	150	63.667	18.113
		Above 10 years	110	68.318	20.535
Management :	1.	Government	35	63.286	16.713
	2.	Private Aided	86	66.977	20.512
	3.	Private Un-aided	135	65.407	19.365
College Sex :	1.	Co-education	240	65.563	19.254
	2.	Women	20	66.500	20.007
University :	1.	Karnataka	85	63.647	21.092
	2.	Bangalore	63	62.619	19.174
	3.	Mysore	29	**74.310**	15.220
	4.	Mangalore	21	60.476	19.420
	5.	Gulburga	41	67.317	14.879
	6.	Kuvempu	21	72.619	20.471

The results in Table—5.14 reveal that teacher education colleges coming under Mysore University have higher mean score on the dimension consideration, than colleges in other Universities.

Principal Influence (PI)

The means and standard deviations of the Organisational Health dimension, Principal Influence, for the whole sample and the sub samples divided on the basis of some selected variables are presented in Table—5.15. The maximum score for this variable is 100.

Table—5.15

Means and Standard Deviations of the Dimension Principal Influence

Variables			No.	Mean	SD
Whole Sample			260	67.558	13.388
Age :		Upto 35 Years	115	66.087	13.967
		Above 35 years	145	68.724	12.840
Sex :	1.	Male: Teacher educators	162	67.870	13.221
	2.	Female: Teacher educators	98	67.041	13.714
Specialisation :		Arts	141	68.865	13.421
		Science	119	66.008	13.238
Designation :		Lecturers/Senior Lecturers	212	67.476	13.076
		Readers/Lecturers Selection Gr.	48	67.917	14.834
Experience :		Upto 10 years	150	66.533	13.842
		Above 10 years	110	68.955	12.673
Management :	1.	Government	35	65.143	11.912
	2.	Private Aided	86	69.302	13.376
	3.	Private Un-aided	135	67.259	13.682
College Sex :	1.	Co-education	240	67.646	13.097
	2.	Women	20	66.500	16.866
University :	1.	Karnataka	85	66.824	13.712
	2.	Bangalore	63	65.318	13.645
	3.	Mysore	29	**71.552**	12.825
	4.	Mangalore	21	68.571	11.307
	5.	Gulburga	41	68.537	14.285
	6.	Kuvempu	21	68.810	11.927

The results in Table—5.15 reveal that teacher education colleges under Mysore University have highest mean score on the dimension Principal Influence than colleges in other Universities.

Resource Support (RS)

The means and standard deviations of the Organisational Health dimension, Resource support, for the whole sample and the sub samples divided on the basis of some selected variables are presented in Table—5.16. The maximum score for this variable is 100.

Table—5.16

Means and Standard Deviations of the Dimension Resource Support

Variables				*No.*	*Mean*	*SD*
Whole Sample				260	66.285	19.290
Age	:		Upto 35 Years	115	60.965	18.134
			Above 35 years	145	70.503	19.195
Sex	:	1.	Male: Teacher educators	162	65.364	20.059
		2.	Female: Teacher educators	98	67.806	17.943
Specialisation	:		Arts	141	67.234	18.837
			Science	119	65.160	19.835
Designation	:		Lecturers/Senior Lecturers	212	65.170	18.711
			Readers/Lecturers Selection Gr.	48	71.208	21.176
Experience	:		Upto 10 years	150	62.493	18.785
			Above 10 years	110	71.455	18.844
Management	:	1.	Government	35	65.086	17.943
		2.	Private Aided	86	74.361	19.081
		3.	Private Un-aided	135	61.467	18.424
College Sex	:	1.	Co-education	240	66.371	19.435
		2.	Women	20	65.250	17.882
University	:	1.	Karnataka	85	61.012	20.152
		2.	Bangalore	63	65.270	19.408
		3.	Mysore	29	77.724	16.146
		4.	Mangalore	21	74.000	14.993
		5.	Gulburga	41	59.878	15.688
		6.	Kuvempu	21	79.667	14.752

The results in Table—5.16 reveal that teacher education colleges under Kuvempu University have highest mean score on the dimension resource support than colleges in other Universities.

Morale (MO)

The means and standard deviations of the Organisational Health dimension, Morale, for the whole sample and the sub samples divided on the basis of some selected variables are presented in Table—5.17. The maximum score for this variable is 100.

Table—5.17

Means and Standard Deviations of the Dimension Morale

Variables				No.	Mean	SD
Whole Sample				260	73.931	16.683
Age	:		Upto 35 Years	115	71.991	16.518
			Above 35 years	145	75.469	16.710
Sex	:	1.	Male: Teacher educators	162	72.500	16.417
		2.	Female: Teacher educators	98	76.296	16.935
Specialisation	:		Arts	141	74.638	15.729
			Science	119	73.092	17.779
Designation	:		Lecturers/Senior Lecturers	212	73.774	16.556
			Readers/Lecturers Selection Gr.	48	74.625	17.399
Experience	:		Upto 10 years	150	73.353	16.134
			Above 10 years	110	74.718	17.448
Management	:	1.	Government	35	69.400	15.674
		2.	Private Aided	86	75.302	17.488
		3.	Private Un-aided	135	74.482	16.457
College Sex	:	1.	Co-education	240	73.229	16.588
		2.	Women	20	**82.350**	15.875
University	:	1.	Karnataka	85	72.400	18.414
		2.	Bangalore	63	74.048	16.432
		3.	Mysore	29	79.241	10.535
		4.	Mangalore	21	74.571	17.218
		5.	Gulburga	41	70.878	17.342
		6.	Kuvempu	21	77.762	14.286

The results in Table—5.17 reveal that women teacher education colleges have higher mean score than colleges on the dimension morale in Co-education colleges.

Academic Emphasis (AE)

The means and standard deviations of the Organisational Health dimension, Academic Emphasis, for the whole sample and the sub samples divided on the basis of some selected variables are presented in Table—5.18. The maximum score for this variable is 100.

Table—5.18

Means and Standard Deviations of the Dimension Academic Emphasis

Variables			*No.*	*Mean*	*SD*
Whole Sample			260	74.227	15.970
Age	:	Upto 35 Years	115	72.296	16.788
		Above 35 years	145	75.759	15.175
Sex	:	1. Male: Teacher educators	162	72.691	17.158
		2. Female: Teacher educators	98	76.765	13.488
Specialisation	:	Arts	141	73.887	16.681
		Science	119	74.630	15.146
Designation	:	Lecturers/Senior Lecturers	212	73.642	16.083
		Readers/Lecturers Selection Gr.	48	76.813	15.360
Experience	:	Upto 10 years	150	73.267	16.464
		Above 10 years	110	75.536	15.248
Management	:	1. Government	35	69.829	17.316
		2. Private Aided	86	77.721	15.074
		3. Private Un-aided	135	73.007	15.872
College Sex	:	1. Co-education	240	73.925	15.957
		2. Women	20	77.850	16.086
University	:	1. Karnataka	85	72.094	18.353
		2. Bangalore	63	74.952	13.168
		3. Mysore	29	76.759	10.446
		4. Mangalore	21	75.048	15.204
		5. Gulburga	41	70.781	16.945
		6. Kuvempu	21	**83.095**	15.956

The results in Table—5.18 reveal that teacher education colleges in Kuvempu University have higher mean score on the dimension academic emphasis than colleges under other Universities.

Quality of Work-Life (QWL)

Quality of Work-Life was studied using Quality of Work-Life inventory. There are five dimensions namely, Autonomy (AT), Personal Growth Opportunity (PSG), Work Speed and Routine (WSR), Work Complexity (WCO), Task Related Interaction (TRI).

Each dimension has 20 as the highest score. As there are five dimensions the maximum possible score for Total Quality of Work-Life will be 100. The means, standard deviations of the whole sample are presented in Table—5.19.

Whole Sample

The means and standard deviations for the whole in the various dimensions of Quality of Work-Life are shown in Table—5.19.

Table—5.19

Means and Standard Deviations of Dimensions of Quality of Work-Life

Dimension	*Mean*	*SD*	*Government*		*Private Aided*		*Private Un-Aided*	
			Mean	*SD*	*Mean*	*SD*	*Mean*	*SD*
Autonomy	12.531	2.090	13.200	2.041	13.035	1.973	12.059	2.036
Personal Growth Opportunity	14.881	2.750	14.743	2.571	14.907	2.965	14.933	2.674
Work Speed and Routine	10.423	2.092	10.514	1.976	10.128	2.146	10.533	2.022
Work Complexity	13.178	2.107	12.943	2.722	13.221	2.060	13.126	1.910
Task Related interaction	14.877	2.647	14.571	2.627	14.977	2.674	15.007	2.561

The results in Table—5.19 reveal that there is no much difference in the components of Quality of Work-Life among the three types of colleges. All of the three types of colleges are more or less at the same level. This is presented in Figure—5.3.

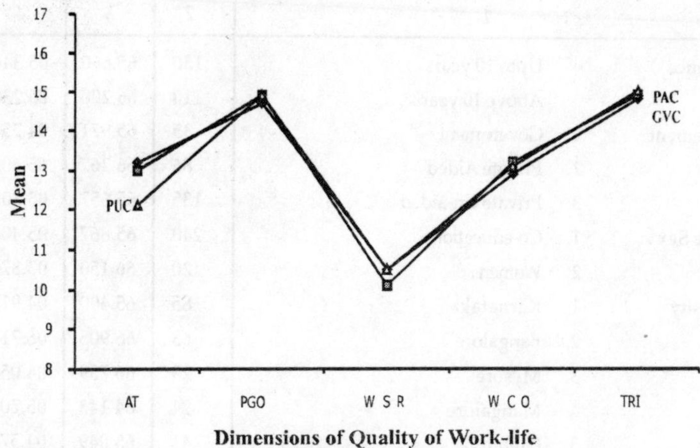

Legend: PAC- Private Aided College
PUC- Private Un-Aided College
GVC- Government College

Fig. 5.3: Teacher Education Colleges under Different Management

The means and standard deviations of the Variable Quality of Work-Life for the whole sample and the sub samples divided on the basis of some selected variables are presented in Table—5.20.

Table—5.20

Means and Standard Deviations of Quality of Work-Life

Variables				*No.*	*Mean*	*SD*
			1	2	3	4
Whole Sample				260	65.889	05.294
Age	:		Upto 35 Years	115	65.365	05.579
			Above 35 years	145	66.303	05.036
Sex	:	1.	Male: Teacher educators	162	65.778	05.097
		2.	Female: Teacher educators	98	66.071	05.626
Specialisation	:		Arts	141	66.135	05.170
			Science	119	65.597	05.444
Designation	:		Lecturers/Senior Lecturers	212	65.797	05.253
			Readers/Lecturers Selection Gr.	48	66.292	05.508

(Table Contd…)

1			2	3	4
Experience	:	Upto 10 years	150	65.660	05.346
		Above 10 years	110	66.200	05.230
Management	:	1. Government	35	65.971	04.756
		2. Private Aided	86	66.267	05.603
		3. Private Un-aided	135	65.657	05.300
College Sex	:	1. Co-education	240	65.867	05.401
		2. Women	20	66.150	03.870
University	:	1. Karnataka	85	65.400	04.912
		2. Bangalore	63	66.905	06.712
		3. Mysore	29	66.759	04.050
		4. Mangalore	21	64.143	05.209
		5. Gulburga	41	65.049	04.577
		6. Kuvempu	21	**67.000**	04.313

The results in Table—5.20 reveal that teacher education colleges in Kuvempu University have highest mean score on Quality of Work-Life than colleges in other Universities.

The means and standard deviations of quality of work life dimensions are presented in the following tables.

Autonomy (AT)

The means and standard deviations of the Quality of Work-Life dimension, Autonomy, for the whole sample and the sub samples divided on the basis of some selected variables are presented in Table—5.21. The maximum possible score is 20.

Table—5.21

Means and Standard Deviations of the Dimension Autonomy

Variables			*No.*	*Mean*	*SD*
1			2	3	4
Whole Sample			260	12.531	2.090
Age	:	Upto 35 Years	115	12.217	2.077
		Above 35 years	145	12.779	2.073

(Table Contd...)

1				2	3	4
Sex	:	1.	Male: Teacher educators	162	12.673	2.141
		2.	Female: Teacher educators	98	12.296	1.991
Specialisation	:		Arts	141	12.610	2.083
			Science	119	12.437	2.102
Designation	:		Lecturers/Senior Lecturers	212	12.514	2.085
			Readers/Lecturers Selection Gr.	48	12.604	2.0131
Experience	:		Upto 10 years	150	12.313	2.040
			Above 10 years	110	12.827	2.128
Management	:	1.	Government	35	13.200	2.041
		2.	Private Aided	86	13.035	1.973
		3.	Private Un-aided	135	12.059	2.036
College Sex	:	1.	Co-education	240	12.558	2.131
		2.	Women	20	12.200	1.508
University	:	1.	Karnataka	85	11.977	2.380
		2.	Bangalore	63	12.857	1.983
		3.	Mysore	29	**13.345**	1.932
		4.	Mangalore	21	12.857	1.526
		5.	Gulburga	41	12.293	2.016
		6.	Kuvempu	21	12.810	1.401

The results in Table—5.21 reveal that teacher education colleges in Mysore University have higher mean score on the dimension Autonomy than colleges in other Universities.

Personal Growth Opportunity (PGO)

The means and standard deviations of the Quality of Work-Life dimension, Personal Growth Opportunity, for the whole sample and the sub samples divided on the basis of some selected variables are presented in the Table—5.22. The maximum possible score is 20.

Table—5.22

Means and Standard Deviations of the Dimension Personal Growth Opportunity

			Variables	*No.*	*Mean*	*SD*
Whole Sample				260	14.881	2.750
Age	:		Upto 35 Years	115	14.774	2.744
			Above 35 years	145	14.966	2.762
Sex	:	1.	Male: Teacher educators	162	14.969	2.749
		2.	Female: Teacher educators	98	14.735	2.760
Specialisation	:		Arts	141	14.936	2.809
			Science	119	14.815	2.690
Designation	:		Lecturers/Senior Lecturers	212	14.854	2.640
			Readers/Lecturers Selection Gr.	48	15.000	3.222
Experience	:		Upto 10 years	150	14.967	2.625
			Above 10 years	110	14.764	2.921
Management	:	1.	Government	35	14.743	2.571
		2.	Private Aided	86	14.907	2.965
		3.	Private Un-aided	135	14.933	2.674
College Sex	:	1.	Co-education	240	14.800	2.766
		2.	Women	20	15.850	2.412
University	:	1.	Karnataka	85	15.212	2.774
		2.	Bangalore	63	14.762	3.135
		3.	Mysore	29	14.655	2.058
		4.	Mangalore	21	13.762	2.095
		5.	Gulburga	41	14.610	2.682
		6.	Kuvempu	21	15.857	2.726

The results in Table—5.22 reveal that teacher education colleges in Kuvempu University have higher means score on the dimension Personal Growth Opportunity than colleges in other Universities.

Workspeed and Routine (WSR)

The means and standard deviations of the Quality of Work-Life dimension, Workspeed and Routine, for the whole sample and the sub samples divided on the basis of some selected variables are presented in Table—5.23. The maximum possible score is 20.

Table—5.23

Means and Standard Deviations of the Dimension Workspeed and Routine

Variables			*No.*	*Mean*	*SD*
Whole Sample			260	10.423	2.092
Age	:	Upto 35 Years	115	10.530	2.206
		Above 35 years	145	10.338	2.001
Sex	:	1. Male: Teacher educators	162	10.488	2.115
		2. Female: Teacher educators	98	10.316	2.059
Specialisation	:	Arts	141	10.312	1.939
		Science	119	10.555	2.261
Designation	:	Lecturers/Senior Lecturers	212	10.481	2.087
		Readers/Lecturers Selection Gr.	48	10.167	2.117
Experience	:	Upto 10 years	150	10.447	2.103
		Above 10 years	110	10.391	2.086
Management	:	1. Government	35	10.514	1.976
		2. Private Aided	86	10.128	2.146
		3. Private Un-aided	135	10.533	2.022
College Sex	:	1. Co-education	240	10.433	2.055
		2. Women	20	10.300	2.557
University	:	1. Karnataka	85	09.988	1.979
		2. Bangalore	63	10.778	2.247
		3. Mysore	29	**11.000**	1.773
		4. Mangalore	21	09.762	1.786
		5. Gulburga	41	10.756	2.010
		6. Kuvempu	21	10.333	2.556

The Results in Table—5.23 reveal that colleges under Mysore University have the highest mean score on the dimension Workspeed and Routine.

Work Complexity (WCO)

The means and standard deviations of the Quality of Work-Life dimension, Work Complexity, for the whole sample and the sub samples divided on the basis of some selected variables are presented in Table—5.24. The maximum possible score is 20.

Table—5.24

Means and Standard Deviations of the Dimension Work Complexity

			Variables	No.	Mean	SD
Whole Sample				260	13.177	2.107
Age	:		Upto 35 Years	115	13.191	1.978
			Above 35 years	145	13.166	2.211
Sex	:	1.	Male: Teacher educators	162	12.796	2.092
		2.	Female: Teacher educators	98	**13.806**	1.988
Specialisation	:		Arts	141	13.135	2.162
			Science	119	13.227	2.048
Designation	:		Lecturers/Senior Lecturers	212	13.165	2.039
			Readers/Lecturers Selection Gr.	48	13.229	2.408
Experience	:		Upto 10 years	150	13.200	2.089
			Above 10 years	110	13.146	2.141
Management	:	1.	Government	35	12.943	2.722
		2.	Private Aided	86	13.221	2.060
		3.	Private Un-aided	135	13.126	1.910
College Sex	:	1.	Co-education	240	13.200	2.102
		2.	Women	20	12.900	2.199
University	:	1.	Karnataka	85	13.059	2.222
		2.	Bangalore	63	13.349	2.273
		3.	Mysore	29	13.241	1.154
		4.	Mangalore	21	13.429	2.315
		5.	Gulburga	41	12.976	1.981
		6.	Kuvempu	21	13.191	2.316

The results in Table—5.24 reveal that female teacher educators have the highest mean score on the dimension Work Complexity.

Task Related Interaction (TRI)

The means and standard deviations of the Quality of Work-Life dimension, Task Related Interaction, for the whole sample and the sub samples divided on the basis of some selected variables are presented in Table—5.25. The maximum possible score is 20.

Table—5.25

Means and Standard Deviations of the Dimension Task Related Interaction

Variables			No.	Mean	SD
Whole Sample			260	14.877	2.647
Age	:	Upto 35 Years	115	14.652	2.602
		Above 35 years	145	15.055	2.677
Sex	:	1. Male: Teacher educators	162	14.852	2.448
		2. Female: Teacher educators	98	14.918	2.959
Specialisation	:	Arts	141	15.142	2.598
		Science	119	14.563	2.680
Designation	:	Lecturers/Senior Lecturers	212	14.783	2.652
		Readers/Lecturers Selection Gr.	48	**15.292**	2.609
Experience	:	Upto 10 years	150	14.733	2.600
		Above 10 years	110	15.073	2.708
Management	:	1. Government	35	14.571	2.627
		2. Private Aided	86	14.977	2.674
		3. Private Un-aided	135	15.007	2.561
College Sex	:	1. Co-education	240	14.875	2.653
		2. Women	20	14.900	2.634
University	:	1. Karnataka	85	15.165	2.853
		2. Bangalore	63	15.159	2.772
		3. Mysore	29	14.517	1.957
		4. Mangalore	21	14.333	2.671
		5. Gulburga	41	14.415	2.470
		6. Kuvempu	21	14.810	2.542

The results in Table—5.25 reveal that Readers have higher mean score on the dimension Task Related Interaction than Lecturers.

Student-Teachers' Involvement in College Activities (SIN)

Whole Sample

The means and standard deviations of the Student-Teachers' Involvement in college activities for the whole sample and the sub samples divided on the basis of some selected variables are presented in Table—5.26. The maximum possible score is 80.

Table—5.26

Means and Standard Deviations of Student Teachers' Involvement in College Activities

Variables			No.	Mean	SD
Whole Sample			260	51.927	7.112
Age	:	Upto 35 Years	115	50.748	7.424
		Above 35 years	145	52.862	6.735
Sex	:	1. Male: Teacher educators	162	51.400	7.302
		2. Female: Teacher educators	98	52.765	6.741
Specialisation	:	Arts	141	52.248	7.198
		Science	119	51.546	7.020
Designation	:	Lecturers/Senior Lecturers	212	51.613	7.263
		Readers/Lecturers Selection Gr.	48	53.313	6.288
Experience	:	Upto 10 years	150	51.347	6.938
		Above 10 years	110	52.718	7.301
Management	:	1. Government	35	52.200	8.145
		2. Private Aided	86	**53.721**	6.817
		3. Private Un-aided	135	50.660	6.883
College Sex	:	1. Co-education	240	52.021	7.203
		2. Women	20	50.800	5.961
University	:	1. Karnataka	85	51.965	7.124
		2. Bangalore	63	53.175	6.987
		3. Mysore	29	53.690	5.977
		4. Mangalore	21	50.333	7.670
		5. Gulburga	41	48.951	7.701
		6. Kuvempu	21	53.000	5.630

The result in Table—5.26 reveal that Student Teachers' Involvement in College Activities, Private Aided Colleges have the highest mean score.

The findings of Descriptive Analysis are presented in the following tables.

Table—5.27

Descriptive Findings of Total Quality Culture

Variable/Dimension	*Highest Mean Score*	*Lowest Mean Score*
Total Quality Culture (Whole sample)	Women Teacher Education Colleges (M= 513.450)	Gulbarga University (M= 458.024)
Environment	Kuvempu University (M= 85.952)	Mysore University (M= 79.069)
Product and Service	Women Teacher Education Colleges (M= 88.600)	Teacher Educators upto years of age (M= 82.713)
Methods	Women Teacher Education Colleges (M= 85.650)	Gulburga University (M= 75.317)
People characteristic	Government Teacher Education Colleges (M= 82.286)	Gulburga University (M= 71.024)
Organisational Structure	Women Teacher Education Colleges (M= 89.700)	Gulburga University (M= 77.268)
Total Quality Mindset	Women Teacher Education Colleges (M= 84.150)	Gulburga University (M= 73.415)

Table—5.28

Descriptive Findings of Organisational Health

Variable/Dimension	*Highest Mean Score*	*Lowest Mean Score*
Organisational Health (whole sample)	Mysore University (M = 532.690)	Gulburga University (M= 472.854)
Institutional Integrity	Mysore University (M= 77.069)	Kuvempu University (M= 66.809)
Initiating Structure	Mysore University (M= 77.069)	Women Teacher Education College (M= 64.500)
Consideration	Mysore University (M= 74.310)	Mangalore University (M= 60.476)
Principal Influence	Mysore University (M= 71.552)	Bangalore University (M= 65.318)
Resource Support	Kuvempu University (M= 79.667)	Gulburga University (M= 59.878)
Morale	Women Teacher Education College (M= 82.350)	Government Teacher Education College (M=69.400)
Academic Emphasis	Kuvempu University (M= 83.095)	Government Teacher Education College (M= 69.829)

Table—5.29

Descriptive Findings of Quality of Work-Life

Variable/Dimension	*Highest Mean Score*	*Lowest Mean Score*
Quality of Work-life (Whole Sample)	Kuvempu University (M = 67.000)	Mangalore University (M= 64.143)
Autonomy	Mysore University (M= 13.345)	Karnataka University (M= 11.977)
Personal Growth Opportunity	Kuvempu University (M= 15.857)	Mangalore University (M= 13.762)
Work Speed and Routine	Mysore University (M= 11.000)	Mangalore University (M= 9.762)
Work Complexity	Female Teacher Educators (M= 13.806)	Male Teacher Educators (M= 12.796)
Task Related Interaction	Teacher Educators Designation with Readers (M = 15.292)	Mangalore University (M= 14.333)

Table—5.30

Discreptive Findings of Student Teachers' Involvement in College Activities

Variable/Dimension	*Highest Mean Score*	*Lowest mean Score*
Student Teacher's Involvement in College Activities (Whole Sample)	Private Aided Colleges (M= 53.721)	Gulbarga University (M= 48.951)

Differential Analysis

The differences between the sub samples in the variables are studied using 'F' and 't' tests as applicable to the number of groups compared. The details are presented in this section.

Total Quality Culture

The results of 't' tests comparing two groups are presented in the following table:

Table—5.31

't' Test Results for the Variable Total Quality Culture

		Groups	*Mean*	*SD*	*t*	*P*	*Significance*
Age	:	Upto 35 years	471.026	75.111	2.06	0.041	<0.05 Significant
		Above 35 years	492.497	93.254			
Sex	: 1.	Male: Teacher educators	481.235	85.450	0.42	0.674	>0.05 Not Significant
	2.	Female: Teacher educators	485.918	87.818			
Specialisation	:	Arts	487.667	84.099	0.95	0.345	>0.05 Not Significant
		Science	477.471	88.686			
Designation	:	Lecturers/ Senior Lecturers	485.043	78.732	0.64	0.526	>0.05 Not Significant
		Reader/Lect. Select. Gr.	473.979	114.135			
Experience	:	Upto 10 years	478.580	74.578	0.92	0.357	>0.05 Not Significant
		Above 10 years	489.027	99.970			
College Sex	: 1.	Co-education	480.463	87.849	2.39	0.024	<0.05 Significant
	2.	Women	513.450	56.385			

The results in Table—5.31 reveal that on Total Quality Culture only teacher educators upto 35 and above 35 years of age and those who are in co-education and women colleges **differ**. Hence, hypothesis that the two groups differ is accepted. Other sub groups based on teacher educators sex, specilisation, designation and experience do not differ. Hence, the hypotheses that the groups differ is not accepted.

Dimension of Total Quality Culture Environment

The results of 't' tests comparing two groups are presented in the following table:

Table—5.32

't' Test Results for the Dimension Environment

		Groups	Mean	SD	t	P	Significance
Age	:	Upto 35 years	80.739	12.964	0.58	0.561	<0.05 Not Significant
		Above 35 years	81.786	16.028			
Sex	: 1.	Male: Teacher educators	81.290	14.339	0.05	0.964	>0.05 Not Significant
	2.	Female: Teacher educators	81.378	15.439			
Specialisation	:	Arts	82.660	13.600	1.58	0.116	>0.05 Not Significant
		Science	79.740	15.885			
Designation	:	Lecturers/ Senior Lecturers	81.561	13.490	0.44	0.664	>0.05 Not Significant
		Reader/Lect. Select. Gr.	80.271	19.440			
Experience	:	Upto 10 years	81.240	13.191	0.10	0.919	>0.05 Not Significant
		Above 10 years	81.436	16.671			
College Sex	: 1.	Co-education	80.971	15.053	1.98	0.058	<0.05 Significant
	2.	Women	85.550	09.400			

The results in Table—5.32 reveal that on the dimension Environment only teacher educators in co-education and women colleges **differ**. Hence, the hypothesis that the two groups differ is accepted. Other sub groups based on teacher educators, age, sex, specialisation, designation and experience do not differ. Hence, the hypotheses that the groups differ are not accepted.

Product and Service

The results of 't' tests comparing two groups are presented in the following table:

Table—5.33

't' Test Results for the Dimension Product & Service

		Groups	*Mean*	*SD*	*t*	*P*	*Significance*
Age	:	Upto 35 years	82.713	12.994	2.35	0.020	**<0.05 Significant**
		Above 35 years	86.924	15.939			
Sex	: 1.	Male: Teacher educators	84.148	15.006	1.29	0.199	>0.05 Not Significant
	2.	Female: Teacher educators	86.571	14.488			
Specialisation	:	Arts	84.851	15.275	0.25	0.803	>0.05 Not Significant
		Science	85.311	14.348			
Designation	:	Lecturers/ Senior Lecturers	85.245	13.601	0.34	0.739	>0.05 Not Significant
		Reader/Lect. Select. Gr.	84.250	19.516			
Experience	:	Upto 10 years	84.373	13.281	0.84	0.400	>0.05 Not Significant
		Above 10 years	86.000	16.733			
College Sex	: 1.	Co-education	84.767	15.226	1.84	0.076	>0.05 Not Significant
	2.	Women	88.600	08.236			

The results in Table—5.33 reveal that on the dimension Product and Service only teacher educators upto 35 years and above 35 years of age **differ**. Hence, the hypothesis that the two groups differ is accepted. Other sub groups based on teacher educators' sex, specialisation, experience, designation and college sex do not differ. Hence, the hypotheses that groups differ are not accepted.

Methods

The results of 't' tests comparing two groups are presented in the following table:

Table—5.34

't' Test Results for the Dimension Methods

Groups			Mean	SD	t	P	Significance
Age	:	Upto 35 years	76.426	15.850	2.25	0.025	**<0.05 Significant**
		Above 35 years	81.048	17.195			
Sex	: 1.	Male: Teacher educators	78.296	17.115	0.89	0.375	>0.05 Not Significant
	2.	Female: Teacher educators	80.174	16.121			
Specialisation	:	Arts	79.028	16.879	0.03	0.980	>0.05 Not Significant
		Science	78.975	16.647			
Designation	:	Lecturers/ Senior Lecturers	79.123	15.632	0.20	0.843	>0.05 Not Significant
		Reader/Lect. Select. Gr.	78.479	21.143			
Experience	:	Upto 10 years	77.587	15.153	1.55	0.123	>0.05 Not Significant
		Above 10 years	80.936	18.588			
College Sex	: 1.	Co-education	78.450	16.888	2.24	0.034	**<0.05 Significant**
	2.	Women	85.850	13.496			

The results in Table—5.34 reveal that on the dimension Methods teacher educators' upto 35 years and above 35 years of age and those working in co-education and women colleges **differ**. Hence, the hypotheses that the two groups differ is accepted. Other sub groups based on teacher educators' sex, specialisation, designation and experience do not differ. Hence, the hypotheses that the groups differ are not accepted.

People Characteristics

The results of 't' tests comparing two groups are presented in the following table:

Table—5.35

't' Test Results for the Dimension People Characteristics

Groups			*Mean*	*SD*	*T*	*P*	*Significance*
Age	:	Upto 35 years	74.078	15.151	2.21	0.028	**<0.05 Significant**
		Above 35 years	78.614	17.884			
Sex	: 1.	Male: Teacher educators	76.932	16.310	0.39	0.697	>0.05 Not Significant
	2.	Female: Teacher educators	76.071	17.781			
Specialisation	:	Arts	77.738	16.562	1.17	0.241	>0.05 Not Significant
		Science	75.269	17.160			
Designation	:	Lecturers/ Senior Lecturers	26.793	16.070	0.32	0.748	>0.05 Not Significant
		Reader/Lect. Select. Gr.	75.792	20.111			
Experience	:	Upto 10 years	75.267	15.102	1.45	0.148	>0.05 Not Significant
		Above 10 years	78.436	18.897			
College Sex	: 1.	Co-education	76.342	17.143	1.13	0.269	<0.05 Significant
	2.	Women	79.800	12.747			

The results in Table—5.35 reveal that on the dimension People Characteristics, teacher educators' up to 35 years and above 35 years of age **differ**. Hence, the hypothesis that the two groups differ is accepted. Other sub groups based on teacher educators' sex, specialisation, designation, experience and college sex do not differ. Hence, the hypotheses that the groups differ are not accepted.

Organisational Structure

The results of 't' tests comparing two groups are presented in the following table:

Table—5.36

't' Test Results for the Dimension Organisational Structure

		Groups	Mean	SD	T	P	Significance
Age	:	Upto 35 years	80.330	15.374	1.19	0.234	>0.05 Not Significant
		Above 35 years	82.814	18.212			
Sex	: 1.	Male: Teacher educators	81.420	16.682	0.35	0.724	>0.05 Not Significant
	2.	Female: Teacher educators	82.204	17.662			
Specialisation	:	Arts	83.135	16.171	1.45	0.147	>0.05 Not Significant
		Science	80.034	17.915			
Designation	:	Lecturers/ Senior Lecturers	82.519	15.588	1.29	0.202	>0.05 Not Significant
		Reader/Lect. Select. Gr.	78.167	22.167			
Experience	:	Upto 10 years	81.760	15.445	0.05	0.962	>0.05 Not Significant
		Above 10 years	81.655	19.051			
College Sex	: 1.	Co-education	81.050	17.346	3.53	0.001	**<0.05 Significant**
	2.	Women	89.700	09.761			

The results in Table—5.36 reveal that on the dimension Organisational Structure only teacher educators' working in co-education and women colleges **differ**. Hence, the hypothesis that the two groups differ is accepted. Other sub groups based on teacher educators' age, sex, specialisation, designation and experience do not differ. Hence, the hypotheses that the groups differ are not accepted.

Total Quality Mindset

The results of 't' tests comparing two groups are presented in the following table:

Table—5.37

't' Test Results for the Dimension Total Quality Mindset

Groups			Mean	SD	t	P	Significance
Age	:	Upto 35 years	76.739	15.450	2.25	0.025	**<0.05 Significant**
		Above 35 years	81.310	17.260			
Sex	: 1.	Male: Teacher educators	79.148	15.837	0.17	0.865	>0.05 Not Significant
	2.	Female: Teacher educators	79.520	17.895			
Specialisation	:	Arts	80.255	16.502	1.02	0.308	>0.05 Not Significant
		Science	78.143	16.734			
Designation	:	Lecturers/ Senior Lecturers	79.802	15.715	0.90	0.373	>0.05 Not Significant
		Reader/Lect. Select. Gr.	77.021	20.130			
Experience	:	Upto 10 years	78.353	15.235	1.03	0.304	>0.05 Not Significant
		Above 10 years	80.564	18.314			
College Sex	: 1.	Co-education	78.883	16.783	1.61	0.121	>0.05 Not Significant
	2.	Women	84.150	13.812			

The results in Table—5.37 reveal that on the dimension Total Quality Mindset teacher educators upto 35 years and above 35 years of age **differ**. Hence, the hypothesis that the two groups differ is accepted. Other sub groups based on teacher educators sex, specialisation, designation, experience and college sex do not differ. Hence, the hypotheses that the groups differ are not accepted.

Organisational Health

The results of 't' tests comparing two groups are presented in the following table:

Table—5.38

't' Test Results for the Variable Organisational Health

		Groups	Mean	SD	t	P	Significance
Age	:	Upto 35 years	473.817	82.268	3.17	0.002	**<0.05 Significant**
		Above 35 years	506.235	81.348			
Sex	: 1.	Male: Teacher educators	485.525	86.545	1.64	0.102	>0.05 Not Significant
	2.	Female: Teacher educators	502.429	76.558			
Specialisation	:	Arts	494.603	84.943	0.57	0.564	>0.05 Not Significant
		Science	488.689	81.275			
Designation	:	Lecturers/ Senior Lecturers	489.623	82.281	0.89	0.375	>0.05 Not Significant
		Reader/Lect. Select. Gr.	501.938	87.207			
Experience	:	Upto 10 years	482.460	81.022	2.14	0.034	**<0.05 Significant**
		Above 10 years	504.764	84.711			
College Sex	: 1.	Co-education	491.929	84.139	0.03	0.980	>0.05 Not Significant
	2.	Women	491.500	72.513			

The results in Table—5.38 reveal that on Organisational Health both teacher educators up to 35 and above 35 years of age and those with experience upto 10 years and above 10 years **differ**. Hence, the hypotheses that the groups differ is accepted. Other sub groups based on teacher educators' sex, specialisation, designation, college sex do not differ. Hence, the hypotheses that the groups differ are not accepted.

Dimensions of Organisational Health

Institutional Integrity

The results of 't' tests comparing two groups are presented in the following table:

Table—5.39

't' Test Results for the Dimension Institutional Integrity

		Groups	*Mean*	*SD*	*t*	*P*	*Significance*
Age	:	Upto 35 years	72.130	12.017	2.13	0.034	**<0.05 Significant**
		Above 35 years	75.297	11.727			
Sex	: 1.	Male: Teacher educators	73.735	12.012	0.28	0.779	>0.05 Not Significant
	2.	Female: Teacher educators	74.163	11.869			
Specialisation	:	Arts	73.383	11.919	0.75	0.452	>0.05 Not Significant
		Science	74.504	11.982			
Designation	:	Lecturers/ Senior Lecturers	74.467	11.695	1.54	1.290	>0.05 Not Significant
		Reader/Lect. Select. Gr.	71.375	12.779			
Experience	:	Upto 10 years	73.847	11.886	0.08	0.938	>0.05 Not Significant
		Above 10 years	73.964	12.061			
College Sex	: 1.	Co-education	74.342	11.456	1.58	0.130	>0.05 Not Significant
	2.	Women	68.550	16.100			

The results in Table—5.39 reveal that on dimension Institutional Integrity both teacher educators up to 35 and above 35 years of age **differ**. Hence, the hypothesis that the two groups differ is accepted. Other sub groups based on teacher educators sex, specialisation, designation, experience and college sex do not differ. Hence, the hyptheses that the groups differ are not accepted.'

Initiating Structure

The results of 't' tests comparing two groups are presented in the following table:

Table—5.40

't' Test Results for the Dimension Initiating Structure

		Groups	*Mean*	*SD*	*t*	*P*	*Significance*
Age	:	Upto 35 years	67.957	17.268	2.03	0.043	**<0.05 Significant**
		Above 35 years	72.276	16.708			
Sex	: 1.	Male: Teacher educators	68.272	18.206	2.72	0.007	**<0.05 Significant**
	2.	Female: Teacher educators	73.827	14.409			
Specialisation	:	Arts	70.106	17.893	0.27	0.789	>0.05 Not Significant
		Science	70.672	16.089			
Designation	:	Lecturers/ Senior Lecturers	69.670	17.152	1.42	0.160	>0.05 Not Significant
		Reader/Lect. Select. Gr.	73.438	16.476			
Experience	:	Upto 10 years	69.300	17.301	1.18	0.238	>0.05 Not Significant
		Above 10 years	71.818	16.697			
College Sex	: 1.	Co-education	70.854	17.096	1.71	0.101	<0.05 Significant
	2.	Women	64.500	15.886			

The results in Table—5.40 reveal that on Initiating Structure only teacher educators up to 35 and above 35 years of age and male and female teacher educators **differ**. Hence, the hypotheses that the groups differ is accepted. Other sub groups based on teacher educators specialisation, designation, experience and college sex do not differ. Hence, the hypotheses that the groups differ are not accepted.

Consideration

The results of 't' tests comparing two groups are presented in the following table:

Table—5.41

't' Test Results for the Dimension Consideration

		Groups	*Mean*	*SD*	*t*	*P*	*Significance*
Age	:	Upto 35 years	62.391	18.759	2.45	0.015	<0.05 **Significant**
		Above 35 years	68.207	19.353			
Sex	: 1.	Male: Teacher educators	65.093	18.943	0.58	0.566	>0.05 Not Significant
	2.	Female: Teacher educators	66.531	19.876			
Specialisation	:	Arts	66.489	19.353	0.78	0.437	>0.05 Not Significant
		Science	64.622	19.213			
Designation	:	Lecturers/ Senior Lecturers	65.425	19.210	0.36	0.718	>0.05 Not Significant
		Reader/Lect. Select. Gr.	66.563	19.736			
Experience	:	Upto 10 years	63.667	18.113	1.90	0.059	>0.05 Not Significant
		Above 10 years	68.318	20.535			
College Sex	: 1.	Co-education	65.563	19.254	0.20	0.842	>0.05 Not Significant
	2.	Women	66.500	20.007			

The results in Table—5.41 reveal that on the dimenion Consideration only teacher educators upto 35 and above 35 years of age **differ**. Hence, the hypothesis that the two groups differ is accepted. Other sub groups based on teacher educators sex, specialisation, designation, experience and college sex do not differ. Hence, the hypotheses that the groups differ are not accepted.

Principal Influence

The results of 't' tests comparing two groups are presented in the following table:

Table—5.42

't' Test Results for the Dimension Principal Influence

	Groups	*Mean*	*SD*	*t*	*P*	*Significance*
Age :	Upto 35 years	66.087	13.967	1.57	0.119	>0.05 Not Significant
	Above 35 years	68.724	12.840			
Sex : 1.	Male: Teacher educators	67.870	13.221	0.48	0.632	>0.05 Not Significant
2.	Female: Teacher educators	67.041	13.714			
Specialisation :	Arts	68.869	13.421	1.72	0.086	>0.05 Not Significant
	Science	66.008	13.238			
Designation :	Lecturers/ Senior Lecturers	67.476	13.076	0.19	0.850	>0.05 Not Significant
	Reader/Lect. Select. Gr.	67.917	14.834			
Experience :	Upto 10 years	66.533	13.842	1.46	0.145	>0.05 Not Significant
	Above 10 years	68.955	12.673			
College Sex : 1.	Co-education	67.646	13.097	0.30	0.770	>0.05 Not Significant
2.	Women	66.500	16.866			

The results in Table—5.42 reveal that on the dimension Principal Influence teacher educators do not differ on all the sub groups. Hence, the hypotheses that the groups differ are not accepted.

Resource Support

The results of 't' tests comparing two groups are presented in the following table:

Table—5.43

't' Test Results for the Dimension Resource Support

		Groups	*Mean*	*SD*	*t*	*P*	*Significance*
Age	:	Upto 35 years	60.965	18.133	4.10	0.000	**<0.05 Significant**
		Above 35 years	70.503	19.195			
Sex	: 1.	Male: Teacher educators	65.364	20.059	1.02	0.310	>0.05 Not Significant
	2.	Female: Teacher educators	67.806	17.943			
Specialisation	:	Arts	67.234	18.837	0.86	0.391	>0.05 Not Significant
		Science	65.160	19.834			
Designation	:	Lecturers/ Senior Lecturers	65.170	18.711	1.82	0.073	>0.05 Not Significant
		Reader/Lect. Select. Gr.	71.208	21.176			
Experience	:	Upto 10 years	62.493	18.784	3.79	0.000	**<0.05 Significant**
		Above 10 years	71.455	18.843			
College Sex	: 1.	Co-education	66.371	19.435	0.27	0.792	>0.05 Not Significant
	2.	Women	65.250	17.882			

The results in Table—5.43 reveal that on the dimension Resource Support only teacher educators upto 35 and above 35 years of age and those having experience up to 10 years and above 10 years **differ**. Hence, the hypotheses that the groups differ is accepted. Other sub groups based on teacher educators sex, specialisation and designation, college sex do not differ. Hence, the hypotheses that the groups differ are not accepted.

Morale

The results of 't' tests comparing two groups are presented in the following table:

Table—5.44

't' Test Results for the Dimension Morale

		Groups	*Mean*	*SD*	*t*	*P*	*Significance*
Age	:	Upto 35 years	71.991	16.518	1.68	0.095	>0.05 Not Significant
		Above 35 years	75.469	16.710			
Sex	: 1.	Male: Teacher educators	72.500	16.417	1.77	0.078	>0.05 Not Significant
	2.	Female: Teacher educators	76.296	16.935			
Specialisation	:	Arts	74.638	15.729	0.74	0.462	>0.05 Not Significant
		Science	73.092	17.779			
Designation	:	Lecturers/ Senior Lecturers	73.774	16.556	0.31	0.758	>0.05 Not Significant
		Reader/Lect. Select. Gr.	74.625	17.398			
Experience	:	Upto 10 years	73.353	16.134	0.64	0.521	>0.05 Not Significant
		Above 10 years	74.718	17.448			
College Sex	: 1.	Co-education	73.229	16.588	2.46	0.022	**<0.05 Significant**
	2.	Women	82.350	15.875			

The results in Table—5.44 reveal on the dimension Morale only teacher educators in women and co-education colleges differ. Hence, the hypothesis that the two groups differ is accepted. Other sub groups based on teacher educators age, sex, specialisation, designation and experience do not differ. Hence, the hypotheses that the groups differ are not accepted.

Academic Emphasis

The results of 't' tests comparing two groups are presented in the following table:

Table—5.45

't' Test Results for the Dimension Academic Emphasis

		Groups	*Mean*	*SD*	*t*	*P*	*Significance*
Age	:	Upto 35 years	72.296	16.788	1.72	0.086	>0.05 Not Significant
		Above 35 years	75.759	15.175			
Sex	: 1.	Male: Teacher educators	72.691	17.158	2.13	0.035	**<0.05 Significant**
	2.	Female: Teacher educators	76.765	13.488			
Specialisation	:	Arts	73.887	16.681	0.38	0.707	>0.05 Not Significant
		Science	74.630	15.146			
Designation	:	Lecturers/ Senior Lecturers	73.642	16.083	1.28	0.205	>0.05 Not Significant
		Reader/Lect. Select. Gr.	76.813	15.360			
Experience	:	Upto 10 years	73.267	16.464	1.15	0.253	>0.05 Not Significant
		Above 10 years	75.536	15.248			
College Sex	: 1.	Co-education	73.925	15.957	1.05	0.305	>0.05 Not Significant
	2.	Women	77.850	16.086			

The results in Table—5.45 reveal that on the dimension Academic Emphasis only male and female teacher educators **differ**. Hence, the hypothesis that the two groups differ is accepted. Other sub groups based on teacher educators age, specialisation, designation, experience, and college sex do not differ. Hence, the hypotheses that the groups differ are not accepted.

Quality of Work-Life

The results of 't' tests comparing two groups are presented in the following table:

Table—5.46

't' Test Results for the Variable Quality of Work-Life

		Groups	*Mean*	*SD*	*t*	*P*	*Significance*
Age	:	Upto 35 years	65.365	5.579	1.41	0.161	>0.05 Not Significant
		Above 35 years	66.303	5.036			
Sex	: 1.	Male: Teacher educators	65.778	5.097	0.42	0.673	>0.05 Not Significant
	2.	Female: Teacher educators	66.071	5.626			
Specialisation	:	Arts	66.135	5.170	0.81	0.417	>0.05 Not Significant
		Science	65.597	5.444			
Designation	:	Lecturers/ Senior Lecturers	65.797	5.253	0.57	0.573	>0.05 Not Significant
		Reader/Lect. Select. Gr.	66.292	5.508			
Experience	:	Upto 10 years	65.660	5.346	0.81	0.416	>0.05 Not Significant
		Above 10 years	66.200	5.230			
College Sex	: 1.	Co-education	65.867	5.401	0.30	0.764	>0.05 Not Significant
	2.	Women	66.150	3.870			

The results in Table—5.46 reveal that on Quality of Work-Life the sub groups do not differ among themselves. Hence, the hypotheses that the groups differ are not accepted.

Dimensions of Quality of Work-Life

Autonomy

The results of 't' tests comparing two groups are presented in the following table:

Table—5.47

't' Test Results for the Dimension Autonomy

Groups			*Mean*	*SD*	*t*	*P*	*Significance*
Age	:	Upto 35 years	12.217	2.077	2.17	0.031	**<0.05 Significant**
		Above 35 years	12.779	2.073			
Sex	: 1.	Male: Teacher educators	12.673	2.141	1.44	0.152	>0.05 Not Significant
	2.	Female: Teacher educators	12.296	1.991			
Specialisation	:	Arts	12.609	2.083	0.66	0.507	>0.05 Not Significant
		Science	12.437	2.102			
Designation	:	Lecturers/ Senior Lecturers	12.514	2.085	0.27	0.792	>0.05 Not Significant
		Reader/Lect. Select. Gr.	12.604	2.131			
Experience	:	Upto 10 years	12.313	2.040	1.96	0.051	>0.05 Not Significant
		Above 10 years	12.827	2.128			
College Sex	: 1.	Co-education	12.558	2.131	0.98	0.334	>0.05 Not Significant
	2.	Women	12.200	1.508			

The results in Table—5.47 reveal that on the dimension Autonomy teacher educators up to 35 years and above 35 years of age **differ**. Hence, the hypothesis that the two groups differ is accepted. Other sub groups based on teacher educators sex, specialisation, designation, experience and college sex do not differ. Hence, the hypotheses that the groups differ are not accepted.

Personal Growth Opportunity

The results of 't' tests comparing two groups are presented in the following table:

Table—5.48

't' Test Results for the Dimension Personal Growth Opportunity

		Groups	*Mean*	*SD*	*t*	*P*	*Significance*
Age	:	Upto 35 years	14.774	2.744	0.56	0.578	>0.05 Not Significant
		Above 35 years	14.966	2.762			
Sex	: 1.	Male: Teacher educators	14.969	2.749	0.66	0.507	>0.05 Not Significant
	2.	Female: Teacher educators	14.734	2.760			
Specialisation	:	Arts	14.936	2.809	0.35	0.723	>0.05 Not Significant
		Science	14.815	2.690			
Designation	:	Lecturers/ Senior Lecturers	14.854	2.640	0.29	0.771	>0.05 Not Significant
		Reader/Lect. Select. Gr.	15.000	3.222			
Experience	:	Upto 10 years	14.967	2.625	0.58	0.564	>0.05 Not Significant
		Above 10 years	14.764	2.921			
College Sex	: 1.	Co-education	14.800	2.766	1.85	0.077	>0.05 Not Significant
	2.	Women	15.850	2.412			

The results in Table—5.48 reveal that on the dimension Personal Growth Opportunity all the sub groups do not differ. Hence, the hypotheses that the groups differ are not accepted.

Workspeed and Routine

The results of 't' tests comparing two groups are presented in the following table:

Table—5.49

't' Test Results for the Dimension Workspeed and Routine

		Groups	*Mean*	*SD*	*t*	*P*	*Significance*
Age	:	Upto 35 years	10.530	2.206	0.73	0.467	>0.05 Not Significant
		Above 35 years	10.338	2.001			
Sex	: 1.	Male: Teacher educators	10.448	2.115	0.64	0.521	>0.05 Not Significant
	2.	Female: Teacher educators	10.316	2.059			
Specialisation	:	Arts	10.312	1.939	0.92	0.359	>0.05 Not Significant
		Science	10.555	2.261			
Designation	:	Lecturers/ Senior Lecturers	10.481	2.087	0.93	0.355	>0.05 Not Significant
		Reader/Lect. Select. Gr.	10.167	2.117			
Experience	:	Upto 10 years	10.447	2.103	0.21	0.832	>0.05 Not Significant
		Above 10 years	10.391	2.086			
College Sex	: 1.	Co-education	10.433	2.055	0.23	0.822	>0.05 Not Significant
	2.	Women	10.300	2.557			

The results in Table—5.49 reveal that on the dimension Work-speed and Routine all the sub groups do not differ. Hence, the hypotheses that the groups differ are not accepted.

Work Complexity

The results of 't' tests comparing two groups are presented in the following table:

Table—5.50

't' Test Results for the Dimension Work Complexity

		Groups	*Mean*	*SD*	*t*	*P*	*Significance*
Age	:	Upto 35 years	13.191	1.977	0.10	0.921	>0.05 Not Significant
		Above 35 years	13.166	2.211			
Sex	: 1.	Male: Teacher educators	12.796	2.092	3.89	0.000	**<0.05 Significant**
	2.	Female: Teacher educators	13.806	1.988			
Specialisation	:	Arts	13.135	2.162	0.35	0.725	>0.05 Not Significant
		Science	13.227	2.048			
Designation	:	Lecturers/ Senior Lecturers	13.165	2.039	0.17	0.865	>0.05 Not Significant
		Reader/Lect. Select. Gr.	13.229	2.408			
Experience	:	Upto 10 years	13.200	2.089	0.21	0.838	>0.05 Not Significant
		Above 10 years	13.146	2.141			
College Sex	: 1.	Co-education	13.200	2.102	0.59	0.562	>0.05 Not Significant
	2.	Women	12.900	2.198			

The results in Table—5.50 reveal that on the dimension. Work Complexity only male and female teacher educators **differ**. Hence, the hypothesis that the two groups differ is accepted. Other sub groups based on teacher educators age, specialisation, designation, experience and college sex do not differ. Hence, the hypotheses that the groups differ are not accepted.

Task Related Interaction

The results of 't' tests comparing two groups are presented in the following table:

Table—5.51

't' Test Results for the Dimension Task Related Interaction

		Groups	Mean	SD	t	P	Significance
Age	:	Upto 35 years	14.652	2.602	1.22	0.222	>0.05 Not Significant
		Above 35 years	15.055	2.676			
Sex	: 1.	Male: Teacher educators	14.852	2.448	0.19	0.852	>0.05 Not Significant
	2.	Female: Teacher educators	14.918	2.959			
Specialisation	:	Arts	15.142	2.598	1.76	0.080	>0.05 Not Significant
		Science	14.563	2.680			
Designation	:	Lecturers/ Senior Lecturers	14.783	2.652	1.22	0.228	>0.05 Not Significant
		Reader/Lect. Select. Gr.	15.292	2.609			
Experience	:	Upto 10 years	14.733	2.600	1.02	0.311	>0.05 Not Significant
		Above 10 years	15.073	2.708			
College Sex	: 1.	Co-education	14.875	2.653	0.04	0.968	>0.05 Not Significant
	2.	Women	14.900	2.634			

The results in Table—5.51 reveal that on the dimension Task Related Interaction all the sub groups do not differ. Hence, the hypotheses that the groups differ are not accepted.

Student Teachers' Involvement in College Activities

The results of 't' tests comparing two groups are presented in the following table:

Table—5.52

't' Test Results for the Variable Student Teachers' Involvement in College Activities

		Groups	Mean	SD	t	P	Significance
Age	:	Upto 35 years	50.748	7.424	2.38	0.018	**<0.05 Significant**
		Above 35 years	52.862	6.735			
Sex	: 1.	Male: Teacher educators	51.420	7.302	1.51	0.132	>0.05 Not Significant
	2.	Female: Teacher educators	52.765	6.741			
Specialisation	:	Arts	52.248	7.198	0.79	0.428	>0.05 Not Significant
		Science	51.546	7.020			
Designation	:	Lecturers/ Senior Lecturers	51.613	7.263	1.64	0.105	>0.05 Not Significant
		Reader/Lect. Select. Gr.	53.313	6.288			
Experience	:	Upto 10 years	51.347	6.938	1.53	0.128	>0.05 Not Significant
		Above 10 years	52.718	7.301			
College Sex	: 1.	Co-education	52.021	7.203	0.86	0.396	>0.05 Not Significant
	2.	Women	50.800	5.961			

The results in Table—5.52 reveal that on Student Teachers' Involvement in College Activities, teacher educators up to 35 years and above 35 years of age **differ**. Hence, the hypothesis that the two groups differ is accepted. Other sub groups based on teacher educators sex, specialisation, experience, designation and college sex do not differ. Hence, the hypotheses that the groups differ are not accepted.

The findings of the differential analyses are presented in the following tables.

Table—5.53

Differential Findings of the Variable Total Quality Culture

Total Quality Culture (Whole Sample)	Teacher Educators Above 35 years of age (M= 492.497)	score better than	Teacher Educators Below 35 years of age (M= 471.026)
	Women Teacher Education Colleges (M= 513.450)	score better than	Co-education Colleges (M= 480.463)
Environment	Women Teacher Education Colleges (M= 85.550)	score better than	Co-education Colleges (M= 80.971)
Product & Service	Teacher Educators Above 35 years of age (M= 86.924)	score better than	Teacher Educators Below 35 years of age (M= 82.713)
Methods	Teacher Educators Above 35 years of age (M= 81.048)	score better than	Teacher Educators Below 35 years of age (M= 76.426)
	Women Teacher Education Colleges (M= 85.850)	score better than	Co-education Colleges (M= 78.450)
People Characteristic	Teacher Educators Above 35 years of age (M= 78.614)	score better than	Teacher Educators Below 35 years of age (M= 74.078)
Organisational Structure	Women Teacher Education Colleges (M= 89.700)	score better than	Co-education Colleges (M= 81.050)
Total Quality Mindset	Teacher Educators Above 35 years of age (M= 81.310)	score better than	Teacher Educators Below 35 years of age (M= 76.739)

Table—5.54

Differential Findings of the Variable Organisational Health

Organisational Health (Whole Sample)	Teacher Educators Above 35 years of age (M= 506.235)	score better than	Teacher Educators Below 35 years of age (M= 473.817)
Institutional Integrity	Teacher Educators Above 35 years of age (M= 75.297)	score better than	Teacher Educators Below 35 years of age (M= 72.130)
Initiating Structure	Teacher Educators Above 35 years of age (M= 72.276)	score better than	Teacher Educators Below 35 years of age (M= 67.957)
	Female Teacher Educators (M= 73.827)	score better than	Male Teacher Educators (M= 68.272)
Consideration	Teacher Educators Above 35 years of age (M= 68.207)	score better than	Teacher Educators Below 35 years of age (M= 62.391)
Resource Support	Teacher Educators Above 35 years of age (M= 70.503)	score better than	Teacher Educators Below 35 years of age (M= 60.965)
	Teacher Educators Above 10 years of experience (M= 71.455)	score better than	Teacher Educators up to 10 years of experience (M= 62.493)
Morale	Teacher educators working in women teacher education colleges (M=82.350)	score better than	Teacher educators working in Co-education colleges (M=73.229)
Academic Emphasis	Female Teacher Educators (M= 76.765)	score better than	Male Teacher Educators (M= 72.691)

Table—5.55

Differential Findings of the Variable Quality of Work-Life

Autonomy	Teacher Educators Above 35 years of age (M= 12.779)	score better than	Teacher Educators Below 35 years of age (M= 12.217)
Work complexity	Female Teacher Educators (M= 13.806)	score better than	Male Teacher Educators (M= 12.796)

Table—5.56

Differential Findings of the Variable Student Teachers' Involvement in College Activities

Student Teachers' Involvement in College Activities	Teacher Educators Above 35 years of age (M= 52.862)	score better than	Teacher Educators Below 35 years of age (M= 50.748)

Analysis of Variance

The analysis of variance is a powerful statistical tool for testing significance of differences between more than two groups in variable(s) at a time. For each variable ANOVA test was used to find out whether three types of managements and six Universities significantly differ. The details are presented in this section.

Total Quality Culture

The differences in the mean scores of the variables of the teacher educators working in different types of management are analysed using 'F' statistics. The results of the variable Total Quality Culture are given below in Table—5.57.

Table—5.57

Results of ANOVA for the Variable Total Quality Culture

Source	*df*	*SS*	*MSS*	*F Ratio*	*F Prob*	*P*
Between groups	3	32386.496	10795.499	1.460	0.2259	> 0.05 Not Significant
Within groups	256	1892597.504	7392.959			
Total	**259**	**1924984.000**				

The results in Table—5.57 reveals that teacher educators working in different type of managements do not vary significantly at 0.05 level with regard to the variable, Total Quality Culture.

Dimensions of Total Quality Culture

Environment

The results for Environment dimension of Total Quality Culture are presented in Table—5.58.

Table—5.58

Results of ANOVA for the Dimension Environment

Source	*Df*	*SS*	*MSS*	*F Ratio*	*F Prob*	*P*
Between groups	3	318.9684	106.323	0.487	0.6917	> 0.05 Not Significant
Within groups	256	55903.8931	218.375			
Total	**259**	**56222.8615**				

The results in Table—5.58 reveal that teacher educators working in different type of managements do not vary significantly at 0.05 level with regard to the dimension Environment of the variable Total Quality Culture.

Product and Service

The results for Product and Service dimension of Total Quality Culture are presented in Table—5.59.

Table—5.59

Results of ANOVA for the Dimension Product and Service

Source	*df*	*SS*	*MSS*	*F Ratio*	*F Prob*	*P*
Between groups	3	1319.747	439.916	2.036	0.1110	> 0.05 Not Significant
Within groups	256	55651.268	217.388			
Total	259	56971.015				

The results in Table—5.59 reveal that teacher educators' working in different type of managements do not vary significantly at 0.05 level of significance with regard to the dimension Product and Service of variable Total Quality Culture.

Methods

The results of Methods dimension of Total Quality Culture are presented in Table—5.60.

Table—5.60

Results of ANOVA for the Dimension Methods

Source	*df*	*SS*	*MSS*	*F Ratio*	*F Prob*	*P*
Between groups	3	1472.935	490.978	1.768	0.1538	> 0.05 Not Significant
Within groups	256	71112.061	277.782			
Total	**259**	**72584.996**				

The results in Table—5.60 reveal that teacher educators working in different type of managements do not vary significantly at 0.05 level of significance with regard to the dimension Methods of the variable Total Quality Culture.

People Characteristics

The results of People Characteristics dimension of Total Quality Culture are presented in Table—5.61.

Table—5.61

Results of ANOVA for the Dimension People Characteristics

Source	*df*	*SS*	*MSS*	*F Ratio*	*F Prob*	*P*
Between groups	3	1530.696	510.232	1.814	0.145	> 0.05 Not Significant
Within groups	256	72011.289	281.294			
Total	**259**	**73541.985**				

The results in Table—5.61 reveal that teacher educators working in different type of managements do not vary significantly at 0.05 level with regard to the dimension People Characteristics of the variable Total Quality Culture.

Organisational Structure

The results of Organisational Structure dimension of Total Quality Culture are presented in Table—5.62.

Table—5.62

Results of ANOVA for the Dimension Organisational Structure

Source	*df*	*SS*	*MSS*	*F Ratio*	*F Prob*	*P*
Between groups	3	1162.062	387.354	1.341	0.262	> 0.05 Not Significant
Within groups	256	73940.877	288.832			
Total	**259**	**75102.939**				

The results in Table—5.62 reveal that teacher educators working in different type of managements do not vary significantly at 0.05 level of significance with regard to the dimension Organisational Structure of the variable Total Quality Culture.

Total Quality Mindset

The results of Total Quality Mindset dimension of Total Quality Culture are presented in Table—5.63.

Table—5.63

Results of ANOVA for the Dimension Total Quality Mindset

Source	*df*	*SS*	*MSS*	*F Ratio*	*F Prob*	*P*
Between groups	3	1353.339	451.113	1.647	1.789	> 0.05 Not Significant
Within groups	256	70100.026	273.282			
Total	**259**	**71453.365**				

The results in Table—5.63 reveal that teacher educators working in different type of managements do not vary significantly at 0.05 level with regard to the dimension Total Quality Mindset of the variable Total Quality Culture.

Organisational Health

The differences in the mean scores of the variables of the teacher educators working in different types of management are analysed using 'F' statistics. The results of ANOVA for the variable organisational health are given in Table—5.64.

Table—5.64

Result of ANOVA for the Variable Organisational Health

Source	*Df*	*SS*	*MSS*	*F Ratio*	*F Prob*	*P*
Between groups	3	54721.832	18240.6108	2.6881	0.0469	< 0.05 Significant
Within groups	256	1737146.364	6785.728			
Total	259	1791868.196				

The results in Table—5.64 reveal that type of teacher educators working in different type of managements vary significantly at 0.05 level with regard to the variable, organisational health. As the 'F' value is significant, pairs of groups are compared for significance of difference using 't' test. The 't' test results are given in Table—5.65.

Table—5.65

Results of 't' Tests for the Variable Organisational Health

Group	*M*	*t*	*P*
Aided Colleges	512.244	2.17	<0.05
Govt. Colleges	476.029		
Un-aided Colleges	483.215	0.43	>0.05
Govt. College	476.029		
Aided Colleges	512.244	1.74	>0.05
Un-aided Colleges	483.215		

The 't' test result in Table—5.65 reveal the teacher educators working in aided and government teacher education colleges significantly differ in their perception of Organisational Health. The aided colleges are higher on Organisational Health when compared to Government Colleges.

Dimensions of Organisational Health

Institutional Integrity

The results for Institutional Integrity dimension of Organisational Health are presented in Table—5.66.

Table—5.66

Results of ANOVA for the Dimension Institutional Integrity

Source	*df*	*SS*	*MSS*	*F Ratio*	*F Prob*	*P*
Between groups	3	480.352	160.117	1.125	0.3394	> 0.05 Not Significant
Within groups	256	36427.844	142.296			
Total	**259**	**36908.196**				

The results in Table—5.66 reveal that teacher educators working in different type of managements do not vary significantly at 0.05 level with regard to dimension institutional integrity of variable Organisational Health.

Initiating Structure

The results for Initiating Structure dimension of Organisational Health are presented in Table—5.67.

Table—5.67

Results of ANOVA for the Dimension Initiating Structure

Source	*df*	*SS*	*MSS*	*F Ratio*	*F Prob*	*P*
Between groups	3	1885.387	628.462	2.189	0.0898	> 0.05 Not Significant
Within groups	256	73504.902	287.129			
Total	**259**	**75390.289**				

The results in Table—5.67 reveal that teacher educators working in different type of managements do not vary at 0.05 level with regard to Initiating Structure dimension of variable Organisational Health.

Consideration

The results for Consideration dimension of Organisational Health are presented in Table—5.68

Table—5.68

Results of ANOVA for the Dimension Consideration

Source	*df*	*SS*	*MSS*	*F Ratio*	*F Prob*	*P*
Between groups	3	356.600	118.867	0.317	0.813	> 0.05 Not Significant
Within groups	256	95863.689	374.468			
Total	**259**	**96220.289**				

The results in Table—5.68 reveal that teacher educators working in different type of managements' do not vary significantly at 0.05 level with regard to dimension Consideration of the variable Organisational Health.

Principal Influence

The results for Principal Influence dimension of Organisational Health are presented in Table—5.69.

Table—5.69

Results of ANOVA for the Dimension Principal Influence

Source	*df*	*SS*	*MSS*	*F Ratio*	*F Prob*	*P*
Between groups	3	637.033	212.345	10187	0.315	> 0.05 Not Significant
Within groups	256	45787.101	178.856			
Total	**259**	**46424.134**				

The results in Table—5.69 reveal that teacher educators working in different type of managements do not vary significantly at 0.05 level with regard to the dimension Principal Influence of the variable of Organisational Health.

Resource Support

The results for Resource Support dimension of Organisational Health are presented in Table—5.70.

Table—5.70

Results of ANOVA for the Dimension Resource Support

Source	*df*	*SS*	*MSS*	*F ratio*	*F Prob*	*P*
Between groups	3	8794.0201	2931.340	8.568	0.0000	< 0.05 Significant
Within groups	256	87580.9184	342.113			
Total	**259**	**96374.9385**				

The results in Table—5.70 reveal that teacher educators working in different type of managements vary significantly at 0.05 level with regard to the dimension Resource Support of the variable Organisational Health. As the 'F' value is significant, pairs of groups are compared for significance of difference using 't' test. The 't' test results are given in Table—5.71.

Table—5.71

Results of 't' Tests for the Dimension Resource Support

Group	*M*	*t*	*P*
Aided Colleges	74.361	2.47	<0.05
Govt. Colleges	65.086		
Unaided Colleges	61.467	1.03	>0.05
Govt. College	65.086		
Aided Colleges	74.361	5.06	<0.05
Unaided Colleges	61.467		

The 't' test result in Table—5.71 reveal the teacher educators working in aided and government teacher education colleges significantly differ, whereas there is no difference between teacher educators working in un-aided and government colleges. Teacher educators working in aided and un-aided teacher education colleges also significantly differ in their perception of Resource Support. The teacher educators of aided teacher education colleges are higher on the perception of Resource Support when compared to government and un-aided colleges.

Morale

The results for Morale dimension of Organisational Health are presented in Table—5.72.

Table—5.72

Results of ANOVA for the Dimension Morale

Source	*df*	*SS*	*MSS*	*F Ratio*	*F Prob*	*P*
Between groups	3	1205.511	401.837	1.451	0.228	> 0.05 Not Significant
Within groups	256	70883.243	276.888			
Total	**259**	**72088.754**				

The results in Table—5.72 reveal that teacher educators working in different type of managements do not vary significantly at 0.05 level with regard to the dimension Morale of the variable Organisational Health.

Academic Emphasis

The results for Academic Emphasis dimension of Organisational Health are presented in Table—5.73.

Table—5.73

Results of ANOVA for the Dimension Academic Emphasis

Source	*df*	*SS*	*MSS*	*F Ratio*	*F Prob*	*P*
Between groups	3	2009.5952	669.865	2.678	0.048	< 0.05 Significant
Within groups	256	64048.0163	250.188			
Total	**259**	**66057.6115**				

The results in Table—5.73 reveal that teacher educators working in different type of managements vary significantly at 0.05 level with regard to dimension Academic Emphasis of the variable Organisational Health. As the 'F' value is significant, pairs of groups are compared for significance of difference using 't' test. The 't' test results are given in Table—5.74.

Table—5.74

Results of 't' Tests for the Dimension Academic Emphasis

Group	*M*	*t*	*P*
Aided Colleges	77.721	2.47	<0.05
Govt. Colleges	69.829		
Un-aided Colleges	73.007	1.06	>0.05
Govt. Colleges	69.829		
Aided Colleges	77.721	2.16	<0.05
Un-aided Colleges	73.007		

The 't' test results in—Table 5.74 reveal the teacher educators working in aided and government teacher education colleges and those working in aided and un-aided colleges significantly differ on the dimension Academic Emphasis. But teacher educators' working in un-aided and government colleges do not differ. The teacher educators of aided colleges are higher on Academic Emphasis when compared to government and un-aided colleges.

Quality of Work-Life

The differences in the mean scores of the variables of the teacher educators' working in different types of management are analysed using 'F' statistics. The results of the variable Quality of Work-Life are given in Table—5.75.

Table—5.75

Results of ANOVA for the Variable Quality of Work-Life

Source	*df*	*SS*	*MSS*	*F Ratio*	*F Prob*	*P*
Between groups	3	24.869	8.2897	0.293	0.830	> 0.05 Not Significant
Within groups	256	7232.896	28.254			
Total	**259**	**7257.765**				

The results in Table—5.75 reveal that teacher educators working in different type of managements do not vary significantly at 0.05 level with regard to the variable Quality of Work-Life.

Dimensions of Quality of Work-Life

Autonomy

The results for Autonomy dimension of Quality of Work-Life are presented in Table—5.76.

Table—5.76

Results of ANOVA for the Dimension Autonomy

Source	*df*	*SS*	*MSS*	*F Ratio*	*F Prob*	*P*
Between groups	3	69.983	23.328	5.6297	0.0009	< 0.05 Significant
Within groups	256	1060.771	4.144			
Total	259	1130.754				

The results in Table—5.76 reveal that teacher educators working in different type of managements vary significantly at 0.05 level with regard to the dimension Autonomy of the variable Quality of Work-Life. As the 'F' value is significant, pairs of groups are compared for significance of difference using 't' test. The 't' test results are given in Table—5.77.

Table—5.77

Results of 't' Tests for the Dimension Autonomy

Group	*M*	*t*	*P*
Aided Colleges	13.035	0.40	>0.05
Govt. Colleges	13.200		
Un-aided Colleges	12.059	2.93	<0.05
Govt. College	13.200		
Aided Colleges	13.035	3.47	<0.05
Un-aided Colleges	12.059		

The 't' test results in Table—5.77 reveal that the teacher educators working in aided and un-aided colleges significantly differ. Teacher educators working in aided and government teacher education colleges do not differ. But teacher educators' working in un-aided and government teacher education colleges significantly differ in Autonomy. The teacher educators of government colleges are high on Autonomy when compared to un-aided colleges, and the teacher educators of aided colleges are high on Autonomy when compared to unaided colleges.

Personal Growth Opportunity

The results for Personal Growth Opportunity dimension of Quality of Work-Life are presented in Table—5.78.

Table—5.78

Results of ANOVA for the Dimension Personal Growth Opportunity

Source	*df*	*SS*	*MSS*	*F Ratio*	*F Prob*	*P*
Between groups	3	6.2123	2.0708	0.2714	0.8460	> 0.05 Not Significant
Within groups	256	1953.0915	7.6293			
Total	**259**	**1959.3038**				

The results in Table—5.78 reveal that teacher educators working in different type of managements do not vary significantly at 0.05 level of significance with regard to the dimension Personal Growth Opportunity of the variable Quality of Work-Life.

Workspeed and Routine

The results for Workspeed and Routine dimension of Quality of Work-Life are presented in Table—5.79.

Table—5.79

Results of ANOVA for the Dimension Workspeed and Routine

Source	*df*	*SS*	*MSS*	*F Ratio*	*F Prob*	*P*
Between groups	3	22.7755	7.592	1.749	0.157	> 0.05 Not Significant
Within groups	256	1110.6860	4.339			
Total	**259**	**1133.4615**				

The results in Table—5.79 reveal that teacher educators working in different type of managements do not vary significantly at 0.05 level of significance with regard to the dimension Workspeed and Routine of the variable Quality of Work-Life.

Work Complexity

The results for Work Complexity dimension of Quality of Work-Life are presented in Table—5.80.

Table—5.80

Results of ANOVA for the Dimension Work Complexity

Source	*df*	*SS*	*MSS*	*F Ratio*	*F Prob*	*P*
Between groups	3	34.315	11.438	2.625	0.0510	> 0.05 Not Significant
Within groups	256	1115.547	4.358			
Total	**259**	**1149.862**				

The results in Table—5.80 reveal that teacher educators working in different type of managements do not vary significantly at 0.05 level with regard to the dimension Work Complexity of the variable Quality of Work-Life.

Task Related Interaction

The results for Task Related Interaction dimension of Quality of Work-Life are presented in Table—5.81.

Table—5.81

Results of ANOVA for the Dimension Task Related Interaction

Source	*df*	*SS*	*MSS*	*F Ratio*	*F Prob*	*P*
Between groups	3	66.544	22.181	3.249	0.022	< 0.05 Significant
Within groups	256	1747.518	6.826			
Total	**259**	**1814.062**				

The results in Table—5.81 reveal that teacher educators working in different type of managements vary significantly at 0.05 level with regard to the dimension Task Related Interaction of the variable Quality of Work-Life. As the 'F' value is significant, pairs of groups are compared for significance of difference using 't' test. The 't' test results are given in Table—5.82.

Table—5.82

Results of 't' Tests for the Dimension Task Related Interaction

Group	*M*	*t*	*P*
Aided Colleges	14.978	0.77	>0.05
Govt. Colleges	14.571		
Un-aided Colleges	15.007	0.87	>0.05
Govt. Colleges	14.571		
Aided Colleges	14.978	0.08	>0.05
Un-aided Colleges	13.126		

The 't' test results in Table—5.82 reveal the teacher educators working in three different types of management do not significantly differ on the dimension Task Related Interaction.

Student Teachers' Involvement in College Activities

The results for Student Teachers' Involvement in College Activities are presented in Table—5.83.

Table—5.83

Results of ANOVA for the Variable Student Teachers' Involvement in College Activities

Source	*df*	*SS*	*MSS*	*F Ratio*	*F Prob*	*P*
Between groups	3	509.634	169.878	3.454	0.017	< 0.05 Significant
Within groups	256	12591.978	49.187			
Total	**259**	**13101.612**				

The results in Table—5.83 reveal that teacher educators working in different type of managements vary significantly at 0.05

level of significance with regard to the variable Student Teachers' Involvement in College Activities. As the 'F' value is significant, pairs of groups are compared for significance of difference using 't' test. The 't' test results are given in Table—5.84.

Table—5.84

Results of 't' Tests for the Variable Student Teachers' Involvement in College Activities

Group	*M*	*t*	*P*
Aided Colleges	53.721	1.07	>0.05
Govt. Colleges	52.200		
Un-aided Colleges	50.659	1.16	>0.05
Govt. Colleges	52.200		
Aided Colleges	53.721	3.17	<0.05
Un-aided Colleges	50.659		

The 't' test results in Table—5.84 reveal that teacher educators working in aided and un-aided colleges significantly differ in their perception of Student Teachers' Involvement in College Activities. But teacher educators working in aided-government and un-aided-government colleges do not significantly differ in their perception of Student Teachers' Involvement in College Activities.

The Student Teachers' of aided colleges are high on involvement in College Activities when compared to Student Teachers' of un-aided colleges.

Change Facilitator Styles of Principals

The three groups of teacher education colleges under Responder, Initiator and Manager Principals have their means in Total Quality Culture as 495.95, 495.92 and 472.67 respectively. The teacher education colleges with Manager Principals significantly differ from the other two groups of teacher education colleges, namely teacher education colleges under Responder and Initiator Principals.

The differences in the mean scores of Total Quality Culture of the teacher educators working in colleges with Principals having different type of Change Facilitator Styles are analysed using 'F' statistics. The results are shown in Table—5.85.

Table—5.85

Results of ANOVA for Change Facilitator Styles of Principals and Total Quality Culture

Source	*df*	*SS*	*MSS*	*F Ratio*	*F Prob*	*P*
Between groups	2	61353.556	30676.778	4.230	0.0156	< 0.05 Significant
Within groups	257	1863630.444	7251.4803			
Total	**259**	**1924984.000**				

The results in Table—5.85 reveal that teacher educators working in colleges with principals having different Change Facilitator Styles vary significantly at 0.05 level of significance with regard to the variable Total Quality Culture.

The difference in the mean scores of Organisational Health of teacher educators working in colleges with principals having different type of Change Facilitator Styles are analysed using 'F' statistics. The results are shown in Table—5.86.

Table—5.86

Results of ANOVA for Change Facilitator Styles of Principals and Organisational Health

Source	*df*	*SS*	*MSS*	*F Ratio*	*F Prob*	*P*
Between groups	2	154943.739	77471.8698	12.163	0.0000	> 0.05 Not Significant
Within groups	257	1636924.456	6369.3559			
Total	**259**	**1791868.195**				

The results in Table—5.86 reveal that teacher educators working in colleges with principals having different Change Facilitator Styles do not vary significantly at 0.05 level with regard to the variable Organisational Health.

The difference in the mean scores of Quality of Work-Life of teacher educators working in colleges with principals having different type of Change Facilitator Styles are analysed by using 'F' statistics. The results are shown in Table—5.87.

Table—5.87

Results of ANOVA for Change Facilitator Styles of Principals and Quality of Work-Life

Source	*df*	*SS*	*MSS*	*F Ratio*	*F Prob*	*P*
Between groups	2	34.1445	17.0722	0.6074	0.5456	> 0.05 Not Significant
Within groups	257	7223.6209	28.1075			
Total	**259**	**7257.7654**				

The results in Table—5.87 reveal that teacher educators working in colleges with principals having different Change Facilitator Styles do not vary significantly at 0.05 level with regard to the variable Quality of Work-Life.

Correlation Analysis

In case of bivariate analyses one has to face questions such as (i) Does there exists an association between the two variables? If so, to what extent? (ii) Is there any cause and effect relationship between two variables? If one increases or decreases, does it affect the other? If yes, to what extent and in which direction. The first question is answered by the use of correlation technique. But the correlation coefficient 'r' usually estimates the degree of closeness of linear relationship between two variables (Y and X). Many apparently unrelated variables rise or fall together. Therefore, it does not answer the second question dealing with cause and effect relationship. How much does it change for a given change in X? What is the shape of the curve connecting Y and X? How accurately can 'Y' be predicted from X? These questions are handled by the regression technique discussed in detail in the next section.

The correlation coefficient is calculated mathematically

$$r = \frac{\sum XY - n\bar{X}\bar{Y}}{\sqrt{\left(\sum X^2 - n\bar{X}^2\right)\left(\sum Y^2 - n\bar{Y}^2\right)}}$$

Where X and Y are two variables X = Mean for the X variable, Y= Mean for Y variable. n = common number of samples.

In the present study correlation analysis was done using the measures of six variables say $X_1 X_2 X_3 X_4 X_5 X_6$ to calculate inter correlations where

X_1 = Total Quality Culture

X_2 = Organisational Health

X_3 = Quality of Work-Life

X_4 = Student Teachers' Involvement in College Activities

X_5 = Change Facilitator Styles of Principals

X_6 = Student Teachers' Commitment to Course

The 45 teacher education colleges formed the sample for the present study. The Karl Pearson's correlation coefficient test was applied. Bivariate correlations between the variables studied are worked out and the details are furnished in this section.

Total Quality Culture and Organisational Health

The correlations between dimensions of Total Quality Culture and Organisational Health are presented in Table—5.88.

Table—5.88

Correlations between Dimensions of Organisational Health and Dimensions of Total Quality Culture

	OH II	*OH IS*	*OH CON*	*OH PI*	*OH RS*	*OH MO*	*OH AE*	*OH TOTAL*
TQC ENV	0.0990	0.189*	0.343*	0.174*	0.342*	0.441*	0.301*	0.392*
TQC PS	0.1020	0.213*	0.322*	0.198*	0.297*	0.332*	0.213*	0.347*
TQCMET	0.0230	0.191*	0.312*	0.0980	0.327*	0.379*	0.346*	0.354*
TQCPEO	0.112	0.212*	0.355*	0.136**	0.327*	0.384*	0.288*	0.378*
TQCOS	0.167*	0.296*	0.438*	0.214*	0.417*	0.516*	0.361*	0.499*
TQCTQM	0.124**	0.226*	0.39*	0.184*	0.352*	0.447*	0.32*	0.424*
TQCTOTAL	**0.125****	**0.264***	**0.429***	**0.198***	**0.409***	**0.496***	**0.364***	**0.475***

Level of Significance: * 0.01 i. e. 1%;

** 0.05 i.e. 5%

Table 5.88 reveals that:

(i) Among the dimensions significant correlations existed between Environment dimension of Total Quality Culture and the following Organisational Health dimensions like Initiating Structure (IS) ($r=0.189, p<0.01$), consideration (CON)($r=0.343, p<0.01$), Principal Influence (PI) ($r=0.174, p<0.01$), Resource Support (RS) ($r=0.342, p<0.01$), Morale (MO) ($r=0.441, p<0.01$) and Academic Emphasis (AE) ($r=0.301, p<0.01$). Hence, the hypothesis that these dimensions are related is accepted. Significant and positive relationship was observed between Environment dimension of Total Quality Culture and total of Organisational Health ($r= 0.392, p<0.01$). The hypothesis that the variable Organisational Health is related to Environment dimension is accepted.

Significant positive relationship was observed between total of Total Quality Culture and total of Organisational Health ($r = 0.475, p<0.01$) ($r=0.125, p<0.05$). The hypothesis that these two variables Total Quality Culture and the Organisational Health are related is accepted.

(ii) Significant positive relationship was observed between Product and Service (PS) dimension of Total Quality Culture and the following dimensions of Organisational Health like Initiating Structure (IS) ($r=0.213, p<0.01$), Consideration (CON) ($r=0.322, p<0.01$), Principal Influence (PI) ($r=0.198, p<0.01$), Resource Support (RS) ($r=0.297, p<0.01$), Morale (MO) ($r=0.332, p<0.01$) and Academic Emphasis (AE) ($r=0.213, p<0.01$); Hence, the hypothesis that these dimensions are related is accepted.

Significant positive relationship was observed between Product and Service (PS) dimension of Total Quality Culture and the total of Organisational Health ($r=0.347, p<0.01$). The Hypothesis that the variable Organisational Health is related to Product and Service dimension is accepted.

(iii) Significant positive relationship was observed between Methods (MET) dimensions of Total Quality Culture and

the following dimensions of Organisational Health like Initiating Structure (IS)($r=0.191$, $p<0.01$), Consideration (CON)($r=0.312$, $p<0.01$), Resource Support (RS) ($r=0.327$, $p<0.01$), Morale (MO)($r=0.379$, $p<0.01$) and Academic Emphasis (AE) ($r=0.346$, $p<0.01$), Hence, the hypothesis that these dimensions are related is accepted.

Significant positive relationship was observed between Methods (MET) dimension of Total Quality Culture and total of variable Organisational Health ($r=0.345$, $p<0.01$). The hypothesis that variable Organisational Health is related to the dimension Methods is accepted.

(iv) Significant positive relationship was observed between People Characteristics (PEO) dimension of Total Quality Culture and following dimensions of Organisational Health like Initiating Structure (IS) ($r=0.212$, $p<0.01$), Consideration (CON) ($r=0.355$, $p<0.01$), Principal Influence (PI) ($r=0.135$, $p<0.01$), Resource Support (RS) ($r=0.327$, $p<0.01$), Morale (MO) ($r=0.384$, $p<0.01$) and Academic Emphasis (AE) ($r=0.288$, $p<0.01$) Hence, the hypothesis that these dimensions are related is accepted.

Significant positive relationship is observed between People Characterstics (PEO) dimension of Total Quality Culture and the total of Organisational Health ($r=0.376$, $p<0.01$). The hypothesis that variable Organisation Health is related to the dimension People Characterstics is accepted.

(v) Significant positive relationship was observed between Organisational Structure (OS) dimension of Total Quality Culture and following dimensions of Organisational Health like Institutional Integrity (II)($r=0.167$, $p<0.01$), Initiating Structure (IS) ($r=0.296$, $p<0.01$), Consideration (CON) ($r=0.438$, $p<0.01$), Principal Influence (PI) ($r=0.214$, $p<0.01$), Resource Support (RS) ($r=0.417$, $p<0.01$), Morale (MO) ($r=0.516$, $p<0.01$) and Academic Emphasis (AE) ($r=0.361$, $p<0.01$). Hence, the hypothesis that these dimensions are related is accepted.

Significant positive relationship was observed between Organisational Structure (OS) dimension of Total Quality Culture and the total of Organisational Health ($r=0.499$, $p<0.01$). The hypothesis that variable Organisational Health is related to the dimension Organisational Structure is accepted.

(vi) Significant positive relationship was observed between Total Quality Mindset (TQM) dimension of Total Quality Culture and following dimensions of Organisational Health like Institutional Integrity (II)($r=0.124$, $p<0.01$), Initiating Structure (IS) ($r=0.226$, $p<0.01$), Consideration (CON) ($r=0.39$, $p<0.01$), Principal Influence (PI) ($r=0.184$, $p<0.01$), Resource Support (RS) ($r=0.352$, $p<0.01$), Morale (MO) ($r=0.447$, $p<0.01$) and Academic Emphasis (AE) ($r=0.32$, $p<0.01$). Hence, the hypothesis that these dimensions are related is accepted

Significant positive relationship was observed between Total Quality Mindset (TQM) dimension of Total Qulity Culture and the total of Organisational Health ($r=0.424$, $p<0.01$). The hypothesis that variable Organisational Health is related to the dimension Total Quality Mindset is accepted.

(vii) Significant and positive relationship was observed between total of Total Quality Culture and following dimensions of Organisational Health like Institutional Integrity (II)($r=0.125$, $p<0.01$), Initiating Structure (IS) ($r=0.264$, $p<0.01$), Consideration (CON) ($r=0.429$, $p<0.01$), Principal Influence (PI) ($r=0.198$, $p<0.01$), Resource Support (RS) ($r=0.409$, $p<0.01$), Morale (MO) ($r=0.496$, $p<0.01$) and Academic Emphasis (AE) ($r=0.364$, $p<0.01$). Hence, the hypothesis that these dimensions are related is accepted.Significant positive relationship was observed between total of Total Quality Culture and total of Organisational Health ($r=0.475$, $p<0.01$). The hypothesis that these two variables Total Quality Culture and Organisation Health are related is accepted.

Total Quality Culture and Quality of Work-Life

The correlations between Total Quality Culture and Quality of Work-Life and their dimensions are presented in Table—5.89.

Table—5.89

Correlations between Dimensions of Total Quality Culture and Dimensions of Quality of Work-Life

	TQC ENV	*TQC PS*	*TQC MET*	*TQC PEO*	*TQC OS*	*TQC TQM*	*TQC TOTAL*
QWL AT	0.0240	-0.0520	-0.0380	-0.0350	-0.0400	-0.0650	-0.0420
QWL PGO	0.366*	0.190	0.402*	0.334*	0.412*	0.405*	0.42*
QWL WSR	*-0.17	-0.0930	-0.115	*-0.17	*-0.25	*-0.201	*-0.199
QWL WCO	0.0770	0.820	0.108	0.0620	0.0930	0.0630	0.0960
QWL TRI	0.332*	0.184*	0.303*	0.301*	0.408*	0.626*	0.369*
QWL TOTAL	**0.199***	**0.0590**	**0.167***	**0.129****	**0.166***	**0.125****	**0.167***

Level of Significance: * 0.01 i. e. 1%

** 0.05 i.e. 5%

Table—5.89 reveals that:

(i) Significant positive relationship was observed between Environment (ENV) dimension of Total Quality Culture (TQC) with Personal Growth Opportunity (PGO) (r=0.3660, p<0.01) and Task Related Interaction (TRI) (r=0.3320, p<0.01) dimensions of Quality of Work-Life. Hence, the hypothesis that these dimensions are related is accepted. But Environment dimension of Total Quality Culture has significantly negative relationship with Workspeed and Routine (WSR) dimensions of Quality of Work-Life (r=-0.1700, p<0.01). Hence, the hypothesis that these dimesions are related is accepted. But the correlation is negative. When Environmental Influence is high Workspeed and Routine is low.

(ii) Product and Service (PS) dimension of Total Quality Culture has a significant positive relationship with Task Related Interaction (TRI) dimension of Quality of Work-Life (r=0.1840, p<0.01). Hence, the hypothesis that these dimensions are related is accepted.

(iii) Methods dimension of Total Quality Culture has a significant negative relationship between Workspeed and Routine dimension of Quality of Work-Life (r=0.3660, p<0.01). Hence the hypothesis that these dimension are related is accepted. But the correlation is negative. When Methods is high Workspeed and Routine is low. Positive relationship was seen between Methods dimension of Total Quality Culture and Personal Growth Opportunity (r=0.4020, p<0.01), Task Related Interaction (r=0.3030, p<0.01) dimensions of Quality of Work-Life. Hence, the hypothesis that these dimension are related is accepted.

Significant positve relationship was observed between Methods dimension of Total Quality Culture and total of Quality of Work-Life (r=0.1679, p<0.01). The hypothesis that variable Quality of Work-Life is related to the dimesion Methods is accepted.

(iv) People Characteristic (PEO) dimension of Total Quality Culture with Workspeed and Routine (WSR) dimension of Quality of Work-Life, have a significant negative relation (r=-0.1700, p<0.01). Hence, the hypothesis that these dimensions are related is accepted. But the correlation is negative. When People Characteristics is high Workspeed and Routine is low. There is a significant positive relationship between People Characteristics of Total Quality Culture and Personal Growth Opportunity (r=0.3340, p<0.01) and Task Related Interaction (r=0.300, p<0.01) dimensions of Quality of Work-Life. Hence the hypothesis that these dimensions are related is accepted.

Significant positive relationship was observed between People characterstics dimension of Total Quality Culture and total of Quality of Work-Life (r=0.1289, p<0.05). The hypothesis that variable Quality of Work-Life is related to People Characterstics dimension of Total Quality Culture is accepted.

(v) A significant negative relationship was observed between Organisational Structure (OS) of Total Quality Culture with Workspeed and Routine (WSR) dimension of Quality of Work-Life ($r=-0.2540$, $p<0.01$). Hence, the hypothesis that these dimensions are related is accepted. But the correlation is negative. When Organisational Structure is high, Workspeed and Routine is low. Positive relationship was seen between Organisational Structure dimension of Total Quality Culture and Personal Growth Opportunity (PGO) ($r=0.0412$, $p<0.01$) and Task Related Interaction (TRI) ($r=0.4080$, $p<0.01$) dimensions of Quality of Work-Life. Hence, the hypothesis that these dimensions are related is accepted.

Significant positive relationship was observed between Organisational Structure dimension of Total Quality Culture and total of Quality of Work-Life ($r=0.1661$, $p<0.01$). The hypothesis that variable Quality of Work-Life is related to Organisational Structure dimension is accepted.

(vi) A significant negative relationship was observed between Total Quality Mindset (TQM) dimension of Total Quality Culture and Workspeed and Routine dimension of Quality of Work-Life ($r=-0.2010$, $p<0.01$). Hence, the hypothesis that these dimensions are related is accepted. But correlation is negative. When Total Quality Mindset is high Workspeed and Routine is low. But a positive significant relation was seen between Total Quality Mindset dimension of Total Quality Culture and Personal Growth Opportunity ($r=0.4050$, $p<0.01$) and Task Related Interaction ($r=0.3260$, $p<0.01$) dimensions of Quality of Work-Life. Hence, the hypothesis that these dimensions are related is accepted.

Significant positive relationship was observed between Total Quality Mindset of Total Quality Culture and total of Quality of Work-Life ($r=0.1250$, $p<0.05$). The hypothesis that variable Quality of Work-Life is related to Total Quality Mindset dimension is accepted.

(vii) The total of Total Quality Culture also has a negative significant relationship with Workspeed and Routine (WSR) dimension of Quality of Work-Life (r=-0.1990, p<0.05). Hence, the hypothesis that the variable Total Quality Culture is related to the dimension Workspeed and Routine is accepted. But the correlation is negative. When Total Quality Culture is high, Workspeed and Routine is low. Positive relationship was seen between Personal Growth Opportunity (PGO) (r=0.4200, p<0.01) and Task Related Interaction (TRI) (r=0.369, p<0.01) and total of Quality of Work-Life (r= 0.1670, p<0.01). Hence, the hypothesis that the variable Total Quality Culture is related to the dimensions Personal Growth Opportunity is accepted.

Significant positive relationship was observed between and total of Total Quality Culture and total of Quality of Work-Life (r=0.1670, p<0.01). The hypothesis that the variable Quality of Work-Life is related to Total Quality Culture is accepted.

Total Quality Culture and Student Teachers' Involvement in College Activities

The correlation between dimensions of Total Quality Culture and Student Teachers' Involvement in College Activities are presented in Table—5.90.

Table—5.90

Correlations between Dimensions of Total Quality Culture and Student Teachers' Involvement in College Activities

	TQC ENV	*TQC PS*	*TQC MET*	*TQC PEO*	*TQC OS*	*TQC TQM*	*TQC TOTAL*
SIN	0.2597*	0.2170*	0.3191*	0.3143*	0.3510*	0.3401*	0.3590*

Level of Significance: * 0.01 i. e. 1%.

Table—5.90 reveals that Student Teachers' Involvement in College Activities has a significant positive relationship with all the dimensions of Total Quality Culture. The hypothesis that the variable Student Teachers' Involvement in College Activities is related to all the dimensions of Total Quality Culture is accepted.

Total Quality Culture and Arts and Science Student Teachers' Commitment to Course

The correlations between dimensions of Total Quality Culture and Arts and Science Student Teachers Commitment to course are presented in Table—5.91.

Table—5.91

Correlations between Dimensions of Total Quality Culture and Arts and Science Student Teachers' Commitment to Course

TQC	*Arts Student teachers' commitment to Course*	*Science Student teachers' commitment to Course*
ENV	0.1080	0.1170
PS	0.0040	0.1710
MET	-0.0550	0.0000
PEO	0.0010	-0.0200
OS	0.1310	0.0250
TQM	-0.0600	0.0790
TOTAL	**0.0220**	**0.0670**

Table—5.91 reveals that there is no significant relationship between Total Quality Culture and Arts and Science Student Teachers' Commitment to Course. Hence, the hypothesis that these variables are related is not accepted.

Organisational Health and Quality of Work-Life

The correlations between dimensions of Organisational Health and Quality of Work-Life are presented in Table—5.92.

Table—5.92

Correlations between Dimensions of Organisational Health and Dimensions of Quality of Work-Life

	OH II	*OH IS*	*OH CON*	*OH PI*	*OH RS*	*OH MO*	*OH AE*	*OH TOTAL*
QWL AT	**-0.146	-0.0240	0.0150	*-0.169	-0.0320	-0.0730	-0.0420	-0.0830
QWL PGO	0.0520	0.135**	0.229*	0.0940	0.178*	0.283*	0.175*	0.239*
QWL WSR	-0.0680	*-0.235	-0.0980	*-0.263	**-0.15	*-0.215	*-0.241	*-0.252
QWL WCO	0.117	0.1010	0.108	0.126**	0.144**	0.151**	0.187*	0.187*
QWL TRI	-0.0190	0.211*	0.277*	0.234*	0.258*	0.423*	0.348*	0.359*
TOTAL	**-0.103**	**0.0490**	**0.155****	**-0.084**	**C.0910**	**0.119**	**0.0950**	**0.0800**

Level of significance: * 0.01 i.e. 1%

** 0.05 i.e. 5%

Table—5.92 reveals the following:

(i) A significant negative relationship is seen betweeen Institutional Integrity (I I) of Organisational Health and Autonomy (AT) ($r=-0.145, p<0.05$). Hence, the hypothesis that these dimensions are related is accepted. But the correlation is negative. When Institutional Integrity is high Autonomy is low.

(ii) A significant negative relationship is seen between Initiating Structure of Organisational Health and Workspeed and Routine (WSR) dimensions of Quality of Work-Life ($r=-0.2350, p<0.01$). Hence, the hypothesis that these dimensions are related is accepted. But the correlation is negative. When Initiating Structure is high Workspeed and Routine is low. A significant positive relationship is seen between Initiating Structure dimension of Organisational Health and Personal Growth Opportunity ($r=0.1350, p<0.05$) and Task Related Interaction dimensions of Quality of Work-Life ($r=0.2110, p<0.01$). Hence, the hypothesis that these dimensions are related is accepted.

(iii) A significant positive relationship was observed between Consideration (CON) dimension of Organisational Health with Personal Growth Opportunity (PGO) ($r=0.2290, p<0.01$) and Task Related Interaction (TRI) ($r=0.2770, P<0.01$) dimensions of Quality of Work-Life. The hypothesis that these dimensions are related is accepted.

Significant positive relationship was observed between Consideration dimension of Organisational Health and total of Quality of Work-Life ($r=0.1550, p<0.01$). The hypothesis that the variable Quality of Work-Life is related to Consideration dimension is accepted.

(iv) A significant negative relationship was observed between Principal Influence dimension of Organisational Health with Autonomy (AT) ($r=-0.1690, p<0.01$) and Workspeed and Routine ($r=-0.2630, p<0.01$) dimensions of Quality Work-Life. Hence, the hypothesis that these dimensions are related is accepted. But the correlation is negative. When Principal Influence is high, Autonomy is low. Significant positive relationships were observed between Work Complexity ($r=0.1260, p<0.05$) and Task Related Interaction dimensions of Quality of Work-Life ($r=0.2340, p<0.01$). Hence, the hypothesis that these dimensions are related is accepted.

(v) A significant positive relationship was observed between Resource Support (RS) of Organisational Health with Personal Growth Opportunity (PGO)($r=0.178, p<0.01$), Work Complexity (WCO)($r=0.144, p<0.05$), and Task Related Interaction (TRI) dimensions of Quality of Work-Life ($r=0.258, p<0.01$). Hence, the hypothesis that these dimensions are related is accepted. And a significant negative relationship was observed between Resource Support of Organisational Health and Workspeed and Routine (WSR) dimension of Quality of Work-Life ($r=-0.15, p<0.05$). Hence, the hypothesis that these dimensions are related accepted. But the correlation is negative. When Resource Support is high, Workspeed and Routine is low.

(vi) A significant positive relationship was observed between Morale (MO) of Organisational Health with Personal Growth Opportunity (PGO) (r=0.283, p<0.01), Work Complexity (WCO) (r=0.151, p<0.05), and Task related interaction dimensions of Quality of Work-Life (r=0.423, p<0.01). Hence, the hypothesis that these dimensions are related is accepted. And there is significant negative relationship between Morale (MO) and Workspeed and Routine (r=-0.215, p<0.01). Hence the hypothesis that these dimensions are related is accepted. But the correlation is negative. When Morale in the Organisation is high, Workspeed and Routine is low.

(vii) There was a positive significant relationship between Academic Emphasis (AE) dimension of Organisational Health and Personal Growth Opportunity (PGO) (r=0.175, p<0.01), Work Complexity (WCO) (r=0.187, p<0.01), and Task Related Interaction dimensions of Quality of Work-Life (TRI) (r=0.348, p<0.01). Hence, the hypothesis that these dimensions are related is accepted. And a negative significant relationship is also observed between Academic Emphasis dimension and Workspeed and Routine (WSR) dimension of Quality of Work-Life (r=-0.241, p<0.01). Hence, the hypothesis that these dimensions are related accepted. But the correlation is negative. When Academic Emphasis is high, Workspeed and Routine is low.

(viii) The Total of Organisational Health has positive significant relationship with Personal Growth Opportunity (PGO)(r=0.239, p<0.01), Work Complexity (WCO) (r=0.187, p<0.01), and Task Related Interaction (TRI) dimension of Quality of Work-Life (r=0.359, p<0.01). The hypothesis that the variable Organisational Health is related to Work Complexity and Task Related Interaction dimensions is accepted. A negative significant relationship was seen between total of Organisational Health and Work Speed and Routine (WSR)(r=-0.252, p<0.01) dimension of Quality of Work-

Life. The hypothesis that the variable Organisational Health is related to Workspeed and Routine dimension is accepted. But the correlation is negative. When Total Quality Culture is high, Workspeed and Routine is low.

Organisational Health and Change Facilitator Styles of Principals

The correlations between dimensions of Organisational Health and Change Facilitator Styles of Principals are presented in Table—5.93.

Table—5.93

Correlations between Dimensions of Organisational Health and Change Facilitator Styles of Principals

OH	*CFS R*	*CFS M*	*CFS I*
II	-0.0800	-0.0640	0.0810
IS	*-0.321	0.0180	0.298*
CON	*-0.25	-0.0220	0.231*
PI	**-0.157	-0.0310	0.22*
RS	*-0.205	0.0030	0.218*
MO	*-0.17	-0.0540	0.217*
AE	-0.12	-0.0330	0.218*
OH TOTAL	***-0.269**	**-0.0330**	**0.302***

Level of significance: * 0.01 i.e. 1%

** 0.05 i.e. 5%

Table—5.93 results clearly indicated that:

(i) Initiating Structure dimension of Organisational Health has a significant negative relationship with Responder Style of Principals ($r=-0.3210$, $p<0.01$). Hence, the hypothesis that the Initiating Structure is related to Responder Style is accepted. But the correlation is negative. When the Organisational Health is high the Responder Change Facilitator Styles of Principal is low. The Initiating Structure dimension of Organisational Health has positively significant relationship with Initiator style. Hence, the hypothesis that Organisational Health is related to Initiator Style of Principals is accepted.

(ii) There is a significant negative relationship between Consideration dimension of Organisational Health with Responder Styles of Principals ($r=-0.2300$, $p<0.01$). Hence, the hypothesis that Consideration dimension is related to Responder Style is accepted. But the correlation is negative. When Consideration is high Responder Style is low. And Consideration dimension of Organisational Health has significant positive relationship with Initiator Styles of Principals ($r=0.2310$, $p<0.01$). Hence, the hypothesis that Consideration dimension is related to Initiator Style is accepted.

(iii) A significant negative relationship is seen between Principal Influence dimension of Organisational Health and Responder Style of Principals ($r=-0.1570$, $p<0.05$). Hence, the hypothesis that Principal Influence dimension is related to Responder Style is accepted. But the correlation is negative. With high Principal Influence the Responder Change Facilitator Style of Principal is low. And Principal Influence dimension of Organisational Health has significant positive relationship with Initiator Style of Principals ($r=0.2200$, $p<0.01$). Hence, the hypothesis that Principal Influence dimension is related to Initiator Style is accepted.

(iv) A significant negative relationship is seen between Resource Support dimension of Organisational Health and Responder Style of Principals ($r=-0.2050$, $p<0.01$). Hence, the hypothesis that Resource Support dimension is related to Responder Style is accepted. But the correlation is negative. When Resource Support is high Responder Style of Change Facilitator Styles of Principals is low. And Resource Support dimension of Organisational Health has significant positive relationship with Initiator Style of Principals ($r=0.2180$, $p<0.01$). Hence, the hypothesis that Resource Support dimension is related to Initiator Style is accepted.

(v) Morale dimension of Organisational Health with Responder Style of Principals ($r=-0.1700$, $p<0.01$), and Academic Emphasis dimension of Organisational Health

with Responder style of Change Facilitator Style of Principal (r=-0.2690, p<0.01) have a significant negative relationship. Hence, hypothesis that these dimensions are related is accepted. But the correlation is negative. When the Morale in the Organisational is high, Responder Change Facilitator Style of Principals is low. The Morale dimension of Organisational Health has significant positive relationship with Initiator Style (r=0.2170, p<0.01) the hypothesis that these dimensions are related accepted. Academic Emphasis dimension and total of Organisational Health also have significant positive relationship with Initiator Style of Principals (r=0.1470, p<0.01). Hence, the hypothesis that the Initiator Style of Principals is related to the variable Organisational Health and its Academic Emphasis dimension is accepted.

Organisational Health and Student Teachers' Involvement in College Activities

The correlations between dimensions of Organisational Health and Student Teachers' Involvement in College Activities are presented in Table—5.94.

Table—5.94

Correlations between Dimensions of Organisational Health and Student Teachers' Involvement in College Activities

	OH II	*OH IS*	*OH CON*	*OH PI*	*OH RS*	*OH MO*	*OH AE*	*OH TOTAL*
SIN	0.0769	0.2455*	0.3778*	0.1933*	0.3584*	0.3288*	0.3621*	0.4550*

Level of Significance: * 0.01 i. e. 1%

Table—5.94 reveal that Student Teachers' Involvement in College Activities has significant positive correlations with all the dimensions of Organisational Health. The hypothesis that the variable Student Teachers' Involvement in College Activities is related to all the dimensions of Organisational Health is accepted.

Quality of Work-Life and Student Teachers' Involvement in College Activities

The correlations between dimensions of Quality of Work-Life and Student Teachers' Involvement in College Activities are presented in Table—5.95.

Table—5.95

Correlations between Dimensions of Quality of Work-Life and Student Teachers' Involvement in College Activities

	QWL AT	*QWL PGO*	*QWL WSR*	*QWL WCO*	*QWL TRI*	*QWL TOTAL*
SIN	0.0386	0.2772*	-0.1306**	0.1195	0.2773*	0.1866*

Level of Significance: * 0.01 i. e. 1%

** 0.05 i.e. 5%

Table—5.95 reveals that there is a negative significant relationship between Student Teachers' Involvement in College Activities and Workspeed and Routine dimension of Quality of Work-Life ($r=-0.1360, p<0.05$). Hence, the hypothesis that the variable Student Teachers' Involvement in College Activities is related to Workspeed and Routine dimension is accepted. But the correlation is negative. When Student Teachers' Involvement in College Activities is high, Workspeed and Routine is low. A positive significant relationships were seen between Student Teachers' Involvement in College Activities and Personal Growth Opportunity ($r=0.2772, p<0.01$), Work Complexity ($r=0.1195, p<0.01$) and Task Related Interaction ($r=0.2773, p<0.01$). The hypothesis that the variable Student Teachers' Involvement in College Activities is related to Personal Growth Opportunity, Work Complexity and Task Related Interaction dimensions of Quality of Work-Life is accepted.

Significant positive relationship was observed between the variable Student Teachers' Involvement in College Activities and the variable total of Quality of Work-Life ($r=0.1866, p<0.01$). The hypothesis that these two variables are related is accepted.

Organisational Health and Student Teachers' Commitment to Course

The correlations between dimensions of Organisational Health and Arts and Science Student Teachers' Commitment to Course are presented in Table—5.96.

Table—5.96

Correlations between Dimensions of Organisational Health and Arts and Science Student Teachers' Commitment to Course

	OH II	*OH IS*	*OH CON*	*OH PI*	*OH RS*	*OH MO*	*OH AE*	*OH TOTAL*
ARTS STC	0.1390	0.0640	-0.0230	-0.0010	0.0360	0.327**	0.1940	0.1250
SCI STC	**-0.318	-0.2460	-0.2480	-0.1240	-0.0930	-0.2220	-0.1420	-0.2500

Level of Significance: * 0.01 i. e. 1%;

** 0.05 i.e. 5%

Table—5.96 reveals that:

(i) There was significant positive relationship between Arts Student Teachers' Commitment to Course and Morale dimension of Organisational Health (r=0.3270, p<0.05). Hence, the hypothesis that the variable Arts Student Teachers' Commitment to Course is related to Morale dimension of Organisational Health is accepted.

(ii) A significant negative relationship was seen between Science Student Teachers' Commitment to Course and Institutional Integrity of dimension of Organisational Health (r=0.3180, p<0.05). The hypothesis that the variable Science Student Teachers' Commitment to Course is related to Institutional Integrity dimension of Organisational Health is accepted. But the correlation is negative. When Science Student Teachers' Commitment to Course is high Institutional Integrity is low.

Significant negative relationship was observed between Science Student Teachers' Commitment to Course with total of Organisational Health (r=-0.2500, p<0.10). The hypothesis that these two variables are related is accepted. But the correlation is negative. When Science Student Teachers' Commitment to Course is high Organisational Health is low.

Quality of Work-Life and Arts and Science Student Teachers' Commitment to Course

The correlations between dimensions of Quality of Work-Life and Arts and Science Student Teachers' Commitment to course are presented in Table—5.97.

Table—5.97

Correlations between Dimensions of Quality of Work-Life and Arts and Science Student Teachers' Commitment to Course

	QWL AT	*QWL PGO*	*QWL WSR*	*QWL WCO*	*QWL TRI*	*QWL TOTAL*
ARTS STC	-0.1800	0.1710	-0.2280	0.0800	0.1340	0.0490
SCI STC	-0.1810	-0.1580	0.0700	0.308**	-0.2000	-0.1410

Level of Significance: ** 0.05 i.e. 5%.

Table—5.97 reveal that, significant positive relationship was seen only between Arts and Science Student Teachers' Commitment to Course and Work Complexity dimension of Quality of Work-Life ($r=0.3080$, $p<0.05$). Hence, the hypothesis that Arts and Science Student Teachers' Commitment to Course is related Work Complexity dimension is accepted.

Regression Analysis

Regression is a statistical tool with the help of which one can predict the unknown values of one variable from known values of other variables. Regression analysis is concerned with the derivation of an appropriate mathematical expression of the functional relationship between variables. This expression is derived for the purpose of predicting values of a dependent variable on the basis of independent variables. Regression analysis is thus designed to examine the relationship of a variable 'Y' to a set of other variables $X_1, X_2, ... X_K$.

The relationship between dependent variable (Y) and the independent variables (X) can be studied through mathematical formulas. The most commonly used linear equation is:

$$Y = b_1X_1 + b_2X_2 \ldots\ldots b_kX_k + b_o$$

Here 'Y' the dependent variable is to be predicted, $X_1, X_2, \ldots\ldots X_K$ are the known variables with which prediction are to be made and $b_1, b_2 \ldots\ldots b_K$ are the coefficients of $X_1, X_2, \ldots\ldots X_K$ variables that are determined from the observed data and b_o is the constant (Y intercept).

The present study considers the Total Quality Culture as the dependent variable and Organisational Health, Quality of Work-Life, Student Teachers' Involvement in College Activities, Change Facilitator Styles of Principals and Student Teachers' Commitment to Course are considered as independent variables.

Multiple Regression

Multiple regression analysis was done taking Total Quality Culture (TQC) as the dependent variable and other variables studied as the independent variables namely, Organisational Health Dimensions, Institutional Integrity (II), Initiating Structure (IS), Consideration (CON), Principal Influence (PI), Resource Support (RS), Morale (MO), Academic Emphasis (AE). Quality of Work-Life Dimensions, Autonomy (AT), Personal Growth Opportunity (PGO), Work Speed and Routine (WSR), Work Complexity (WCO), Task Related Interaction (TRI) and the Variable Student Teachers' Involvement (SIN) in College Activities. The regression equations were computed for the whole sample and for sub samples divided on the basis of Universities, type of management and sex of the college.

Whole Sample

The regression was first computed using the whole sample data. The variables significantly contributing to the variance in the Total Quality Culture in the decreasing order are Personal Growth Opportunity (PGO), Morale (MO), Resource Support (RS), Initiating Structure (IS) and Student Teachers' Involvement in activities (SIN) as indicated by the Beta Coefficients.

Table—5.98

Relevant Statistics of Regression Analysis for the Whole Sample

Variables	*B*	*SEB*	*Beta*	*T*	*Significant*	*R*
PGO	11.452326	1.619107	0.365368	7.073	0.0000	
MO	1.615066	0.319663	0.32544	5.052	0.0000	
RS	0.892534	0.290627	0.199707	3.071	0.0024	0.667
IS	-0.670286	0.319884	-0.132649	2.095	0.0371	
SIN	1.352334	0.652921	0.111566	2.071	0.0393	
Constant	110.958558	32.883285		3.374	0.0009	

Equation

Y = 110.958 + 11.452 + 1.615 + 0.893-0.670 + 1.352

(TQC) (PGO) (MO) (RS) (IS) (SIN)

University Wise

Karnatak University

The variables significantly contributing to the variance in the Total Quality Culture in the decreasing order are Resource Support (RS), Personal Growth Opportunity (PGO), Student Teachers' Involvement in Activities (SIN), and Task Related Interaction (TRI) as indicated in the Beta Coefficients.

Table—5.99

Relevant Statistics of Regression Analysis for Karnatak University

Variables	*B*	*SEB*	*Beta*	*T*	*Significant*	*R*
RS	1.630601	0.326092	0.416027	5.000	0.0000	
PGO	11.721770	2.607813	0.411623	4.495	0.0000	
SIN	3.219908	0.958836	0.290417	3.358	0.0012	0.747
TRI	-5.398939	2.505067	-0.195014	-2.155	0.0342	
Constant	135.015922	48.090787		2.808	0.0063	

Equation

Y = 135.0159-1.631 + 11.722 + 3.219 + 5.399

(TQC) (RS) (PGO) (SIN) (TRI)

Bangalore University

The variables significantly contributing to the variance in the Total Quality Culture in the decreasing order are Morale (MO) and Personal Growth Opportunity (PGO) as indicated in the Beta Coefficients.

Table—5.100

Relevant Statistics of Regression Analysis for Bangalore University

Variables	*B*	*SEB*	*Beta*	*T*	*Significant*	*R*
MO	3.001795	0.624716	0.475386	4.805	0.0000	
PGO	12.166463	3.274234	0.367622	3.716	0.0004	0.675
Constant	69.743072	57.978863		1.203	0.2337	

Equation

Y = 69.743-3.002 + 12.166

(TQC) (MO) (PGO)

Mysore University

The variables significantly contributing to the variance in the Total Quality Culture in the decreasing order are Morale (MO) and Resource Support (RS) as indicated in the Beta Coefficients.

Table—5.101

Relevant Statistics of Regression Analysis for Mysore University

Variables	*B*	*SEB*	*Beta*	*T*	*Significant*	*R*
MO	7.314025	1.738998	0.889791	4.206	0.0003	
RS	-2.941778	1.134583	-0.548535	-2.593	0.0154	0.639
Constant	123.280627	99.457076		1.240	0.2262	

Equation

Y = 123.281 + 7.314-2.942

(TQC) (MO) (RS)

Mangalore University

The variables significantly contributing to the variance in the Total Quality Culture in the decreasing order are Morale (MO), Personal Growth Opportunity (PGO) and Institutional Integrity (II) as indicated in the Beta Coefficients.

Table—5.102

Relevant Statistics of Regression Analysis for Mangalore University

Variables	*B*	*SEB*	*Beta*	*T*	*Significant*	*R*
MO	2.427265	0.439212	0.641005	5.526	0.0000	
PGO	14.193172	3.674357	0.456140	3.863	0.0012	0.884
II	1.543998	0.611907	0.293544	2.523	0.0219	
Constant	-2.948572	77.301523		-0.038	0.9700	

Equation

Y = 2.948-2.427 + 14.193 + 1.544

(TQC) (MO) (PGO) (II)

Gulbarga University

The variables significantly contributing to the variance in the Total Quality Culture in the decreasing order are Personal Growth Opportunity (PGO) and Morale (MO) as indicated in the Beta Coefficients.

Table—5.103

Relevant Statistics of Regression Analysis for Gulbarga University

Variables	*B*	*SEB*	*Beta*	*T*	*Significant*	*R*
PGO	16.242980	3.603121	0.516694	4.508	0.0001	
MO	1.900118	0.557252	0.390820	3.410	0.0016	0.754
Constant	86.041771	53.590770		1.606	0.1167	

Equation

Y = 86.042-16.243 + 1.900
(TQC) (PGO) (MO)

Kuvempu University

The variables significantly contributing to the variance in the Total Quality Culture in the decreasing order are Personal Growth Opportunity (PGO), Work Complexity (WCO), Institutional Integrity (II), Student Teachers' Involvement in College Activities (SIN) and Workspeed and Routine (WSR) as indicated in the Beta Coefficients.

Table—5.104

Relevant Statistics of Regression Analysis for Kuvempu University

Variables	*B*	*SEB*	*Beta*	*T*	*Significant*	*R*
PGO	21.005403	2.437502	0.879262	8.618	0.0000	
WCO	13.048407	3.115326	0.464036	4.188	0.0008	
II	-2.030708	0.580069	-0.328081	-3.501	0.0032	0.951
SIN	-3.564559	1.355888	-0.308227	-2.629	0.0190	
WSR	-6.903026	2.326122	-0.270983	-2.968	0.0096	
Constant	397.151706	83.017718		4.784	0.0002	

Equation

Y = 397.152-21.005 + 13.048 + 2.031 + 3.565 + 6.903
(TQC) (PGO) (WCO) (II) (SIN) (WSR)

General Observation: In Universities the highly contributing variables to the variance in Total Quality Culture (TQC) are Morale (MO) and Personal Growth Opportunity (PGO).

Type of Management Wise

Government Teacher Education Colleges

The variables significantly contributing to the variance in the Total Quality Culture in the decreasing order are Student Teachers' Involvement in College Activities (SIN), Personal Growth Opportunity (PGO), and Work Complexity (WCO) as indicated in the Beta Coefficients.

Table—5.105

Relevant Statistics of Regression Analysis for Government Colleges

Variables	*B*	*SEB*	*Beta*	*T*	*Significant*	*R*
SIN	4.470438	1.113272	0.529036	4.016	0.0003	
PGO	14.055457	3.364970	0.524973	4.177	0.0002	0.780
WCO	9.837499	3.239838	0.389037	3.036	0.0048	
Constant	-58.699794	92.041735		-0.638	0.5283	

Equation

Y = 58.699 + 4.470-14.055 + 9.837

(TQC) (SIN) (PGO) (WCO)

Private Aided Colleges

The variables significantly contributing to the variance in the Total Quality Culture in the decreasing order are Morale (MO) and Personal Growth Opportunity (PGO) as indicated in the Beta Coefficients.

Table—5.106

Relevant Statistics of Regression Analysis for Private Aided Colleges

Variables	*B*	*SEB*	*Beta*	*T*	*Significant*	*R*
MO	2.668714	0.520658	0.450232	5.126	0.0000	
PGO	12.423146	3.070944	0.355341	4.045	0.0001	0.669
Constant	87.022486	48.715433		1.786	0.0777	

Equation

Y = 87.023-2.669 + 12.423

(TQC) (MO) (PGO)

Private Un-aided Colleges

The variables significantly contributing to the variance in the Total Quality Culture in the decreasing order are Personal Growth Opportunity (PGO), Resource Support (RS) and Morale (MO) as indicated in the Beta Coefficients.

Table—5.107

Relevant Statistics of Regression Analysis for Private Unaided Colleges

Variables	*B*	*SEB*	*Beta*	*T*	*Significant*	*R*
PGO	11.743348	1.859276	0.404517	6.316	0.0000	
RS	1.198613	0.309449	0.284444	3.873	0.0002	0.714
MO	1.276435	0.356134	0.270567	3.584	0.0005	
Constant	138.301965	30.834690		4.485	0.0000	

Equation

Y = 138.302-11.743 + 1.199 + 1.276

(TQC) (PGO) (RS) (MO)

General Observations: In Type of Management the highly contributing variables to the variance in Total Quality Culture (TQC) are Personal Growth Opportunity (PGO), Morale (MO) and Student Teachers' Involvement in College Activities (SIN).

College Sex Wise

Co-Education

The variables significantly contributing to the variance in the Total Quality Culture in the decreasing order are Personal Growth Opportunity (PGO), Morale (MO), Resource Support (RS) and Student Teachers' Involvement in College Activities (SIN) as indicated in the Beta Coefficients.

Table—5.108

Relevant Statistics of Regression Analysis for Co-Education Colleges

Variables	*B*	*SEB*	*Beta*	*T*	*Significant*	*R*
PGO	11.353831	1.743321	0.357470	6.513	0.0000	
MO	1.405021	0.332084	0.265302	4.231	0.0000	
RS	0.631421	0.281015	0.139691	2.247	0.0256	0.653
SIN	1.392263	0.701428	0.114150	1.985	0.0483	
Constant	95.202636	34.334740		2.773	0.0060	

Equation

Y = 95.203-11.354 + 1.405 + 0.631 + 1.392

(TQC) (PGO) (MO) (RS) (SIN)

Women Colleges

The variables significantly contributing to the variance in the Total Quality Culture in the decreasing order are Morale (MO), and Work Complexity (WCO) as indicated in the Beta Coefficients.

Table—5.109

Relevant Statistics of Regression Analysis for Women Colleges

Variables	*B*	*SEB*	*Beta*	*T*	*Significant*	*R*
MO	2.764508	0.560360	0.778353	4.933	0.0001	
WCO	-11.505813	4.047137	-0.448534	-2.843	0.0112	0.781
Constant	434.217749	59.728660		7.270	0.0000	

Equation

Y = 434.218-2.765 + 11.506

(TQC) (MO) (WCO)

General Observation: In Co-education Colleges the highly contributing variables to the variance in Total Quality Culture (TQC) are Personal Growth Opportunity (PGO) and Morale (MO). In Women Colleges highly contributing variables to the variance in Total Quality Culture (TQC) are Morale (MO) and Work Complexity (WCO).

Factor Analysis

Nineteen variables were put in factor analysis and the results regarding the groupings of variables under each factor extracted for the whole sample and for the various universities are compared and details are furnished in Table—5.110.

Whole Sample

Factor:	I	II	III	IV
Eigen Value	7.306	2.301	1.479	1.188
% of Variance	38.500	12.100	7.800	6.300
Cumulative %	38.500	50.060	58.400	64.600

Table—5.110

Results of (varimax) Rotated Factor Matrix

	Factor 1	*Factor 2*	*Factor 3*	*Factor 4*
TQM	0.896			
MET	0.877			
OS	0.876			
PEO	0.870			
ENV	0.818			
PS74	0.795			
IS		0.816		
CON		0.803		
AE		0.774		
RS		0.772		
MO		0.718		
PI		0.567		
SIN		0.467		
WSR			0.763	
TRI			0.647	
PGO			0.529	
WCO			0.509	
AT				0.754
II				0.485

Factor 1

The following dimensions of Total Quality Culture have high loadings on the 1st factor:

1. Total Quality Mind Set (TQM)
2. Methods (MET)
3. Organisational Structure (OS)
4. People Characteristic (PEO)
5. Environment (ENV)
6. Product and Service (PS)

The above dimensions of Total Quality Culture have high loading on factor 1. The factor may therefore be called Total Quality Culture. The factor explains 38.5 % of variance.

Factor 2

The following dimensions of Organisational Health and Student Teachers' Involvement in College Activities have high loadings on the 2nd factor:

1. Initiating Structure (IS)
2. Consideration (CON)
3. Academic Emphasis (AE)
4. Resource Support (RS)
5. Morale (MO)
6. Principal Influence (PI)
7. Student Teachers' Involvement in College Activities (SIN)

The above dimensions of Organisational Health and Student Teachers' Involvement in College Activities have high loadings on factor 2. The factor may therefore be called Organisational health. The factor explains 12.1 % of variance.

Factor 3

The following dimensions of Quality of Work-Life have high loadings on the 3rd factor.

1. Workspeed and Routine (WSR)
2. Task Related Interaction (TRI)
3. Personal Growth Opportunity (PGO)
4. Work Complexity (WCO)

The above dimensions of Quality of Work-Life have high loadings on factor 3. The factor may therefore be called Quality of Work-Life. The factor explains 7.8% of variance.

Factor 4

The following dimensions of Quality of Work-Life (AT) and Organisational Health (II) have high loading on the 4th factor.

1. Autonomy (AT)
2. Institutional Integrity (II)

The above dimensions of Quality of Work-Life and Organisational Health have high loadings on factor 4. The factor may therefore be called as Institutional Autonomy. The factor explains 6.3% of variance.

University-Wise

Factor Analysis for Karnatak University

Factor:	*I*	*II*	*III*	*IV*	*V*
Eigen Value	7.794	2.373	1.876	1.188	1.131
% of Variance	41.000	12.500	9.900	6.300	6.000
Cumulative %	41.000	53.500	63.400	69.600	75.600

Table—5.111

Results of Rotated Factor Matrix for Karnatak University

	Factor 1	*Factor 2*	*Factor 3*	*Factor 4*	*Factor 5*
MET	0.878				
PEO	0.854				
PS	0.844				
TQM	0.839				
OS	0.798				
ENV	0.766				
SIN	0.484				
AE		0.845			
IS		0.844			
CON		0.803			
MO		0.778			
RS		0.691			
PI		0.535			
WSR			0.781		
WCO			0.691		
PGO			0.688		
TRI			0.664		
AT				0.901	
II					0.913

Factor 1

The following dimensions of the variable Total Quality Culture and the Variable Student Teachers' Involvement in College Activities (SIN) have high loadings on the 1st factor.

1. Methods (MET)
2. People Characteristic (PEO)
3. Products and service (PS)
4. Total Quality Mindset (TQM)
5. Organisational Structure (OS)
6. Environment (ENV)
7. Student Teachers' Involvement in College Activities (SIN)

The above dimensions of Total Quality Culture and Student Teachers' Involvement in College Activities have high loadings on factor 1. The factor may therefore be called Total Quality Culture. The factor may be called Total Quality Culture and Student Teachers' Involvement in College Activities. The factor explains 41.0% of variance.

Factor 2

The following dimensions of the Organisational Health have high loadings on the 2nd factor:

1. Academic Emphasis (AE)
2. Initiating Structure (IS)
3. Consideration (CON)
4. Morale (MO)
5. Resource Support (RS)
6. Principal Influence (PI)

The above dimensions of Organisational Health have high loadings on factor 2, the factor may therefore be called Organisational Health. The factor explains 12.5% of variance.

Factor 3

The following dimensions of Quality of Work-Life have high loadings on the 3rd factor:

1. Work Speed and Routine (WSR)
2. Work Complexity (WCO)
3. Personal Growth Opportunity (PGO)
4. Task Related Interaction (TRI)

The above dimensions of Quality of Work-Life have high loadings on factor 3. The factor may therefore be called Quality of Work-Life. The factor explains 9.9% of variance.

Factor 4

The following dimensions of variable Quality of Work-Life has high loading on the 4th factor.

1. **Autonomy (AT)**

The above dimension of Quality of Work-Life has high loading on factor 4. The factor may therefore be called as Institutional Autonomy. The factor explains 6.3% of variance.

Factor 5

The following dimensions of Organisational Health has high loading on 5th factor.

1. **Institutional Integrity (II)**

The above dimension of Organisational Health has high loading on factor 5. The factor may therefore be called as Institutional Integrity. The factor explains 6% of variance.

Bangalore University

Factor Analysis for Bangalore University

Factor:	*I*	*II*	*III*	*IV*	*V*
Eigen Value	8.027	2.189	1.573	1.198	1.029
% of Variance	42.200	11.500	8.300	6.300	5.400
Cumulative %	42.200	53.800	62.000	68.400	73.800

Table—5.112

Results of Rotated Factor Matrix for Bangalore University

	Factor 1	*Factor 2*	*Factor 3*	*Factor 4*	*Factor 5*
PEO	0.916				
MET	0.914				
TQM	0.914				
OS	0.871				
PS	0.814				
ENV	0.802				
IS		0.796			
RS		0.763			
CON		0.759			
PI		0.731			
PGO			0.762		
TRI			0.697		
SIN			0.676		
AT			0.631		
WSR				0.785	
I I				0.685	
MO				0.494	
AE				0.455	
WCO					0.918

Factor 1

The following dimensions of Total Quality Culture have high loadings on the 1st factor.

1. People Characteristic (PEO)
2. Methods (MET)
3. Total Quality Mindset (TQM)
4. Organisational Structure (OS)
5. Product and Service (PS)
6. Environment (ENV)

The above dimensions of Total Quality Culture have high loadings on factor 1. The factor may therefore be called Total Quality Culture. The factor explains 42.2% variance.

Factor 2

The following dimensions of Organisational Health have high loadings on the 2nd factor:

1. Initiating Structure (IS)
2. Resource Support (RS)
3. Consideration (CON)
4. Principal Influence (PI)

The above dimensions of Organisational Health have high loadings on factor 2. The factor may therefore be called Organisational Health. The factor explains 11.5% of variance.

Factor 3

The following dimensions of Quality of Work-Life have high loadings on the 3rd factor:

1. Personal Growth Opportunity (PGO)
2. Task Related Interaction (TRI)
3. Student Teachers' Involvement in College Activities (SIN)
4. Autonomy (AT)

The above dimensions of Quality of Work-Life and the variable Student Teachers' Involvement in College Activities have high loadings on factor 3. The factor may therefore be called Quality of Work-Life and Student Teachers' Involvement in College Activities. The factor explains 8.3% of variance.

Factor 4

The following dimensions of Quality of Work-Life (WSR) and the remaining dimensions of Organisational Health (II, MO, AE) and have high loadings on factor 4.

1. Workspeed and Routine (WSR)
2. Institutional Integrity (II)

3. Morale (MO)
4. Academic Emphasis (AE)

The above dimension of Quality of Work-Life and dimensions of Organisational Health have high loadings on factor 4. The factor may therefore be called Organisational Health and Workspeed and Routine. The factor explains 6.3% of variance.

Factor 5

The following dimension of the variable Quality of Work-life has high loading on 5th factor:

1. Work Complexity (WCO)

The above dimension of Quality of Work-Life (QWL) has high loading on factor 5. The factor may therefore be called Work Complexity. The factor explains 5.4% of variance.

Mysore University

Factor Analysis of Mysore University

Factor:	*I*	*II*	*III*	*IV*
Eigen Value	6.363	3.942	2.417	1.30615
% of Variance	33.500	20.700	12.700	6.90000
Cumulative %	33.500	54.200	67.000	73.80000

Table—5.113

Results of Rotated Factor Matrix for Mysore University

	Factor 1	*Factor 2*	*Factor 3*	*Factor 4*
1	2	3	4	5
TQM	0.951			
OS	0.930			
PS	0.888			
MET	0.868			
ENV	0.823			
PEO	0.712			
IS		0.901		

(Table Contd...)

1	2	3	4	5
RS		0.889		
AE		0.876		
CON		0.860		
MO		0.781		
PI		0.724		
WCO			0.785	
PGO			0.762	
WSR			0.653	
AT			0.616	
TRI			0.556	
II				0.779
SIN				0.414

Factor 1

The following dimensions of the variable Total Quality Culture have high loadings on 1st factor.

1. Total Quality Mindset (TQM)
2. Organisational Structure (OS)
3. Products and Service (PS)
4. Methods (MET)
5. Environment (ENV)
6. People Characteristic (PEO)

The above dimensions of Total Quality Culture have high loading on factor 1. The factor may therefore be called Total Quality Culture. The factor explains 33.5% of variance.

Factor 2

The following dimensions of Organisational Health have high loadings on 2nd factor.

1. Initiating Structure (IS)
2. Resource Support (RS)
3. Academic Emphasis (AE)

4. Consideration (CON)
5. Morale (MO)
6. Principal Influence (PI)

The above dimensions of Organisational Health have high loadings on factor 2. The factor may therefore be called Organisational Health. The factor explains 20.7% of variance.

Factor 3

The following dimensions of the variable Quality of Work-Life have high loadings on factor 3.

1. Work Complexity (WCO)
2. Personal Growth Opportunity (PGO)
3. Workspeed and Routine (WSR)
4. Autonomy (AT)
5. Task Related Interaction (TRI)

The above dimensions of Quality of Work-Life have high loadings on factor 3. The factor may therefore be called Quality of Work-Life. The factor explains 12.7% of variance.

Factor 4

The following dimension of Organisational Health and the variable Student Teachers' Involvement in College Activities have high loadings on the 4th factor:

1. Institutional Integrity (II)
2. Student Teachers' Involvement in College Activities (SIN)

The above dimensions of Organisational Health and variable Student Teachers' Involvement in College Activities have high loadings on factor 4. The factor may therefore be called Institutional Integrity and Student Teachers' Involvement in College Activities. The factor explains 6.9% of variance.

Mangalore University

Factor analysis for Mangalore University

Factor:	*I*	*II*	*III*	*IV*	*V*
Eigen Value	7.535	3.114	1.947	1.366	1.084
% of Variance	39.700	16.400	10.200	7.200	5.700
Cumulative %	39.700	56.000	66.300	73.500	79.200

Table—5.114

Results of Rotated Factor Matrix for Mangalore University

	Factor 1	*Factor 2*	*Factor 3*	*Factor 4*	*Factor 5*
MET	0.907				
OS	0.890				
PEO	0.875				
ENV	0.858				
TQM	0.857				
PRI	0.656				
PGO	0.617				
AE	0.583				
WCO	0.576				
PS	0.471				
PI		0.852			
RS		0.819			
CON		0.801			
SIN		0.717			
MO		0.649			
WSR			0.902		
IS			0.724		
AT				0.927	
II					0.891

Factor 1

The following dimensions of Total Quality Culture (MET, OS, PEO, ENV, TQM, PS), dimension of Organisational Health (AE) and dimensions of Quality of Work -Life (TRI, PGO, WCO) have high loadings on 1st factor.

1. Methods (MET)
2. Organisational Structure (OS)
3. People Characteristic (PEO)
4. Environment (ENV)
5. Total Quality Mindset (TQM)
6. Task Related Interaction (TRI)
7. Personal Growth Opportunity (PGO)
8. Academic Emphasis (AE)
9. Work Complexity (WCO)
10. Product and Service (PS)

The above dimensions of Total Quality Culture, Quality of Work-Life and Organisational Health have high loadings on factor 1. The factor may therefore be called Total Quality Culture and Quality of Work-Life. The factor explains 39.7% of variance.

Factor 2

The following dimensions of Organisational Health (PI, RS, CON, MO) and variable Student Teachers' Involvement in College Activities have high loadings on 2nd factor.

1. Principal Influence (PI)
2. Resource Support (RS)
3. Consideration (CON)
4. Student Teachers' Involvement in College Activities (SIN)
5. Morale (MO)

The above dimensions of Organisational Health and variable Student Teachers' Involvement in College Activities have high loadings on factor 2. The factor may therefore be called as Organisational Health and Student Teachers' Involvement in College Activities. The factor explains 16.4% of variance.

Factor 3

The following dimensions of variable Quality of Work-Life (WSR) and Organisational Health (IS) have high loadings on 3rd factor:

1. Work Speed and Routine (WST)
2. Initiating Structure (IS)

The above dimensions of Quality of Work-Life and Organisational Health have high loadings on factor 3. The factor explains 10.2% of variance and it may be named Workspeed and Routine and Initiating Structure.

Factor 4

The following dimension of the variable Quality of Work-Life has high loading on the 4th factor:

1. Autonomy (AT)

The above dimension of Quality of Work-Life has high loading on factor 4. The factor explains 7.2% of variance and it may be named Autonomy.

Factor 5

The following dimension of Organisational Health has high loading on 5th factor:

1. Institutional Integrity (II)

The above dimension of Organisational Health has high loading on factor 5. The factor explains 5.7% of variance and it may be named as Institutional Integrity.

Gulbarga University

Factor analysis for Gulbarga University

Factor:	*I*	*II*	*III*	*IV*	*V*
Eigen Value	6.757	2.473	1.861	1.378	1.166
% of Variance	35.600	13.000	9.800	7.300	6.100
Cumulative %	35.600	48.600	58.400	65.600	71.800

Table—5.115

Results of Rotated Factor Matrix for Gulburga University

	Factor 1	*Factor 2*	*Factor 3*	*Factor 4*	*Factor 5*
OS	0.881				
ENV	0.876				
MET	0.859				
TEO	0.836				
TQM	0.827				
PS	0.797				
PGO	0.719				
AE		0.813			
RS		0.677			
MO		0.669			
IS		0.660			
CON		0.598			
AT			0.764		
I I			0.705		
WCO			0.698		
TRI			0.657		
PI				0.719	
WSR					0.722
SIN					0.678

Factor 1

The following dimensions of Total Quality Culture (OS, ENV, MET, PEO, TQM, PS) and Quality of Work-Life dimension (PGO) have high loadings on 1st factor.

1. Organisational Structure (OS)
2. Environment (ENV)
3. Methods (MET)
4. People Characteristic (PEO)
5. Total Quality Mindset (TQM)
6. Product and Service (PS)
7. Personal Growth Opportunity (PGO)

The above dimensions of Total Quality Culture and one dimension of Quality of Work-Life have high loadings on factor 1. Therefore the factor may be called Total Quality Culture and Personal Growth Opportunity. The factor explains 35.6% of variance.

Factor 2

The following dimensions of the variable Organisational Health have high loading on 2nd factor:

1. Academic Emphasis (AE)
2. Resource Support (RS)
3. Morale (MO)
4. Initiating Structure (IS)
5. Consideration (CON)

The above dimensions of Organisational Health have high loadings on factor 2. The factor may therefore be called as Organisational Health. The factor explains 13.0% of variance.

Factor 3

The following dimensions of Quality of Work-Life and one dimension of Organisational Health (II) have high loadings on 3rd factor.

1. Autonomy (AT)
2. Institutional Integrity (II)
3. Work Complexity (WCO)
4. Task Related Interaction (TRI)

The above dimensions of Quality of Work-Life and Organisational Health high loadings on factor 3. The factor may therefore be called Quality of Work-Life and Institutional Integrity. The factor explains 9.8% of variance.

Factor 4

The following dimension of the variable Organisational Health have high loading on 4th factor:

1. Principal Influence (PI)

The above dimension of Organisational Health has high loadings on the factor 4. The factor may therefore be called as Principal Influence. The factor explains 7.3% of variance.

Factor 5

The following dimensions of the variable Quality of Work-Life (WSR) and Student Teachers' Involvement in College Activities have high loading on 5th factor.

1. Workspeed and Routine (WSR)
2. Student Teachers' Involvement in College Activities (SIN)

The above dimensions of Quality of Work-Life and variable Student Teachers' Involvement in College Activities have high loadings on factor 5. The factor may be called Workspeed and Routine and Student Teachers' Involvement in College Activities. The factor Workspeed and Routine explains 6.1% of variance.

Kuvempu University

Factor analysis for Kuvempu University

Factor:	*I*	*II*	*III*	*IV*
Eigen Value	9.116	2.441	1.990	1.380
% of Variance	48.000	12.800	10.500	7.300
Cumulative %	48.000	60.800	71.300	78.600

Table—5.116

Results of Rotated Factor Matrix for Kuvempu University

	Factor 1	*Factor 2*	*Factor 3*	*Factor 4*
1	2	3	4	5
TQM	0.919			
PEO	0.893			
PGO	0.864			
MET	0.847			
ENV	0.807			
PS	0.805			

(Table Contd...)

1	2	3	4	5
OS	0.786			
MO	0.541			
CON		0.893		
IS		0.849		
II		0.667		
TRI		0.586		
SIN		0.580		
RS		0.571		
AE		0.568		
WCO			0.902	
PI			0.880	
AT				0.813
WSR				0.662

Factor 1

The following dimensions of Total Quality Culture (TQM, PEO, MET, ENV, PS, OS), Quality of Work-Life dimensions (PGO) and Organisational Health dimension (MO) have high loading on 1st factor.

1. Total Quality Mindset (TQM)
2. People Characteristic (PEO)
3. Personal Growth Opportunity (PGO)
4. Methods (MET)
5. Environment (ENV)
6. Product and Service (PS)
7. Organisational Structure (OS)
8. Morale (MO)

The highest loadings on the Total Quality Culture dimension Total Quality Mindset explain is 0.919. The factor Total Quality Culture explains 48.0% of variance.

Factor 2

The following dimensions of the variable Organisational Health (CON, IS, II, RS, AE), dimensions of Quality of Work-Life

(TRI) and Student Teachers' Involvement in College Activities have high loadings on 2nd factor.

1. Consideration (CON)
2. Initiating Structure (IS)
3. Institutional Integrity (II)
4. Task Related Interaction (TRI)
5. Student Teachers' Involvement in College Activities (SIN)
6. Resource Support (RS)
7. Academic Emphasis(AE)

The above dimensions of Quality of Work-Life, Organisational Health and Student Teachers' Involvement in College Activities have high loadings on factor 2. The factor Quality of Work-Life explains 12.8% of variance.

Factor 3

The following dimension of the variable Quality of Work-Life (WCO) and Organisational Health (PI) have high loadings on 3rd factor.

1. Work Complexity (WCO)
2. Principal Influence (PI)

The above dimensions of Quality of Work-Life and Organisational Health have high loadings on factor 3. The factors may therefore be called Work Complexity and Principal Influence. The factor explains 10.5% of variance.

Factor 4

The following dimensions of the variable Quality of Work-Life have high loadings on 4th factor:

1. Autonomy (AT)
2. Work Speed and Routine (WSR)

The above dimensions of Quality of Work-Life have high loadings on factor 4. The factor may therefore be called as Autonomy and Workspeed and Routine. The factor explains 7.3% of variance.

Comparison of Factors in Six Universities

Factor I

1. Common variables significantly contributing to factor one in all the six Universities are; Karnatak, Bangalore, Mysore, Mangalore, Gulburga and Kuvempu as shown below.

   (i) Methods (MET)

   (ii) People Characteristic (PEO)

   (iii) Total Quality Mindset (TQM)

   (iv) Organisational Structure (OS)

   (v) Environment (ENV)

Unique variables are Student's Involvement in College Activities, Task Related Interaction, Academic Emphasis, Work Complexity and Morale.

2. Common variables significantly Contributing to Factor I in five Universities are:

   (i) Products and Service (PS)

   (ii) Environment (ENV)

   (iii) Methods (MET)

   (iv) People Characteristic (PEO)

   (v) Organisational Structure (OS)

   (vi) Total Quality Mindset (TQM)

Unique Variables are Task Related Interaction, Academic Emphasis, Work Complexity, Student Teachers' Involvement in College Activities and Morale.

3. Common variables significantly contributing to Factor I in four Universities are:

   Methods, People Characteristics, Total Quality Mindset, Organisational Structure, Environment, Product and Service.

Unique Variables are Student Teachers' Involvement in College Activities, Academic Emphasis, Work Complexity and Task Related Interaction.

4. Common variables significantly contributing to Factor I in three Universities are:
   - *(i)* Personal Growth Opportunity (PGO)
   - *(ii)* Methods (MET)
   - *(iii)* People Characteristics (PEO)
   - *(iv)* Total Quality Mindset (TQM)
   - *(v)* Organisational Structure (OS)
   - *(vi)* Environment (ENV)
   - *(vii)* Product and service (PS)

   Unique Variables are Task Related Interaction, Academic Emphasis, Work Complexity, Morale and Student Teachers' Involvement in College Activities.

5. Common variables significantly contributing to Factor I in two Universities are:

   Methods, People Characteristics, Product and Service, Total Quality Mindset, Organisational Structure, Environment and Personal Growth Opportunity.

   Unique Variables are Student Teachers' Involvement in College Activities, Morale, Work Complexity, Academic Emphasis, Task related Interaction.

6. Unique variables significantly contributing to Factor I in one University are:
   - *(i)* Academic Emphasis } Mangalore University
   - *(ii)* Work Complexity } Mangalore University
   - *(iii)* Morale – Kuvempu University
   - *(iv)* Student Teachers' Involvement in College Activities: – Karnatak University

Factor II

1. Common variables significantly contributing to Factor II in all six Universities are:

(i) Consideration (CON)

(ii) Resource Support (RS)

Unique Variables are Institutional Integrity, Task Related Interaction.

2. Common variables significantly contributing to Factor II in five Universities are:

 (i) Resource Support (RS)

 (ii) Initiating Structure (IS)

3. Common variables significantly contributing to Factor II in four Universities are;

 (i) Academic Emphasis (AE)

 (ii) Principal Influence (PI)

 (iii) Morale (MO)

 (iv) Consideration (CON)

 (v) Initiating Structure (IS)

4. Common variables significantly contributing to Factor II in three Universities are;

 (i) Morale (MO)

 (ii) Resource Support (RS)

 (iii) Initiating Structure (IS)

 (iv) Academic Emphasis (AE)

5. Common variables significantly contributing to Factor II in two Universities are;

 (i) Student Teachers' Involvement in College Activities (SIN)

 (ii) Consideration (CON)

 (iii) Resource Support (RS)

6. Unique variables significantly contributing to Factor II in one University that is Kuvempu University are:

 (i) Institutional Integrity (II)

 (ii) Task Related Interaction (TRI)

Factor III

1. Common variables significantly contributing to Factor III in all six Universities are:
   - *(i)* Workspeed and Routine (WSR)
   - *(ii)* Work Complexity (WCO)
   - *(iii)* Personal Growth Opportunity (PGO)
   - *(iv)* Task Related Interaction (TRI)

Unique Variables are Student Teachers' Involvement in College Activities, Initiating Structure, Institutional Integrity and Principal Influence.

1. Common variables significantly contributing to Factor III in five Universities are nil.
2. Common variables significantly contributing to Factor III in four Universities are:
   - *(i)* Work Complexity (WCO)
   - *(ii)* Task Related Interaction (TRI)
3. Common variables significantly contributing to Factor III in three Universities are:
   - *(i)* Personal Growth Opportunity (PGO)
   - *(ii)* Autonomy (AT)
   - *(iii)* Workspeed and Routine (WSR)
   - *(iv)* Task Related Interaction (TRI)
   - *(v)* Work Complexity (WCO)
4. Common variables significantly contributing to Factor III two Universities like Karnatak and Mysore Universities are;
   - *(i)* Work Complexity (WCO)
   - *(ii)* Personal Growth Opportunity (PGO)
   - *(iii)* Workspeed and Routine (WSR)
   - *(iv)* Autonomy (AT)
   - *(v)* Task Related Interaction (TRI)

5. Unique variables significantly contributing to Factor III in different Universities are;

   (i) Student Teachers' Involvement in College Activities (SIN) – Bangalore University

   (ii) Initiating Structure (IS) – Mangalore University

   (iii) Principal Influence (PI) – Kuvempu University

   (iv) Institutional Integrity (II) – Karnatak University

Factor IV

Unique variables significantly contributing to Factor IV in all six Universities are:

(i) Morale (MO)

(ii) Academic Emphasis (AE)

(iii) Student Teachers' Involvement in College Activities (SIN)

(iv) Principal Influence (PI)

1. Common variables significantly contributing to Factor IV in five Universities are nil.

2. Common variables significantly contributing to Factor IV in four Universities are nil.

3. Common variables significantly contributing to Factor IV in three Universities are:

   (i) Autonomy (AT)

4. Common variables significantly contributing to Factor IV in two Universities are:

   (i) Workspeed and Routine (WSR)

   (ii) Autonomy (AT)

   (iii) Institutional Integrity (II)

   Unique variables significantly contributing to Factor IV in some Universities are:

   (i) Morale
   (ii) Academic Emphasis
   (iii) Student Teachers' Involvement in College activities } Bangalore University

   – Mysore University

   (iv) Principal Influence – Gulburga University

Factor V

1. Common variables significantly contributing to Factor V two Universities are:

   (i) Institutional Integrity } Karnatak University, Mangalore University

Unique variables significantly contributing to Factor five different Universities are:

(i) Work Complexity (WCO)–Bangalore University

(ii) Workspeed and Routine (WSR) } Gulbarga University

(iii) Student Teachers Involvement in College Activities (SIN) } Gulbarga University

Conclusion

Details of data analyses at various levels involving uni, bi, and multi variables using appropriate statistics are given in this chapter. A summary of findings and the implications of the findings for the teacher education colleges, teacher educators and administrators are given in the next chapter.

6

Retrospects and Prospects

Introduction

This chapter is the concluding part of the research report. It gives a brief summary of the study starting with the objectives, the methodology and the major findings. The suggestions are offered for further research studies.

The Problem

The present investigation is entitled as "Correlates of Total Quality Culture in Teacher Education Colleges". No doubt that every one is interested in knowing how Total Quality Culture in each teacher education college can be achieved by regulating some correlated factors. A teacher education college can be having good Total Quality Culture only when it achieves its objectives using the available human resources efficiently and economically.

The present study aims at identifying certain variables responsible for Total Quality Culture in teacher education colleges that account for growth and development, and prosperity of the institutional life.

Objectives

The main objective of the study is to identify the correlates of total quality culture. The study also aims at analysing the relationship of six variables in developing the total quality culture in teacher education colleges.

Hypotheses

The following hypotheses are formulated based on the objectives of the study.

DIFFERENTIAL HYPOTHESES

Hypothesis 1

Teacher educators of different age groups differ in their perception of Total Quality Culture as a whole and in the following dimensions of Total Quality Culture:

(a) Environment
(b) Product and Service
(c) Methods
(d) People Characteristics
(e) Organisational Structure
(f) Total Quality Mindset

Hypothesis 2

Teacher educators of different age groups differ in their perception of Organisational Health as a whole and in the following dimensions of Organisational Health:

(a) Institutional Integrity
(b) Initiating Structure
(c) Consideration
(d) Principal Influence
(e) Resource Support
(f) Morale
(g) Academic Emphasis

Hypothesis 3

Teacher educators of different age groups differ in their perception of Quality of Work-Life as a whole and in the following dimensions of Quality of Work-Life:

(a) Autonomy
(b) Personal Growth Opportunity

(c) Workspeed and Routine

(d) Work Complexity

(e) Task-Related Interaction

Hypothesis 4

Teacher educators of different age groups differ in their perception of Student Teachers' Involvement in the College Activities

Hypothesis 5

Men and Women teacher educators differ in their perception as a whole and in the dimensions of following variables:

(a) Total Quality Culture

(b) Organisational Health

(c) Quality of Work-Life

(d) Student Teachers' Involvement in College Activities

Hypothesis 6

Teacher educators with different specialisation differ in their perception as a whole and in the dimensions of the following variables:

(a) Total Quality Culture

(b) Organisational Health

(c) Quality of Work-Life

(d) Student Teachers' Involvement in College Activities

Hypothesis 7

Teacher educators with different designations differ in their perception as a whole and in the dimensions of the following variables:

(a) Total Quality Culture

(b) Organisational Health

(c) Quality of Work-Life

(d) Student Teachers' Involvement in College Activities

Hypothesis 8

Teacher educators with different years of teaching experience differ in their perception as a whole and in the dimensions of the following variables:

(a) Total Quality Culture

(b) Organisational Health

(c) Quality of Work-Life

(d) Student Teachers' Involvement in College Activities

Hypothesis 9

Teacher educators working in different college sex differ in their perception of as a whole and in the dimensions of the following variables:

(a) Total Quality Culture

(b) Organisational Health

(c) Quality of Teachers' College Activities

(d) Student Teachers' Involvement in College Activities

CORRELATIONAL HYPOTHESES

The correlational hypothesis of the study are stated below;

Hypothesis 1

Total Quality Culture and its dimensions significantly correlate with:

(a) Organisational Health and its dimensions

(b) Quality of Work-Life and its dimensions

(c) Student Teachers' Involvement in College Activities

(d) Student Teachers' Commitment to Course

Hypothesis 2

Organisational Health and its dimensions significantly correlate with:

(a) Quality of Work-Life and its dimensions

(b) Student Teachers' Involvement in College Activities

(c) Student Teachers' Commitment to Course

(d) Change Facilitators Styles of Principals

Hypothesis 3

Quality of Work-Life and its dimensions significantly correlates with:

(a) Student Teachers' Involvement in College Activities

(b) Student Teachers' Commitment to Course

Methodology

The present study adopted normative survey (ex-post-facto) technique and the data were collected from principals, teacher educators and student teachers from teacher education colleges.

Sample

The data was collected from nine hundred student teachers and two hundred and sixty teacher educators and forty principals from forty five teacher education colleges coming under six universities in Karnataka State.

Tools

The following tools were administered to student teachers, teacher educators and Principals of teacher education colleges.

1. Total Quality Culture (Teacher Educators and Principals)
2. Organisational Health (Teacher Educators)
3. Quality of Work-Life (Teacher Educators)
4. Student Teachers Involvement in College Activities (Teacher Educators)
5. Student Teachers' Commitment to Course (Student Teachers)
6. Change Facilitator Styles of Principals (Teacher Educators)

Data Analyses

For the analysis of data collected, descriptive, differential, one-way ANOVA, correlation, multivariate and factor analysis statistics were used.

Major Findings

The major findings of the study are enumerated as follows.

Findings of Descriptive Analysis:

1. In types of management especially government teacher education colleges have higher mean scores on the variable Total Quality Culture with regard to the dimension People characteristics (M=82.286).

2. Women teacher education colleges have higher mean scores on the variable Total Quality Culture with regard to the following dimensions;
   (i) Product and Service (M = 88.600)
   (ii) Methods (M = 85.650)
   (iii) Organisational Structure (M = 89.700)
   (iv) Total Quality of Mindset (M=84.150)

3. Teacher education colleges in Kuvempu University have higher mean score on the variable Total Quality Culture with regard to the dimension Environment (M=85.952).

4. In types of management especially Aided teacher education colleges have higher mean score on Institutional Integrity dimension of Organisational Health (M=75.143).

5. Teacher education colleges in Mysore University have higher mean score on the whole sample of the variable Organisational Health. (M=532.690).

6. In types of management especially aided teacher education colleges have higher mean score on Institutional Integrity Dimension of Organisational Health (M=75.143).

7. Women teacher education colleges have higher mean score on the variable Organisational Health with regard to the dimension Morale (M=82.350).

8. Teacher education colleges in Mysore University have higher mean score on the variable Organisational Health with regard to the following dimensions:

(i) Initiating Structure (M = 77.069)

(ii) Consideration (M = 74.310)

(iii) Principal Influence (M = 71.552)

9. Teacher education colleges in Kuvempu University have higher mean score on the variable Organisational Health with regard to the following dimensions:

   (i) Resource Support (M=79.667)

   (ii) Academic Emphasis (M=83.095)

10. In types of management teacher education colleges have no much difference on the dimensions of Quality of Work-Life.

11. Teacher educators designated as Readers have higher mean score on the variable Quality of Work-Life with regard to the dimension Task Related Interaction (M=15.292).

12. Teacher education colleges in Kuvempu University has higher mean score on the variable Quality of Work-Life with regard to the dimension Personal Growth Opportunity (M=15.857).

13. Teacher education colleges in Mysore University have higher mean score on the variable Quality of Work-Life with regard to the dimension Autonomy (M=13.345).

14. Female teacher educators have higher mean score on Work Complexity dimension of Quality of Work-Life (M= 13.806).

15. Private aided colleges have higher mean score on the variable Student Teachers' Involvement in College Activites (M=53.721).

Findings of Differential Analysis

A. Significant difference in their perception exists in Total Quality Culture between:

   (a) Teacher educators who are above 35 years of age (Mean=492.697) and Teacher educators who are below 35 years of age (Mean=471.026).

(b) Women teacher education colleges (Mean=513.450) and Co-education colleges (Mean=480.463).

B. Significant difference in their perception exists in Organisational Health between:

Teacher educators who are above 35 years of age (Mean=506.235) and Teacher educators who are below 35 years of age (Mean=473.817).

C. Significant difference in their perception exists in quality of Work-Life dimension, Autonomy between

(a) Teacher educators who are above 35 years of age (Mean=12.779) and Teacher educators who are below 35 years of age (Mean=12.217).

(b) Significant difference in their perception exists in work complexity dimension of quality of Work-Life between female teacher educators (Mean=13.806) and Male teacher educators (Mean=12.796).

D. Significant difference in their perception exists in Student Teachers' Involvement in College Activities between:

Teacher educators who are above 35 years of age (Mean=52.862) and Teacher educators who are below 35 years of age (Mean=50.748).

Findings of One Way Analysis of Variance (ANOVA)

1. Teacher educators working in different types of management do not vary significantly at 0.05 level of significance with regard to the variable Total Quality Culture. The ANOVA results are explained in Table—5.57 (F=0.2259) in the analysis chapter.
2. Teacher educators working in different type of managements vary significantly at 0.05 level with regard to the variable Organisational Health. The 'F' value is (0.0469). The ANOVA and 't' test results are explained in Tables—5.64 and 5.65 in the analysis chapter. The 't' test results in Table—5.65 reveals that teacher educators working in aided and government teacher education colleges significantly differ in their perception of Organisational Health. The aided colleges are higher on Organisational Health when compared to government colleges.

(i) The teacher educators working in different types of management vary significantly at 0.05 level with regard to the dimension, Resource support. The F value is (0.0000). The ANOVA and 't' test results are explained in Table—5.70 and 5.71 in the analysis chapter. The 't' test results in Table—5.71 reveals that the teacher educators working in aided and government teacher education colleges significantly differ in their perception of Resource Support, whereas teacher educators working in unaided and government teacher education colleges do not differ. The teacher educators of aided teacher education colleges are higher on the perception of Resource Support dimension of Organisational Health when compared to government and un-aided colleges.

(ii) The teacher educators working in different types of management vary significantly at 0.05 level with regard to the dimension, Academic Emphasis. The F value is (0.048). The ANOVA and 't' test results are explained in Tables—5.73 and 5.74 in the analysis chapter. The 't' test results in Table—5.74 reveals that the teacher educators working in aided and government teacher education colleges and those working in aided and un-aided teacher education colleges significantly differ in their perception of Academic Emphasis. The teacher educators of aided colleges are higher on Academic Emphasis dimension of Organisational Health when compared to government and un-aided colleges.

3. Teacher educators working in different type of managements do not vary significantly at 0.05 level in their perception of Quality of Work-Life. The 'F' value is (0.830) not significant, the ANOVA results are explained in Table 5.75.

(i) The teacher educators working in different types of management vary significantly at 0.05 level with regard to the dimension Autonomy of the variable Quality of Work-Life. The 'F' value is (0.0009). The ANOVA and 't' test results are explained in Tables—5.76 and 5.77 in the analysis chapter. The 't' test results in Table—5.77 reveals that the teacher educators working in aided and un-aided teacher education colleges and un-aided and government teacher education colleges significantly differ in their perception of Autonomy. But those working in aided and government teacher education colleges do not differ in their perception of Autonomy. Teacher educators of government colleges are high on Autonomy dimension of Quality of Work-Life when compared to un-aided colleges, and the teacher educators of aided colleges are high on Autonomy when compared to un-aided colleges.

(ii) The teacher educators working in different types of management do not vary significantly at 0.05 level with regard to the variable Quality of Work-Life. The 'F' value (0.0510) is not significant. The ANOVA results are explained in Table—5.75 in the analysis chapter.

(iii) The teacher educators working in different types of management vary significantly at 0.05 level with regard to the dimension Task related interaction of the variable Quality of Work-Life. The 'F' value is (0.022). The ANOVA and 't' test results are explained in Tables—5.81 and 5.82 in the analysis chapter. The 't' test results in Table—5.82 reveals that the teacher educators working in different type of management do not differ in their perception of Task Related Interaction.

4. The teacher educators working in different types of management vary significantly at 0.05 level with regard to the variable Student Teacher Involvement in College Activities. The 'F' value (0.017) is significant. The ANOVA and 't' test results are explained in Tables—5.83 and 5.84 in the analysis chapter. The 't' test results in Table—5.84 reveals that the teacher educators working in aided and un-aided colleges significantly differ but those working in aided-government and un-aided government teacher education colleges do not significantly differ in their perception of Student Teachers' Involvement in College Activities. The Student Teachers' of Aided Colleges are high on Involvement in College Activities when compared to Student Teachers of un-aided colleges.

5. The three groups of teacher education colleges under Responder, Initiator and Manager Principals have their means in Total Quality Culture as 495.95, 495.92 and 472.67 respectively. The teacher education colleges with Manager Principals significantly differ from the other two groups of teacher education colleges, namely teacher education colleges under Responder and Initiator Principals.
6. The differences in the mean scores of Total Quality Culture of the teacher educators working in colleges with Principals having different type of change facilitator styles are analysed using 'F' statistics are explained in the Analysis chapter. The F value (0.0156) is significant. The ANOVA results are explained in Table—5.85 in the analysis chapter. The results reveal that teacher educators working in colleges with principals having different Change Facilitator Styles vary significantly at 0.05 level of significance with regard to the variable Total Quality Culture.
7. The teacher educators working in colleges with Principals having different Change Facilitator Styles do not vary significantly at 0.05 level with regard to the variable Organisational Health. The results are shown in Table—5.86 in the analysis chapter.
8. The teacher educators working in colleges with Principals having different type of Change Facilitator Styles do not vary significantly at 0.05 level with regard to the variable Quality of Work-Life. The results are shown in Table—5.87 in the analysis chapter.

Findings of Correlation Analysis

A. The correlations between dimensions of Total Quality Culture and Organisational Health are presented in Table—5.88 in the analysis chapter. The findings are presented as follows.

   (i) Among the dimensions significant correlations existed between Environment dimension of Total Quality Culture and the following Organisational Health dimensions like Initiating Structure (IS) ($r=0.189, p<0.01$), consideration (CON)($r=0.343, p<0.01$), Principal Influence (PI) ($r=0.174, p<0.01$), Resource Support (RS)

(r=0.342, p<0.01), Morale (MO) (r=0.441, p<0.01), and Academic Emphasis (AE) (r=0.301, p<0.01). Significant and positive relationship was observed between Environment dimension of Total Quality Culture and total of Organisational Health (r= 0.392, p<0.01). The hypothesis that the variable Organisational Health is related to Environment dimension is accepted.

Significant positive relationship was observed between total of Total Quality Culture and total of Organisational Health (r = 0.475, p<0.01) (r=0.125, p<0.05).

(ii) Significant positive relationship was observed between Product and Service (PS) dimension of Total Quality Culture and the following dimensions of Organisational Health like Initiating Structure (IS) (r=0.213, p<0.01), Consideration (CON) (r=0.322, p<0.01), Principal Influence (PI) (r=0.198, p<0.01), Resource Support (RS) (r=0.297, p<0.01), Morale (MO) (r=0.332, p<0.01), Academic Emphasis (AE) (r=0.213, p<0.01).

Significant positive relationship was observed between Product and Service (PS) dimension of Total Quality Culture and the total of Organisational Health (r=0.347, p<0.01).

(iii) Significant positive relationship was observed between Methods (MET) dimensions of Total Quality Culture and the following dimensions of Organisational Health like Initiating Structure (IS)(r=0.191, p<0.01), Consideration (CON)(r=0.312, p<0.01), Resource Support (RS) (r=0.327, p<0.01), Morale (MO)(r=0.379, p<0.01) and Academic Emphasis (AE) (r=0.346, p<0.01).

(iv) Significant positive relationship was observed between Methods (MET) dimension of Total Quality Culture and total of variable Organisational Health (r=0.345, p<0.01).

Significant positive relationship was observed between People Characteristics (PEO) dimension of Total Quality Culture and following dimensions of Organisational Health like Initiating Structure (IS) (r=0.212, p<0.01), Consideration (CON) (r=0.355, p<0.01), Principal

Influence (PI) ($r=0.135, p<0.01$), Resource Support (RS) ($r=0.327, p<0.01$), Morale (MO) ($r=0.384, p<0.01$) and Academic Emphasis (AE) ($r=0.288, p<0.01$).

Significant positive relationship is observed between People Characteristics (PEO) dimension of Total Quality Culture and the total of Organisational Health ($r=0.376, p<0.01$). The hypothesis that variable Organisation Health is related to the dimension People Characteristics is accepted.

(v) Significant positive relationship was observed between Organisational Structure (OS) dimension of Total Quality Culture and following dimensions of Organisational Health like Institutional Integrity (II)($r=0.167, p<0.01$), Initiating Structure (IS) ($r=0.296, p<0.01$), Consideration (CON) ($r=0.438, p<0.01$), Principal Influence (PI) ($r=0.214, p<0.01$), Resource Support (RS) ($r=0.417, p<0.01$), Morale (MO) ($r=0.516, p<0.01$) and Academic Emphasis (AE) ($r=0.361, p<0.01$).

Significant positive relationship was observed between Organisational Structure (OS) dimension of Total Quality Culture and the total of Organisational Health ($r=0.499, p<0.01$).

(vi) Significant positive relationship was observed between Total Quality Mindset (TQM) dimension of Total Quality Culture and following dimensions of Organisational Health like Institutional Integrity (II)($r=0.124, p<0.01$), Initiating Structure (IS) ($r=0.226, p<0.01$), Consideration (CON) ($r=0.39, p<0.01$), Principal Influence (PI) ($r=0.184, p<0.01$), Resource Support (RS) ($r=0.352, p<0.01$), Morale (MO) ($r=0.447, p<0.01$) and Academic Emphasis (AE)($r=0.32, p<0.01$).

Significant positive relationship was observed between Total Quality Mindset (TQM) dimension of Total Quality Culture and the total of Organisational Health ($r=0.424, p<0.01$).

(vii) Significant and positive relationship was observed between total of Total Quality Culture and following

dimensions of Organisational Health like Institutional Integrity (II)(r=0.125, p<0.01), Initiating Structure (IS) (r=0.264, p<0.01), Consideration (CON) (r=0.429, p<0.01), Principal Influence (PI) (r=0.198, p<0.01), Resource Support (RS) (r=0.409, p<0.01), Morale (MO) (r=0.496, p<0.01) and Academic Emphasis (AE) (r=0.364, p<0.01).

Significant positive relationship was observed between total of Total Quality Culture and total of Organisational Health (r=0.475, p<0.01).

B. The correlations between dimensions of Total Quality Culture and Quality of Work-Life are presented in Table—5.89 in the analysis chapter. The findings are presented as follows.

(i) A significant positive relationship was observed between Environment (ENV) dimension of Total Quality Culture (TQC) with Personal Growth Opportunity (PGO)(r=0.3660, p<0.01) Task Related Interaction (TRI) (r=0.3320, p<0.01) dimensions of Quality of Work-Life. Hence, the hypothesis that these dimensions are related is accepted. But Environment dimension of Total Quality Culture has significantly negative relationship with Workspeed and Routine (WSR) dimension of Quality of Work-Life (r=-0.1700, p<0.01). But the correlation is negative. When Environmental Influence is high Workspeed and Routine is low.

(ii) Product and Service (PS) dimension of Total Quality Culture has a significant positive relationship with Task Related Interaction (TRI) dimension of Quality of Work-Life (r=0.1840, p<0.01).

(iii) Methods dimension of Total Quality Culture has a significant negative relationship between Work-speed and Routine dimension of Quality of Work-Life (r=0.3660, p<0.01). But the correlation is negative. When Methods is high Workspeed and Routine is low. Positive relationship was seen between Methods dimension of Total Quality Culture and Personal Growth Opportunity (r=0.4020, p<0.01), Task Related Interaction (r=0.3030, p<0.01) dimensions of Quality of Work-Life.

Significant positive relationship was observed between Methods dimension of Total Quality Culture and total of Quality of Work -Life (r=0.1679, p<0.01).

(iv) People Characteristic (PEO) dimension of Total Quality Culture with Workspeed and Routine (WSR) dimension of Quality of Work-Life, have a significant negative relation (r=-0.1700, p<0.01). But the correlation is negative. When People Characteristics is high Workspeed and Routine is low. There is a significant positive relationship between People Characteristics of Total Quality Culture and Personal Growth Opportunity (r=0.3340, p<0.01) and Task Related Interaction (r=0.300, p<0.01) dimensions of Quality of Work-Life.

Significant positive relationship was observed between People characteristics dimension of Total Quality Culture and total of Quality of Work-Life (r=0.1289, p<0.05).

(v) A significant negative relationship was observed between Organisational Structure (OS) of Total Quality Culture with Workspeed and Routine (WSR) of Quality of Work-Life (r=-0.2540, p<0.01). But the correlation is negative. When Organisational Structure is high, Workspeed and Routine is low. Positive relationship was seen between Organisational Structure of Total Quality Culture and Personal Growth Opportunity (PGO) (r=0.0412, p<0.01) and Task Related Interaction (TRI) (r=0.4080, p<0.01). But correlation is negative. When People Characteristics is high Workspeed and Routine is low.

Significant positive relationship was observed between Organisational Structure dimension of Total Quality Culture and total of Quality of Work-Life (r=0.1661, p<0.01). The hypothesis that variable Quality of Work-Life is related to Organisational Structure dimension is accepted.

(vi) A significant negative relationship was observed between Total Quality Mindset (TQM) dimension of Total

Quality Culture and Workspeed and Routine dimension of Quality of Work-Life (r=-0.2010, p<0.01). But correlation is negative. When Total Quality Mindset is high Workspeed and Routine is low. But a positive significant relation was seen between Total Quality Mindset dimension of Total Quality Culture and Personal Growth Opportunity (r=0.4050, p<0.01) and Task Related Interaction (r=0.3260, p<0.01) dimensions of Quality of Work-Life.

Significant positive relationship was observed between Total Quality Mindset of Total Quality Culture and total of Quality of Work-Life (r=0.1250, p<0.05). The hypothesis that variable Quality of Work-Life is related to Total Quality Mindset dimension is accepted.

(vii) The total of Total Quality Culture also has a negative significant relationship with Workspeed and Routine (WSR) dimension of Quality of Work-Life (r=-0.1990, p<0.05). But the correlation is negative. When Total Quality Culture is high, Workspeed and Routine is low. Positive relationship was seen between Personal Growth Opportunity (PGO) (r=0.4200, p<0.01) and Task Related Interaction (TRI) (r=0.369, p<0.01) and Total of Quality of Work-Life (r= 0.1670, p<0.01).

Significant positive relationship was observed between and total of Total Quality Culture and total of Quality of Work-Life (r=0.1670, p<0.01). The hypothesis that the variable Quality of Work-Life is related to Total Quality Culture is accepted.

C. The correlations between dimensions of Total Quality Culture and Student Teachers' Involvement in College Activities are presented in Table—5.90 in the analysis chapter. The findings are presented as follows.

The Student Teachers' Involvement in College Activities has a significant positive relationship with all the dimensions of Total Quality Culture.

D. The correlations between dimensions of Total Quality Culture and Arts and Science Student Teachers' Commitment to

Course are presented in Table—5.91 in the analysis chapter. The findings are presented as follows.

There is no significant relationship between Total Quality Culture and Arts and Science Student Teachers' Commitment to Course.

E. The correlations between dimensions of Organisational Health and Quality of Work-Life are presented in Table—5.92 in the analysis chapter. The findings are presented as follows.

(i) A significant negative relationship is seen between Institutional Integrity (I I) of Organisational Health and Autonomy (AT) (r=-0.145, P<0.05). Hence, the hypothesis that these dimensions are related is accepted. But the correlation is negative. When Institutional Integrity is high Autonomy is low.

(ii) A significant negative relationship is seen between Initiating Structure of Organisational Health and Workspeed and Routine (WSR) dimensions of Quality of Work-Life (r=-0.2350, p<0.01). But the correlation is negative. When Initiating Structure is high Workspeed and Routine is low. A significant positive relationship is seen between Initiating Structure dimension of Organisational Health and Personal Growth Opportunity (r=0.1350, p<0.05) and Task Related Interaction dimensions of Quality of Work-Life (r=0.2110, p<0.01).

A significant positive relationship was observed between Consideration (CON) dimension of Organisational Health with Personal Growth Opportunity (PGO) (r=0.2290, p<0.01), Task Related Interaction (TRI) (r=0.2770, p<0.01) dimensions of Quality of Work-Life.

Significant positive relationship was observed between Consideration dimension of Organisational Health and total of Quality of Work-Life (r=0.1550, p<0.01).

(iii) A significant negative relationship was observed between Principal Influence dimension of Organisational Health with Autonomy (AT) (r=-0.1690,

$p<0.01$) and Workspeed and Routine ($r=-0.2630$, $p<0.01$) dimensions of Quality Work-Life. But the correlation is negative. When Principal Influence is high, Autonomy is low. Significant positive relationships were observed between Work Complexity ($r=0.1260$, $p<0.05$) and Task Related Interaction dimensions of Quality of Work-Life ($r=0.2340$, $p<0.01$).

(iv) A significant positive relationship was observed between Resource Support (RS) of Organisational Health with Personal Growth Opportunity (PGO)($r=0.178$, $p<0.01$), Work Complexity (WCO)($r=0.144$, $p<0.05$), and Task Related Interaction (TRI) dimensions of Quality of Work-Life ($r=0.258$, $p<0.01$). And a significant negative relationship was observed between Resource Support of Organisational Health and Workspeed and Routine (WSR) dimension of Quality of Work-Life ($r=-0.15$, $p<0.05$). But the correlation is negative. When Resource Support is high, Workspeed and Routine is low.

(v) A significant positive relationship was observed between Morale (MO) of Organisational Health with Personal Growth Opportunity (PGO) ($r=0.283$, $p<0.01$), Work Complexity (WCO) ($r=0.151$, $p<0.05$), and Task related interaction dimensions of Quality of Work-Life ($r=0.423$, $p<0.01$). And there is significant negative relationship between Morale (MO) and Workspeed and Routine ($r=-0.215$, $p<0.01$). But the correlation is negative. When Morale in the Organisation is high, Workspeed and Routine is low.

(vi) There was a positive significant relationship between Academic Emphasis (AE) dimension of Organisational Health and Personal Growth Opportunity (PGO) ($r=0.175$, $p<0.01$), Work Complexity (WCO) ($r=0.187$, $p<0.01$), and Task Related Interaction dimensions of Quality of Work-Life (TRI) ($r=0.348$, $p<0.01$). And a negative significant relationship is also observed between Academic Emphasis dimension and Workspeed and Routine (WSR) dimension of Quality of

Work-Life ($r=-0.241$, $p<0.01$). But the correlation is negative. When Academic Emphasis is high, Workspeed and Routine is low.

(vii) The Total of Organisational Health has positive significant relationship with Personal Growth Opportunity (PGO)($r=0.239$, $p<0.01$), Work Complexity (WCO) ($r=0.187$, $p<0.01$), and Task Related Interaction (TRI) dimension of Quality of Work-Life ($r=0.359$, $p<0.01$). A negative significant relationship was seen between total of Organisational Health and Workspeed and Routine (WSR)($r=-0.252$, $p<0.01$) dimension of Quality of Work-Life. The hypothesis that the variable Organisational Health is related to Workspeed and Routine dimension is accepted. But the correlation is negative. When Total Quality Culture is high, Workspeed and Routine is low.

F. The correlations between dimensions of Organisational Health and Change Facilitator Styles of Principals are presented in Table—5.93 in the analysis chapter. The findings are presented as follows.

(i) Initiating Structure dimension of Organisational Health has a significant negative relationship with Responder Style of Principals ($r=-0.3210$, $p<0.01$). But the correlation is negative. When the Organisational Health is high the Responder Change Facilitator Style of Principal is low. The Initiating Structure dimension of Organisational Health has positively significant relationship with Initiator style.

(ii) There is a negative significant relationship between Consideration dimension of Organisational Health with Responder Styles of Principals ($r=-0.2300$, $p<0.01$). But the correlation is negative. And Consideration dimension of Organisational Health has significant positive relationship with Initiator Styles of Principals ($r=0.2310$, $p<0.01$).

(iii) A significant negative relationship is seen between Principal Influence dimension of Organisational Health

and Responder Style of Principals ($r=-0.1570$, $p<0.05$). But the correlation is negative. With high Principal Influence the Responder Change Facilitator style of Principal is low. And Principal Influence dimension of Organisational Health has significant positive relationship with Initiator Style of Principals ($r=0.2200$, $p<0.01$).

(iv) Significant negative relationship is seen between Resource Support dimension of Organisational Health and Responder Style of Principals ($r=-0.2050$, $p<0.01$). But the correlation is negative. When Resource Support is high Responder Change Facilitator Styles of Principals is low. And Resource Support dimension of Organisational Health has significant positive relationship with Initiator Styles of Principals ($r=0.2180$, $p<0.01$).

(v) Significant negative relationship is seen on Morale dimension of Organisational Health with Responder Style of Principals ($r=-0.1700$, $p<0.01$), and Academic Emphasis dimension of Organisational Health with Responder style of Change Facilitator Styles of Principals ($r=-0.2690$, $p<0.01$). But the correlation is negative. When the Morale in the Organisation is high, Responder Change Facilitator Style of Principals is low. When Academic Emphasis is high Responder Change Styles of Principals is low. But the Morale dimension of Organisational Health has positive relationship with Initiator Style ($r=0.2170$, $p<0.01$). Academic Emphasis dimension and total of Organisational Health also have positive relationship with Initiator Styles of Principals ($r=0.1470$, $p<0.01$). When Academic Emphasis in the Organisation is high, Responder Style of Principals is low.

G. The correlations between dimensions of Organisational Health and Student Teachers' Involvement in College Activities are presented in Table—5.94 in the analysis chapter. The findings are presented as follows.

The Student Teachers' Involvement in College Activities has significant positive correlations with all the dimensions of Organisational Health.

H. The correlations between dimensions of Quality of Work-Life and Student Teachers' Involvement in College Activities are presented in Table—5.95 in the analysis chapter. The findings are presented as follows.

There is a negative significant relationship between Student Teachers' Involvement in College Activities and Workspeed and Routine dimension of Quality of Work-Life (r=-0.1360, p<0.05). But the correlation is negative. When Student Teachers' Involvement in College Activities is high, Workspeed and Routine is low. A positive significant relationships were seen between Student Teachers' Involvement in College Activities and Personal Growth Opportunity (r=0.2772, p<0.01), Work Complexity (r=0.1195, p<0.01) and Task Related Interaction (r=0.2773, p<0.01).

Significant positive relationship was observed between the variable Student Teachers' Involvement in College Activities and the variable total of Quality of Work-Life (r=0.1866, p<0.01).

I. The correlations between dimensions of Organisational Health and Student Teachers' Commitment to Course are presented in Table—5.96 in the analysis chapter. The findings are presented as follows.

(i) There was significant positive relationship between Arts Student Teachers' Commitment to Course and Morale dimension of Organisational Health (r=0.3270, p<0.05).

(ii) A significant negative relationship was seen between Science Student Teachers' Commitment to course and Institutional Integrity of dimension of Organisational Health (r= 0.3180, p<0.05). But the correlation is negative. When Science Student Teachers' Commitment to Course is high Institutional Integrity is low.

Significant negative relationship was observed between Science Student Teachers' Committment to Course is related to total of Organisational Health (r=-0.2500, p<0.10). But the correlation is negative. When Science Student Teachers' Commitment to Course is high Organisational Health is low.

J. The correlations between dimensions of Quality of Work-Life and Arts and Science Student Teachers' Commitment to Course are presented in Table—5.97 in the analysis chapter. The findings are presented as follows.

Significant positive relationship was seen only between Arts and Science Student Teachers' Commitment to Course and Work Complexity dimension of Quality of Work-Life (r=0.3080, p<0.05).

Findings of Regression Analysis

(i) For the Entire Sample

Equation

Y = 110.958 + 11.452 + 1.615 + 0.893-0.670 + 1.352

(TQC) (PGO) (MO) (RS) (IS) (SIN)

(ii) University wise regression equations are given below.

Karnatak Unversity

Equation

Y = 135.0159-1.631 + 11.722 + 3.219 + 5.399

(TQC) (RS) (PGO) (SIN) (TRI)

Bangalore University

Equation

Y = 69.743-3.002 + 12.166

(TQC) (MO) (PGO)

Mysore University

Equation

Y = 123.281 + 7.314-2.942

(TQC) (MO) (RS)

Mangalore University

Equation

Y = 2.948-2.427 + 14.193 + 1.544

(TQC) (MO) (PGO) (II)

Gulburga University

Equation

Y = 86.042-16.243 + 1.900

(TQC) (PGO) (MO)

Kuvempu University

Equation

Y = 397.152-21.005 + 13.048 + 2.031 + 3.565 + 6.903

(TQC) (PGO) (WCO) (II) (SIN) (WSR)

The results reveal that in universities the highly contributing variable to the variance in Total Quality Culture is Morale and Personal Growth Opportunity.

(iii) Types of Management Wise

The regression equations of different types of management are given below.

Government Teacher Education Colleges

Equation

Y = 58.699 + 4.470-14.055 + 9.837

(TQC) (SIN) (PGO) (WCO)

Private Aided Colleges

Equation

Y = 87.023-2.669 + 12.423

(TQC) (MO) (PGO)

Private Un-aided Colleges

Equation

Y = 138.302-11.743 + 1.199 + 1.276

(TQC) (PGO) (RS) (MO)

In type of management the highly contributing variable to the variance in Total Quality Culture (TQC) is Personal Growth Opportunity (PGO), Morale (MO) and Student Teachers' Involvement in College Activities (SIN).

(iv) College Sex Wise

The regression equations of different college sex are given below.

Co-education Colleges

Equation

Y = 95.203-11.354 + 1.405 + 0.631 + 1.392

(TQC) (PGO) (MO) (RS) (SIN)

Women Colleges

Equation

Y = 434.218-2.765 + 11.506

(TQC) (MO) (WCO)

Conclusion

In college sex especially in co-education colleges the highly contributing variable to the variance in Total Quality Culture (TQC) is Personal Growth Opportunity (PGO) and Morale (MO). In Women Colleges highly contributing variable to the variance in Total Quality Culture (TQC) is Morale (MO) and Work Complexity (WCO).

Findings of Factor Analysis

Varimax rotation is done for the whole group and secondary teacher education colleges coming under six universities are extracted and compared. It is found that there is not much difference in the factor structure for the various sub groups. From each factor common variables and unique variables significantly contributing to six universities are explained as below.

Factor I

It is observed that common variables significantly contributing to factor I in all six universities are related to dependent variable Total Quality Culture. Some of the unique variables which, have direct relationship with Total Quality Culture are Academic Emphasis, Work complexity, Morale, Student Teachers' Involvement in College Activities and Task Related Interaction.

Factor II

It is observed that common variables significantly contributing to factor II in all six universities are Consideration and Resource Support. They are known to be Managerial dimensions of Organisational Health. They have direct influence on enhancement of Total Quality Culture in all secondary teacher education colleges. There are some unique variables significantly contributing to factor II in six universities, they are Institutional Integrity, Task Related Interaction, both of them are highly influencing Total Quality Culture in Kuvempu University.

Factor III

It is found that common variables significantly contributing to factor III in all secondary teacher education colleges coming under six universities are Workspeed and Routine, Work Complexity, Personal Growth Opportunity and Task Related Interaction have direct influence on Total Quality Culture. There are some unique variables significantly contributing to factor III in all universities are Student Teachers' Involvement in College Activities and Principal Influence. It reveals that to attain a better Total Quality Culture in an institution there should be good Quality of Work-Life and Organisational Health.

Factor IV

It is also found that only unique variables have significantly contributed to this factor in all six universities they are Morale, Academic Emphasis, Principal Influence and Student Teachers'

Involvement in College Activities. This indicates that institutional Total Quality Culture fully depends on relationship of these unique variables.

Factor V

It is observed that common variable significantly contributing to this factor is Institutional Integrity. This variable has direct influence in two universities like Karnatak University and Mangalore University. Some unique variables are also significantly contributed in different universities like work complexity in Bangalore University, Workspeed and Routine and Student Teachers' Involvement in College Activities in Gulburga University.

Implications

The modern world is one in which the only constant is change. Change is a precarious matter. Implementing Total Quality Culture in secondary teacher education colleges requires coping with change in positive and constructive manner. Secondary teacher education institutions' culture must be redesigned so as to be consistent with the Total Quality Culture. That helps to create a congenial atmosphere for Total Quality Management. Organisational Health, Quality of Work-Life, Student Teacher's Involvement in College Activities, Student Teacher's Commitment to Course and Change Facilitator Styles of Principals are the main factors that will promote Quality Culture in a teacher education college.

The findings of the study, as reported earlier in chapter V, and the earlier section of this chapter indicates that co-education colleges need to adopt measures to inculcate quality culture principles and maintain healthy organisational conditions, sustain better Quality of Work-Life and provide scope for more and more Student Teachers' Involvement in College Activities.

Teacher educators below 35 years of age need to understand and live the message of Total Quality Culture, Organisational Health and Quality of Work-Life. However to create a continuous improvement in culture, Principals have to trust their staff and to delegate powers to make decisions at the appropriate levels and entrust responsibility for ensuring quality within their own sphere.

Staff need the freedom to operate within a framework of clear and known corporate goals.

In case of co-education secondary teacher education colleges to promote Total Quality Culture, apart from the changing the behaviour of staff, it also requires a change in the way in which institutions are managed and led. The latter is characterized by the understanding that people produce quality. Two things are required for staff to produce quality. First, staff needs a suitable environment in which to work. They need the tools of the occupation and they need to work with systems and procedures which are simple and which aid them in doing their jobs. To do a good job staff needs encouragement and recognition of their success and achievement. They need leaders who can appreciate their achievements and coach them to greater success. The motivation to do a good job comes from a leadership style and an atmosphere, which hightens self-esteem and empowers the individual.

In different Universities the highly contributing values to the variance in Total Quality Culture is Morale and Personal Growth Opportunity. They have more influence on Total Quality Culture than other variables. Morale is a sum of individual sentiments, centered around feelings of well-being and satisfaction. It has direct and powerful influence on total quality culture in all six Universities. So, for all the teacher educators working in secondary teacher education colleges coming under different Universities workshops or crash courses should be organised for improvement of their Morale. Personal Growth Opportunity for teacher educators also play a crucial role in the enhancement of Total Quality Culture. To provide opportunities for increasing Personal Growth teacher educators need career advancement programs which are to be conducted by the Universities.

In aided, un-aided and government secondary teacher education colleges, Morale of the staff can be improved by creating pleasant working conditions; A sense of belongingness, a fair treatment, a sense of achievement, a feeling of importance, a part in policy formulation must be provided for the improvement of Morale in teacher educators.

In order to provide opportunities for Personal Growth for teacher educators working in different types of management, they are to be encouraged and supported in their efforts to learn new skills, techniques and methods. In-service training workshops and seminars are to be conducted periodically by the Universities.

In women secondary teacher education colleges highly influencing variables to Total Quality Culture are Morale and Work Complexity. In order to improve these, special training programs may be chalked out to improve those qualities in teacher educators.

Conclusion

For the last few years no research on Total Quality Culture has been conducted in the field of secondary teacher education program. The major concern in secondary teacher education course should be educational excellence for which teacher education colleges have to become Total Quality Driven, Enjoying Healthy Conditions and Quality of Work-Life. Student Teachers' Active Involvement in College Activities and their Commitment to the Academic Excellence and the Principal as an ardent Change Facilitator would go a long way in making the college quality conscious and quality borne.

Total Quality Culture is also correlated with Organisational Health. A healthy organisation is one that not only survives in its environment, but continues to grow and prosper over the long term. Now a days most of the secondary teacher education organisations have become ineffective and unhealthy in their condition. Most of them lack in innovativeness, autonomy, adaptation, and problem solving adequacy that deal with the organisation needs for growth and change.

Another contributing factor to Total Quality Culture is Quality of Work-Life. It is defined as "the quality of the relationship between employees and the total working environment with human dimensions". The goal of Quality of Work-Life is the creation of Organisational Conditions that foster individual learning and development, that provide individuals with substantial influence and control over what they do and how they are to do it, and that provides individuals with interesting and meaningful work that serves as a source of personal satisfaction and a means to valued personal rewards. In case of most of the secondary teacher education colleges, teacher educators Quality of Work-Life dimensions like Personal Growth Opportunity and Institutional Autonomy are not at satisfactory levels. Teacher educators may be provided apportunities to learn new skills, methods and techniques to keep up with changes and new developments in their specialisation. They also need some freedom in taking their own decisions about their work.

In most of the secondary teacher education colleges student teachers do not have involvement in college activities. To make student teachers' involve in college activities, variety of need based activities are to be designed and they are to be motivated to involve in those activities.

To create an enduring institutional Quality Culture, another important contributor is Student Teachers' Commitment to Training Course. This is based on their loyalty to the college work, work effort put by them, work attitudes, their engagements in course work, active participation in co-curricular activities conducted in the college as well as in practicing schools where they are deputed for internship period. To improve these qualities all the teacher education colleges should facilitate the guidance and orientation programs for student teachers.

Another most important facilitator of institutional Quality Culture is leadership behaviour of Principals. It is nothing but a process of directing and influencing the task related activities of a group of staff members in that institution. The main role of Principals is related to the facilitation of alternative programs. The three styles of the Principals were 'Responder', 'Manager', and 'Initiator'. The Initiators are those who effect more successful changes in their colleges. It is found that in most of the secondary teacher education colleges Principals behaviour is based on managerial style. In some colleges Principals are Responders, but in a very few colleges Principals are Initiators. So there is a need of proper leadership skills training for the Principals working in various colleges. Then only they can put efforts in raising the status of Quality Culture in their college.

Suggestions for Further Research

1. The present study is undertaken only in Secondary Teacher Education Colleges. The study may be extended to Primary Teacher Education Colleges and to general Arts and Science Colleges.
2. The study can also be extended to Primary Schools and Higher Secondary Schools.
3. The study may be extended by including some other variables such as Facilities available In Colleges, Teacher Educators' Innovativeness, Teacher Educators' Performance Appraisal, Time-on-Task, Teacher Educators' Commitment, Job Satisfaction and so on.

Bibliography

Adams, E.A. (1993). Organisational Leadership and its Impact on School Effectiveness: A Case Study of Sixty Schools Within a Suburban School District. *Dissertation Abstracts International*, 54 (06), December, p. 2001-A.

Alkire, G. J. (1995). The Principal as a Cultural Leader and the Change Process: Elements and Tools that Contribute to Shaping the Elementary School's Organisational Culture. *Dissertation Abstracts International*, 56(11), May, p. 4211-A.

Astone, B. (2000). Commitment to College: What it Means and How it Changes, From the Community College Student Perspective. *Dissertation Abstracts International*, 61(7), January, p. 2569-A.

Babione, S. P. (1995). A Study on Interaction between Organisational Culture and Process of Continuous Quality Improvement in the Community College Environment. *Dissertation Abstracts International*, 57(1), July, p. 38-A.

Barlosky, M. and Lawton, S. (1995). *Developing Quality Schools*. Toranto: Kodak Canada Inc.

Barnes, K. M. (1994). The Organisational Health Of Middle Schools, Trust, and Decision Participation (Work Environment). *Dissertation Abstracts International*, 55(06), December, p. 1427-A.

Barry, T.J. (1996). *Excellence Is A Habit*: How to Avoid Quality Burnout, New Delhi: BenJonston Publishing Co.

Bauerly, K. M. E. (1997). The Implementation of Total Quality Management Principles in Minnesota Schools: Evidence from the Field. *Dissertation Abstracts International*, 58(08), February, p. 2913-A.

Baughman, K. S. (1995). The Contributing Effect of Organisational Health to Organisational Climate in Explaining Public Secondary School Teacher Job Satisfaction (Work Atmosphere). *Dissertation Abstracts International*, 56(05), November, p. 1589-A.

Becky, H. L. and Priscilla, N. W. (1984). *Occupational Index Scale*. The Department of Human Development and Family Life, Alabama: University of Alabama.

Becker, H.S. (1960). Notes on the Concept of Commitment. *American Journal of Sociology*, 66, pp. 32-40.

Binkley, D. K. (1997). Implementing the Total Quality Management Philosophy in an Elementary School. *Dissertation Abstracts International*, 58(5), November, p.1590-A.

Bourland, S.S. (1988). The Influence of Organisational Health on Four Elementary Schools Participating in the Effective Schools Research Program. *Dissertation Abstracts International*, 50(02), August, p. 355-A.

Burroughs, G.E.R. (1975). *Design and Analysis in Educational Research*. Oxford: Alden and Mowbrany Limited.

Campbell, J.P., and Pritchard, R.D. (1977). *Motivation theory in industrial and Organisational Psychology*. In M.D. Dunnette (Ed.), Handbook of Industrial and Organisational Psychology. Chicago: Rand McNally.

Carey, T. R. (1998). Total Quality Management in Higher Education: Why it Works? Why it Does Not? *Dissertation Abstracts International*, 59(01), July, p. 31-A.

Chaffee, E. and Sherr, L. (1992), Quality Transforming Post Secondary Education *ASHE-ERIC Higher Education Report*, 3, p. 1.

Chang, S.L. (1996). Organisational Culture and Total Quality Management. *Dissertation Abstracts International*, 57(4), October, p. 1726-A.

Chenoweth, W. F. (1997). Organisational Culture in School Districts: a Phenomenological Perspective. *Dissertation Abstracts International*, 58(6), December, p. 1995-A.

Chirichello, M. P. (1997). A Study of the Preferred Leadership Styles of Principals and the Organisational Climates in Successful Public Elementary Schools in New Jersey. *Dissertation Abstracts International*, 58(3), September, p.659-A.

Colegrove, D. J. (1999). Total Quality Management at a South West School District: A Case Study of Practicing Educators. *Dissertation Abstracts International*, 60(11), May, p. 3850-A.

Critchley, E. S. (1999). The Nature and Extent of Student Involvement in Educational Policy Making in Canadian School Systems. *Dissertation Abstracts International*, 61(01), July, p. 37-A.

Davis, D. K. (1997). The Relationship between West Virginia Early and Middle School Principals' Leadership Style and School Culture as Perceived by Faculty. *Dissertation Abstracts International*, 58(07), January, p. 2475-A.

Deming, W.E. (1951). "Managerial System". In: Voehl, Frank (1992). *Total Quality: Principle and Practice within Organisation. Coral Springs*, Fla.: Strategy Associates, pp. III, 91.

Dhiman, S. K. (1995). Leadership Implications of Total Quality Management in Higher Education. *Dissertation Abstracts International* 56(7), January, p. 278.

Edward, S. (1996). *Total Quality Management in Education*. London Kogan Page Ltd.

Elliott, D. G. (1997). Teacher Perceptions and Total Quality Management Teaching Strategies. *Dissertation Abstracts International*, 59(02), August, p. 406-A.

Etzioni, A. (1975). *A Comparative Analysis of Complex Organisations* (2nd Ed.). New York: Free Press.

Evans, R.L. (1988). Teachers Perceptions of Principals Change Facilitator Styles in Schools that Differ According to Effectiveness and Socioeconomic Context. *Dissertation Abstracts International*, 49(08), February, p. 2039-A.

Finkelstein, R. (1999). The Effects of Organisational Health and Pupil Control Ideology on the Achievement and Alienation of High School Students. *Dissertation Abstracts International*, 59(11), May, p. 4018-A.

Flam, E.J. (1997). The Principal's Role in Educational Change. *Dissertation Abstracts International*, 58(06), December, p. 1998-A.

Ford, M. G. (1998). A Multi-Site Case Study of Total Quality Management within a Texas School District. *Dissertation Abstracts International*, 59(04), October, p. 1022-A.

Franklin, I. (1975). A Study of Organisational Climate and Teacher Morale in College of Education in Gujarat. In M.B. Buch (Ed.), *Secondary Survey of Research in Education Baroda*: Society for Educational Research and Development.

Frueauff, R. L. (1998). Organisational Health and the Influences that Enable and Constrain the Development of Healthy Schools. *Dissertation Abstracts International*, 59(02), August, p. 382-A.

Garret, H.E. (1971). *Statistics in Psychology and Education* Bombay: Vakils Feffer and Simons Private Ltd.

Gatto, C. C. (1997) A Description of the Influence of Culture on the Change Process at Central High. Dissertation Abstracts International, 58 (12), June, p. 45015-A.

Gene, E. H. and William, L. R. (1983) Three Change Facilitator Styles; How Principals Affect Improvement Efforts, *American Edition Research Association*, April, p. 3155.

Giard, J. (1994). Relationships between the Components of Student Involvement and Educational Outcomes with the Prospect of Improving Achievement in Québec Cégeps. *Dissertation Abstracts International*, 56(7), January, p. 330.

Gilmer, B. (1966). *Industrial Psychology (2nd Ed.)*. New York: McGraw-Hill.

Gordon, J.M. (1996). Readiness for Change Among Urban School Principals: Leadership Style and Other Potential Influences. *Dissertation Abstracts International*, 57(10), April, p. 4202-A.

Grachek, L. K. (1998). An Examination of the Relationships between Value Conflict, Quality of Work-Life, Job satisfaction and Job Retention Among County Human Service Workers in the State of Ohio. *Dissertation Abstracts International*, 59(08), February, p. 3209-A.

Guilford, J.P. and Fruchter, B. (1973). *Fundamental Statistics in Psychology and Education*. New York: McGraw Hill.

Gupta, S. (1977). A Study of Some Selected Inputs for Improving Education of Secondary School Teachers (B.Ed. Level) in Punjab. In M.B. Buch (Ed.), *Secondary Survey of Research in Education*. Baroda: Society for Educational Research and Development.

Hall, J. E. and Guzman, F. M. (1984). Sources of Leadership for Change in High Schools. *ERIC* (150), p. 25.

Hall, R.H. (1991) *Organisations Structure Process and Outcomes*. New Jersey: Printice Hall.

Halpin, A.W., and Croft, D.B. (1963). *The Organisational Climate of Schools*. Chicago: Midwest Administration Center of the University of Chicago.

Halpin, A.W., and Croft, D.B. (1962, August). *The Organisational Climate of Schools*. Washington: DC:U.S. Office of Education.

Hillman, A. L. (1995). Total Quality Reform (TQR): Restructuring Teacher Education Through the Infusion of Technology and Total Quality Management. *Dissertation Abstracts International*, 57(02), August, p. 530-A.

Holt, K. E. (1999). Relationship between the Organisational Health of Selected Public Schools in Texas and Strategies for Communicating with the Public. *Dissertation Abstracts International*, 60(07), January, p. 2306-A.

Hoy, W.K., and Feldman, J.A. (1981). Organisational Health: The Concept and its Measure. *Journal of Research and Development in Education*, 20, pp. 30-38

Hoy, W.K., and Miskel, C.G. (1987). *Educational Administration: Theory, Research, and Practice (3rd Ed.)*. New York: Random House.

Hrebiniak, L.G., and Alutto, J. A. (1972). Personal and Role-related Factors in the Development of Organisational Commitment. *Administrative Science Quarterly*, 18, 555-573.

Huling, A.L., Hall.J.E. and Guzman, F. M. (1985). High School Principals; Their Role in Guiding Change. In M.B. Buch (Ed.), *Fourth Survey of Research in Education*. New Delhi: National Council of Educational Research and Training.

Jeannett, D. A. (1995). Organisational Health and Leadership in Educational Administration. *Dissertation Abstracts International*, 56(09), March, p. 3393-A.

Jerome, S.A. (1997). *Quality in Education. An Implementation Handbook*. USA: St. Lucie Press, Inc.

Joffres, C. E. (1998). Beyond Organisational Commitment: Selected Elementary School Teachers' Work Commitments. *Dissertation Abstracts International*, 59(07), January, p .2272.

John, W. (2000). Managing Professional Development in Schools, London: Routledge. Pub. Ltd.,

Jones, M. T.(1998). The Relationship of Organisational Commitment to the Organisational Culture of High Schools. *Dissertation Abstracts International*, 59(04), October, p.1026-A.

Joseph, B. J. (1997). The Relationship between the Quality of School Life and Students' Perception of Power in Middle School. *Dissertation Abstracts International*, 58(12), June, p. 4509-A.

Juran, J. (1989). *The Quality Control Handbook*, Ten Steps to Quality, In: Voehl, Frank (1992). *Total Quality: Principle and Practice Within Organisation*. Coral Springs, Fla.: Strategy Associates, pp. II, 55.

Kadyschuk, R. (1997). Teacher Commitment: A Study of the Organisational Commitment, Professional Commitment, and Union Commitment of Teachers in Public Schools in Saskatchewan. *Dissertation Abstracts International*, 58(12), June, p. 4510-A.

Kahn, R. L. (1974). The Work Module: A Proposal for the Humanisation of Work. In J.O. Toole (Ed.) *Work and the Quality of Life* (pp. 118-145) Cambridge: MIT Press.

Katz, R. (1978). Job Longevity as a Situational Factor in Job Satisfaction. *Administrative Science Quarterly*, 23, pp. 204-233.

Kehoe, J. F. (1995). An Investigation of the Relationship between the Organisational Structure of the Middle School and School Health. *Dissertation Abstracts International*, 55(12), June, p. 3701-A.

Kells, P. (1994). Perceptions of Quality of Working Life in two Ontario Colleges of Applied Arts and Technology. *Dissertation Abstracts International*, 56(7), January, p. 398.

Kothari Education Commission (1966), *Government of India Document*. New Delhi: Ministry of Education.

Kottkamp, R.B., Mulherin, J.A., and Hoy, W.K. (1987). Secondary School Climate: A Revision of the OCDQ. *Educational Administration Quarterly*, 23, pp. 31-48.

Kyle, L. D. (1995). Visionary Leadership and Total Quality Management in Higher Education Administration. *Dissertation Abstracts International* 56(08), February, p. 2955-A.

Larkin, D. (1994). Faculty Integration in International Schools: An Application of the Organisational Health Inventory to the East Asia Regional Council of Overseas Schools. *Dissertation Abstracts International*, 56(03), September, p. 782-A.

Leonard, P. E. (1997). Understanding the Dimensions of School Culture: An Investigation in to Educators Value Orientations and Value Conflicts. *Dissertation Abstracts International*, 59(07), January, p. 2274-A.

Leou, M. J. (1997). A Study of Beginning Teachers and Learning in the Work Place. *Dissertation Abstracts International*, 58(5), November, p. 1664-A.

Litwin, G.H. and Stringer, R.A. (1968). *Motivational and Organisational Climate*. Boston, MA: Graduate School of Business Administration, Harvard University.

Lok, P. (1997). The Influence of Organisational Culture, Sub Culture, Leadership Style and Job Satisfaction on Organisational Commitment. *Dissertation Abstracts International*, 59(08), February, p. 3078-A.

Malhotra, M.M. (1993). *Quality Improvement in Technical Education and Training* in M. M. Malhotra (Ed.) *Collection of Papers on Excellence in Technical Education*. Chandigarh; Technical Teachers' Training Institute.

Mazula, C. M. (1996). Pupil Control Orientation and Organisational Health in Special Education Schools: A Comparative Analysis. New Brunswick: *Disseration Abstracts International*, 57(11), May, p. 4613-A.

McCullough, Y.J. (1994). A Comparative Analysis of Leadership Qualities of African, American, Anglo-American and Hispanic American Principals Reading School Effectiveness in Selected Urban Secondary Schools. *Dissertation Abstracts International*, 55(12), June, p. 3703-A.

McDonald, D. J. (1996). Total Quality Management: A Case Study of the Cherry Hill Public Schools, Cherry Hill, New Jersey. *Dissertation Abstracts International*, 57(11), May, p. 4613-A.

McGregor, D. (1960). *The Human Side of Enterprise*. New York: Mc Graw-Hill.

Mckenzie, D.E. (1983). Research for School Improvement: An Appraisal of Some Recent Trends. *Educational Researcher*, 12(4), pp. 5-17.

McMillan, J. M. (1998). Total Quality Management in Higher Education: A Study of Senior Administrators' Perceptions about Total Quality Management in Institutions of Higher Education in Ohio. *Dissertation Abstracts International*, 59(07), January, p. 2276-A.

Meyer, J. and Rowan, B. (1978). 'Institutionalised Organisations': Formal Secondary Education, London, Ruotledge and Kegan Paul.

Millard, D. A. (1998). Perspective of leaders in Educational Change. *Dissertation Abstracts International*, 59(07), January, p. 2277-A.

Miles, M.B. (1965). Education and Innovation: The Organisation in Context. In M. Abbott and J. Lovell (Eds.), *Changing Perspectives in Educational Administration* (pp. 54-72). Auburn, AL: Auburn University.

Mistry, D.H. (1985). The Quality School Life as a Function of Organisational Climate and Pupil Control Indeology. In M.B.Buch (Ed.), *Fourth Survey of Research in Education*. New Delhi: National Council of Educational Research and Training.

Mouritsten, M. L. (1997). The Development and Application of a Model Total Quality Education Approach in Utha School District. *Dissertation Abstracts International*, 58(11), May, p. 4145-A.

Mowday, R.T., and Steers, R.M. (1979). The Measures of Organisational Commitment. *Journal of Vocational Behaviour*, 14, pp. 224-247.

Mowday, R. T., Porter, L.M., & Steers, R.M. (1982). *Employee-Organisation Linkages: The Psychology of Commitment, Absenteeism, and Turnover*. New York: Academic Press.

National Policy on Education (1986). *Government of India Document* Delhi: Ministry of Human Resource Development.

Nielson, D. (1997). Student Involvement in Graduate Education: Comparison of African, American and White Students. *Dissertation Abstracts International*, 58(08), February, p. 3039-A.

Obisesan, A. A. (1998). Quality Management and System Change in Three Suburban Public School Districts. *Dissertation Abstracts International*, 59(07), January, p. 2279-A.

Pace, C.R. and Stern, G.C. (1958). An Approach to the Measure of Psychological Characteristics of College Environment. *Journal of Educational Psychology*, 49, pp. 269-277.

Palmer, R.E. (1996). The Relationship between Principals Leadership Style and Faculty Perception of Principals Effectiveness. *Dissertation Abstracts International*, 56(09), March, p. 3400-A

Parsons, T., Bales, R.F. and Shils, E.A. (1953). *Working Papers in the Theory of Action*. Glencoe, I.L.; Free Press.

Parsons, C. (1994). Quality Improvement in Education. *Case Studies in Schools, Colleges and Universities*. London: David Fulton Pub. Ltd.

Paul, C.L.(1998). The Relationship between the Principles of Total Quality Management and School Climate, School Culture, and Teacher Empowerment. *Dissertation Abstracts International*, 59(08), February, p. 2803-A.

Pletnick, G. K. (1997). A Relationship between the Leadership Styles of Middle School Principals and the Stages of Development of Interdisciplinary Teams. *Dissertation Abstracts International*, 58(3), September, p. 681-A.

Podgurski, T.P. (1991). School Effectiveness as it Relates to Groups Consensus and Organisational Health of Elementary Schools. *Dissertation Abstracts International*, 52(03), September, p. 769-A.

Porter, L.W., Steers, R.M., Mowday, R.T. and Boulian, B.V. (1974). Organisational Commitment, Job Satisfaction and Turnover among Psychiatric Technicians. *Journal of Applied Psychology*, 59, pp. 603-609.

Ralph G. L. and Douglas H. S. (1994). Total Quality in Higher Education Florida St. Lucie Press.

Rhodes, L.A. (1992). *Educational Leadership* (GEDL), 49(6), March, pp. 76-80.

Richardson, C. M. (1999). Perceptions of the Preparedness of Teacher Educator Students for Teaching: A Case Study. *Dissertation Abstracts International*, 60(05), November, p.1441-A.

Robinson, B. M. (1996). Total Quality Management in Education: The Empowerment of School Community. *Dissertation Abstracts International*, 57(4), October, p. 1428-A.

Rodgers, C. G. (1998). Teacher Perceptions of Total Quality Management Practices in Elementary Schools. *Dissertation Abstracts International*, 59(10), April, p. 3709-A.

Ronne Berg, J. S. (2000). The Urban School Leader as a Change Agent: Case Studies of Three Urban School Principals. *Dissertation Abstracts International*, 61(01), July, p. 50-A.

Rossmiller, R A. (1992), The Secondary School Principal and Teachers' Quality of Work-Life. *Educational Management and Administration*. 20(3), July, pp. 132-46.

Rutherford, W.L. (1983). *Three Change Facilitator Styles: How Principals Affect Improvement Efforts'*. Montreal: American Educational Research Association.

Sallis, E. (1996). Total Quality Management in Education (Edn 2nd). London: Kogan Page Limited.

Sashkin, M. and Joseph, J. L. (1984). Quality of Work-Life Scale. In William Pfeiffer and Leonard D. Goodstein, *Annual Hand book of Group Facilitators*, San Diego: San Diego.

Sharma, D.K. (1982). A Study of Management of Education Systems with Special Reference to Decision-making and Organisational Health. In M.B.Buch (Ed.), *Third Survey of Research in Education*. New Delhi: National Council of Educational Research and Training.

Shear, R. G. (1997). Measuring Student Involvement and Participation in Decision-Making Public Schools. *Dissertation Abstracts International*, 58(4), October, p. 1243-A.

Smith, B. (1994). Teacher Quality of Work-Life According to Teacher: The Case of High Schools. *Dissertation Abstracts International*, 55(04), October, p. 826-A.

Stevens, I. E.(1997). A Comparison of Organisational Culture between Academic Affairs Administrators and Student Affairs Administrators at Selected Institutions of Higher Education. *Dissertation Abstracts International*, 59(02), August, p. 391-A.

Sweeney, M. A. (1997). The Effects of Self-Determination Training on Student Involvement in the IEP Process. *Dissertation Abstracts International*, 58(3), September, p. 821-A.

Tagiuri, R. (1968). The Concept of Organisational Climate. In R. Tagiuri and G.W. Litwin (Eds.), *Organisational Climate; Explorations of a Concept (pp.1-32)*. Boston, MA: Division of Research, Graduate School of Business Administration, Harvard University.

Thomas, C. D. (1997). Perceived Levels of Success of a Total Quality Management Program in an Institution of Higher Learning. *Dissertation Abstracts International*, 58(09), March, p. 3389-A.

Thomas, S. (1987). *The Principalship—A Reflective Practice Perspective, Texas Trinity University*.

Tolbart, C. W. (1997). Principals as Change Agents. *Dissertation Abstracts International*, 58(5), November, p. 1534-A.

Tribus, M. (1990). The Three Systems of Total Quality. In: Vohel, Frank (1992). *Total Quality: Principles and Practices within Organisations*. Coral Springs, Fla.: Strategy Associates, pp. IV, 20.

Tulsi, P.K. (1998). Total Quality Management in Higher Education. *University News*, 36(25), June, pp. 5-8.

Turan, S. (1998). A Study of Organisational Climate and Organisational Commitment in Human Organisations. *Dissertation Abstracts International*, 59(04), October, p.1038-A.

Udupa, S.R. (1992). Quality Circles: *Progress Through Participation*. New Delhi: Tata McGraw-Hill Publishing Co.

University Education Commission (1950). *Government of India Document*. New Delhi: Ministry of Education.

Watson, J. R. (2000). Total Quality Education: a School District's Beliefs, Behaviours, and Outcomes. *Dissertation Abstracts International*, 61(01), July, p. 53-A.

Whitty, G. (1992). Quality Control in Teacher education. *British Journal of Educational Studies*, XXXX (1), February, pp. 38-48.

Weick, K. (1976). Educational Organisations as Loosely Coupled Systems. *Administrative Science Quarterly*, 21, pp. 1-19.

Weiner, Y. (1982). Commitment in Organisations: A Normative Review. *Academy of Management Review*. 7, pp. 418-425.

Wenbourna, D.L.P. (1996). Perceptions of Principal Change Facilitator Style in California Distinguished Schools and Non-Distinguished Schools. *Dissertation Abstracts International*, 57(11), May, p. 4620-A.

Index

S